NORTH CAROLINA
STATE BOARD OF COMMUNITY COLLEGES
LIBRARIES
ASHEVILLE-BUNCOMBE TECHNICAL COMMUNITY COLLEGE

UNDERSTANDING OLDER ADULTS

UNDERSTANDING OLDER ADULTS

An Experiential Approach to Learning

VALERIE L. REMNET
University of Southern California

Foreword by
David A. Peterson

Lexington Books
D.C. Heath and Company
Lexington, Massachusetts/Toronto

Library of Congress Cataloging-in-Publication Data

Remnet, Valerie L.
  Understanding older adults.

  Includes index.
  1. Gerontology—Study and teaching (Higher)—
United States. 2. Experiential learning—United
States. 3. Social work with the aged—Study and
teaching (Higher)—United States. I. Title.
HQ1065.U5R384   1989   306.2'6'07   86-45995
ISBN 0-669-14825-3 (alk. paper)

Copyright © 1989 by Valerie L. Remnet

All rights reserved. No part of this publication may be reproduced
or transmitted in any form or by any means, electronic or mechanical,
including photocopy, recording, or any information storage or retrieval
system, without permission in writing from the publisher.

This restriction on reproduction notwithstanding, instructors
wishing to reproduce individual exercises in this publication for
classroom use with their students are hereby given permission to do so.

Published simultaneously in Canada
Printed in the United States of America
Text design by Joyce C. Weston
Casebound International Standard Book Number: 0-669-14825-3
Library of Congress Catalog Card Number 86-45995

The paper used in this publication meets the minimum requirements of
American National Standard for Information Sciences—Permanence of
Paper for Printed Library Materials, ANSI Z39.48-1984. ∞™

88 89 90 91 92 8 7 6 5 4 3 2 1

*To my husband, Jack,
and in memory of Jessie Barclay*

Contents

Foreword ix
Preface xi
Acknowledgments xvii
1. Introduction to an Experiential Approach to Learning   1

Part 1: Perceptions of Aging   11
2. Anticipating Your Future Self   13
3. Needs and Services: Optimum Fit   29
4. First Impressions   45

Part 2: Physical Aging   55
5. Pacing and Patience   57
6. Developing Trust   67
7. A Surprise Snack   83
8. Maintaining Mobility   97
9. Skin Sensitivity   107

Part 3: Environmental Changes   119
10. Home Assessment   121
11. Relocation   143

Part 4: Psychosocial Considerations   159
12. Recognition Day   161
13. Reminiscing   171
14. Family Interactions   191
15. An Unexpected Role   205

Appendix: Answer Key for Activities   217
References   221
Index   235
About the Author   237

Foreword

THE RAPID development of research in gerontology and geriatrics has resulted in an explosion of publications related to aging, older people, service delivery, and public policy on the elderly. Accompanying this growth over the past twenty years has occurred the creation of gerontology instructional programs now available in nearly half of the three thousand or more institutions of higher education in the United States. These instructional programs run the gamut from gerontology degrees at the associate, bachelor's, and master's levels to noncredit workshops, general and specialized conferences, and public lectures dealing with aspects of the later stages of life.

The vast majority of instruction is conducted in traditional educational formats; that is, lectures, discussions, and field work offered to students who are seeking knowledge, attitudes, and skills related to aging. While most of the instruction is general, some is intended to assist practitioners to design and offer services to older persons. Because the instruction is often didactic rather than experiential, it has not always been successful in aiding current and future practitioners to appreciate aging, gain empathy for older people, or fully experience various aspects of physical or mental change.

Publications in the field of aging have likewise taken a traditional approach. Most describe the research and summarize the conclusions, without devoting much space to the application of this knowledge for the students and professionals who read them.

This book breaks new ground by focusing on the learner and the instructional process rather than the gerontological content. As an alternative to providing extensive information on aging and its attributes, the book offers a means of experiencing aspects of the aging process and sharing that experience with others, a result that can be as important as just gaining knowledge. Although each chapter provides background content, the chief purpose of the book is to offer experiences that allow the learner to gain a new and deeper appreciation of some aspect of aging. Through this method, the learner is aided in integrating insights and gaining a deeper understanding of some portion of the aging process.

The book is unusual because it is not a text in the normal sense of the word. Nor is it a monograph, fiction, or biography. It is rather a handbook consisting of a set of exercises for use by instructors who desire a new approach, who wish to go beyond the understanding that comes from the lecture, and who seek student learning that will appreciate, value, empathize, and experience aging.

The approach is unique and so is vulnerable to comment that it is not like other publications in this area. This conclusion is accurate, and that is to the book's credit rather than to its detriment. While gerontology publications and instruction have grown in number, they have experienced relatively little innovation. Practically every course is taught in the same way with the same texts. While this may lead to consistent outcomes, it does not encourage alternative approaches or lead to evaluation of creative instructional ideas. This book provides that opportunity. While its approach may not appeal to every instructor, it will be very valuable for those of us who believe that involvement, innovation, and understanding can be facilitated in alternative ways that are interesting and creative.

David A. Peterson, Ph.D.
Director, School of Gerontology and
Associate Dean, Andrus Gerontology
Center, University of Southern California

Preface

AS EDUCATORS, our ongoing challenge is to create optimum learning experiences for our students. I have found this to be particularly challenging in gerontology and geriatrics because, in addition to presenting factual information about the processes of aging and the state of older people in our society, we also need to address the issue of ageism, or the prejudices and stereotypes too frequently applied to the elderly. This requires that students have an opportunity to examine their attitudes and biases that can affect their behaviors toward older people. Given this need for cognitive (knowledge) and affective (emotional) learning, it is apparent that gerontological curricula should include both in a holistic approach.

Over the years, I have developed the experiential learning activities in this handbook as a means to meet this educational challenge. They are based on three adult education principles. First, the process of these activities promotes active rather than passive learning. Secondly, because the students draw on their own experiences, either from the past or from the activity itself, to discuss a topic related to the aging process or elderly people, it has more meaning for them. Third, the debriefing process facilitates group interaction, which promotes learning.

One purpose of these activities is to have the participants recognize aging as normal, lifelong process in which we all participate. This recognition that aging is a personal process helps to begin to break down the barrier between "we who are studying aging" and "they who are aged." This, in turn, facilitates the students' rejection of ageism, acceptance of their own aging, and development of understanding and empathy for older adults.

Overall, the participants' evaluations of these educational activities have been positive. They have reported increased understanding of aging, enhanced self-awareness and appreciation of older people, and positive proposed behavior changes toward the elderly. These positive responses from a wide range of multidisciplinary students, professionals, and other service providers have encouraged me to develop this instructor's handbook as a means to promote teachers' increased interest in and use of this experiential approach to learning in gerontological education.

Organization and Content

Chapter 1 introduces an experiential approach to learning and explains why it is effective in gerontological education. It describes how this approach integrates the cognitive and affective domains of learning to facilitate the students' enhancing their understanding of aging and elderly individuals. The chapter includes the essential components of the experiential activities: the instructor as facilitator and role model, the appropriate type of activity, the process of group discussion and debriefing, and the development of empathy.

The activities in this handbook are organized by chapters and are divided into four major parts: perceptions of aging, physical aging, environmental changes, and psychosocial considerations.

Part 1: Perceptions of Aging

These activities focus on ways to develop the participants' awareness of the multiple and interrelated factors that contribute to their attitudes and perceptions about aging and the aged. This enhancement of self-awareness is important because it can serve to motivate students to consciously monitor their perceptions for accuracy. In this way, they can reduce their biases, enhance their ability to remain more objective, and therefore respond more optimally and empathetically to the needs of the elderly.

Chapter 2 focuses on normal aging and its variations for different individuals as a means to sensitize participants to their perceptions of self and of older adults in society. Chapters 3 and 4 help students understand how their selective perceptions can influence their behaviors toward the elderly. This, in turn, can increase their self-monitoring abilities during the process of working with older adults.

Part 2: Physical Aging

These activities focus on physical changes associated with aging and their psychosocial implications. Though some physical changes are inevitable as people progress through the life cycle, the effect of these changes is very individual. Those who work with older adults need to be not only knowledgeable about general age-related changes but also sensitive to how these changes can have individual effects on elderly people's physical and psychosocial functioning. This combined knowledge and sensitivity can enhance the health care and service providers' ability to motivate older adults to take a proactive approach to maintaining their own optimum functioning as well as to help them compensate for inevitable changes.

Chapter 5 gives participants an opportunity to increase their appreciation of the importance of pacing and patience in working with the elderly and to enhance their knowledge of ways to help older adults compensate for their slower reaction time. Chapters 6 and 7 use simulated sensory impairments as a means to enhance the learners' sensitivity to the effect of reduced sensory input, the resultant feelings of dependency, and the importance of developing trust in the helping relationship. Chapter 8 focuses on heightening the participants' awareness of the effect of musculoskeletal changes on older people's mobility and on increasing their understanding of ways to minimize these changes. Chapter 9 gives the students an experience to increase their understanding of the importance of good skin care for the elderly and ways to promote it.

Part 3: Environmental Changes

These activities focus on environmental changes associated with the later years. These changes include those that can occur in older people's homes as well as in actual relocations.

The elderly's home environment can reflect change and continuity that need to be assessed. Changes in the safety of the physical environment can occur because of deferred maintenance and older adults' declining ability to negotiate it effectively. Continuity in their psychosocial environment can provide links to the past and the security of the familiar in the present. Those who work with older adults need to be aware of the significance of these changes and continuities so they can help the elderly create or re-create an optimum environment in which to live.

Chapter 10 gives students an opportunity to enhance their appreciation of the value of a home assessment visit. First, they practice using a framework designed to facilitate their conducting a home assessment by doing one in their mind's eye. Then, if in keeping with the objectives of the class, they can do an actual home visit with an elderly person. Chapter 11 focuses on heightening the participants' awareness of the psychosocial aspects involved in the relocation process and ways to facilitate a positive move for older adults.

Part 4: Psychosocial Considerations

These activities focus on psychosocial aspects of the later years, including the importance of maintaining individuality, recognizing the value of life experiences, and understanding the intergenerational family system.

Everyone needs individual recognition throughout the life cycle. However, as people grow older, there may be reduced social opportunities to receive such recognition. Thus, those who interact with the elderly need to appreciate the importance of using every appropriate opportunity to give individual recognition to them. This not only enhances older people's psychosocial functioning, it also deepens caregivers' appreciation of them as unique individuals. Another means to gain further understanding of the elderly is to view them as an integral part of their family system. This view also provides those who work with the elderly information that will help them to be supportive to the intergenerational family.

Chapter 12 gives participants an opportunity to increase their awareness of the importance of giving individual recognition to elderly people and to increase their knowledge of ways to provide such recognition. Chapter 13 offers students an opportunity to learn the value of reminiscing as another important way to give older adults individual recognition. First, they are guided through a reminiscence of an experience in their own lives. Then, if in keeping with the objectives of the class, they can conduct a reminiscing session with an elderly person. This chapter also includes an example of an inservice training session on reminiscing titled "Reminiscing over the Holidays." It can be used as an extra activity or as an illustration of reminiscing to review and discuss with your class.

Chapter 14 focuses on the family as a "system in process" and the interaction patterns of its members. This approach gives the students an opportunity to explore an intergenerational family system and ways to examine it. Chapter 15 offers learners an occasion to increase their appreciation of the effect of an unexpected caregiving role being thrust on a family member and their knowledge of ways to help the intergenerational family handle it.

Use of the Activities

I hope that you will find the format of the activities useful as you review, edit, and "shape" them to reflect your own teaching style. Taking the time to personalize the activities contributes to their success, as does pretesting them with supportive colleagues. I would like to comment briefly on some of the parts.

The learning objectives have been designed to provide a way to evaluate the participants' growth in knowledge, increase in understanding, awareness and/or sensitivity, and behavioral change. Thus, each activity reflects a holistic approach to learning by addressing the cognitive and affective components of learning and resultant behavior change. The last objective for each activity which relates to behavior change requests that the students give at least one example of how the activity will affect their interactions with older adults. This objective is based on adult learning theory, which suggests that when learners set their own objectives for behavioral change, they are more likely to follow through. As with all learning objectives, these self-selected objectives should be in quantitative behaviors so that they can be measured, and realistic so that they can be accomplished. Depending on the availability of time, there are two ways to help participants check out the feasibility of their proposed objectives. First, as they are completing their evaluations, you can ask them to include in their response to the question on proposed interactions with older adults, how, when, where, and with whom they intend to accomplish their objectives. Secondly, you can have them divide up into pairs and discuss them. Both of these methods can promote the follow-through process. In addition to doing evaluations immediately following the activities, in ongoing projects or classes, follow-up assessments can be done periodically.

I have listed the categories of people whom I think would benefit most from each activity. Some activities are appropriate for everyone who interacts with older people. Other exercises have been designed with certain groups in mind, such as providers of health care. However, only you, as the instructor, can make the final decision, for you know the backgrounds and needs of your students.

Generally speaking, class size influences the frequency and quality of student interactions. For many of the exercises I recommend breaking into small discussion groups before debriefing as a class.

Time is important in the experiential learning process. The times I have suggested for each activity are subject to many variables, including class size, background of participants, group dynamics of the class and related issues that arise and are timely to discuss. You can extend or contract the time for group discussion and class debriefing depending on your time constraints. However, it is important to remember to take the time to give recognition to the value of each experience shared by the students.

The examples of participants' responses I have included in the debriefing section are representative of those I've received over the years. I never begin the debriefing with them; rather I let the participants share their experiences first. Then, if there is a premature lull in the sharing, I will select a few examples not yet mentioned and ask if anyone experienced these feelings, as had some previous participants. This adds to the discussion of similarities and differences of any given experience related to aging.

Use of the Book

The activities in this handbook can be useful to teachers in the field of educational gerontology who are looking for a variety of creative options that will add an affective learning component to their curriculum.

They can be used by instructors in academic settings, including behavioral sciences, social work, medical and allied health, and religion.

They can be useful to inservice educators in mental health, hospitals, home health and long-term care settings, and social service agencies.

They can be used by workshop leaders who provide training to volunteers and caregivers in community settings such as churches and service organizations.

The exercises in this handbook represent my efforts to respond to the need for innovative approaches to gerontological education. The purpose of these activities is to offer the students experiences to gain a greater understanding of some of the processes of aging and a deeper appreciation of and empathy toward older people.

I hope these activities not only will be useful to you in your teaching but also will challenge you to create your own. Much more needs to be done in the development and evaluation of this experiential approach to the study of aging. I invite you to join me in addressing this need.

Acknowledgments

I WISH to express my appreciation to my colleagues Helen Dennis, project director at the Conference Board, New York; David Peterson, associate dean of the Andrus Gerontology Center, University of Southern California; Vicki Plowman, associate director of communication at the Rehabilitation, Research and Training Center on Aging, Rancho Los Amigos Medical Center; Kristen Smith, nursing home administrator and consultant on aging for the Evangelical Lutheran Church in America; and Gwen Uman, gerontological nurse practitioner and adjunct assistant professor, School of Education, University of Southern California for their reviews of the manuscript, constructive comments, and ongoing encouragement during the development of this handbook. A special thank you is extended to Rita Ivens for her excellent preparation of the manuscript and her professional commitment to this book.

I would like to thank the many people who have participated in these activities over the years, shared their thoughts and feelings about their experiences and, in the process, enhanced our humanitarianism. Their responses to these activities have encouraged me to continue using the experiential teaching/learning approach.

It is hard to know where the ideas for developing these activities originated. Possible sources include my experiences as a student, brainstorming with colleagues, comments from participants, wise words from elderly people, or ideas that occurred while I was digging up weeds in my back yard. To those people whom I can identify, I have acknowledged in the appropriate activity. To them, and to all the others whom I am unable to identify, I give my thanks.

1 Introduction to an Experiential Approach to Learning

Aging, Ageism, and Attitudes

1. Aging

Aging and the aged are increasingly important issues in American society because of the growth of the older population. In 1980, there were 24 million older people living in the United States. By 1990 there will be 28 million, and by the year 2020 there will be 40 million (Atchley 1987). The fastest growing segments of this older population are the seventy-five-plus and eighty-five-plus age groups (Butler and Lewis 1982). These numbers have major implications because of the increasing need for health care and other supportive services as people grow older.

The challenge is to provide this needed care and service in the most effective and economical ways. An overall approach is the development of an interrelated support system including professionals, paraprofessionals, volunteers and family caregivers who would work with the elderly to enhance their ability to function optimally in an environment of their choice. The overall goal of this approach is to maintain quality of life for older people.

An essential component in the plan to assist the elderly in the maintenance of quality lives is the people who interact with them. First, there must be enough of them. Secondly, these supportive people need to have the knowledge, skills, and attitudes that will help them understand each elderly person as a unique individual and prepare them to provide these older people with a balance of care and challenge.

2. Ageism

More educational institutions, health care facilities, and other community agencies are responding to this educational need of people who interact with the elderly. However, a barrier impedes the recruitment of individuals into the field of gerontology, the effectiveness of educational offerings, and the provision of optimum care and services to the elderly. This barrier is ageism, or the prejudices and stereotypes applied to older people strictly on the basis of age (Butler and Lewis 1982). Because prejudices and stereotypes reflect people's attitudes, the need to change these attitudes in a more positive direction is obvious.

Austin's (1985) findings of a positive shift in Americans' attitudes toward older people is encouraging. However, educators in the health care and service professions report the need for a proactive approach to attitudinal change. They suggest that gerontology curricula include creative teaching and learning methods that will encourage students to examine their attitudes toward aging and the aged and increase their understanding of and empathy for the elderly (Benson 1982; Brower 1981; Galbraith and Suttie 1987; Heller and Walsh 1976; Holtzman, Beck, and Ettinger 1981). Before any educational attempt is made to modify attitudes, it is relevant to review a definition of attitudes, how they develop, and their principal components.

3. Attitudes

Values and beliefs contribute to the development of attitudes. Values pertain to the way things "should be." They are always with us, guiding our decisions and judgments of ourselves and others regarding right and wrong, good or bad, desirable or objectionable. Values are broad, general, and abstract. Beliefs are convictions about the way things "are." They consist of general knowledge and assumptions acquired through our interactions with the environment and other people. Beliefs are expressions of what people think about an issue, object, or person (Muldary 1983).

Attitudes have a significant influence on perceptions. Perceptions are based on an individual's cognitive processes, which give recognition and meaning to people, objects, or events based on sensory input. Attitudes are important because they predispose individuals to react in a given and consistent way toward a specific target. Though attitudes are not the only determinants of actions, they do exert a strong influence on verbal and nonverbal behavior and the kinds of situations and values a person chooses.

All attitudes are learned. Based on his review of studies in attitude development, Tyler (1949) reported on three means by which people develop attitudes. The most frequent is through assimilation from the environment—things that are taken for granted, points of view held by family and friends. This assimilation can be unintentional or intentional. The next most common is from the emotional effects of personal experiences. The third is through direct intellectual processes in which a person sees the implications of behavior. Thus, it is evident that attitudes are learned responses that reflect complex relationships among assimilation, past experiences, and present environmental situations.

The general view today is that attitudes consist of three basic components: cognitive, affective, and behavioral (Glass and Knott 1982; Klausmeier and Goodwin 1975; Muldary 1983). The cognitive (intellectual) component includes beliefs and factual information about the identified person, object, or event. If the information is inadequate or incorrect it can result in stereotyping. The affective (emotional) component of attitudes consists of feelings connected with the identified target. These feelings can vary in intensity depending on the person's target-related experiences. The behavioral (predisposition to action) component of attitudes consists of avoidance-approach behaviors along a continuum. Attitudes learned by any means influence the direction of response along the continuum. A negative attitude would be toward avoidance behaviors; a favorable attitude would move toward approach behaviors. The stronger the attitude, the more the motivation to act in a given direction.

Given the basic and interrelated components of attitudes and the process of their development, it is apparent how ageism with its stereotyping has developed in America's youth-oriented society. The need to change ageist attitudes is vital because stereotyping negates understanding older people as unique individuals. Without such understanding from the people in their health care and service support systems, the elderly's quality of life will be compromised.

4. Attitudinal Change

Attitudes are emotionally toned predispositions to react in a consistent way, either favorably or unfavorably toward a person, object, or event, and are relatively enduring. However, because they are learned, they can be shaped and changed. Based on their literature review, Glass and Knott (1982) reported that there appeared to be three primary ways in which attitudes can be formed or changed: through more knowledge, through direct experiences with the attitude objects, and through interactions with others.

Many studies have supported this report. They have concurred that when a gerontological curriculum includes information regarding the processes of aging; selected, supervised direct contact with the relatively well elderly; and an opportunity for debriefing their experiences with peers and their teacher, the students had a positive attitudinal change toward older people (Boren, Johnson, and Pawlson 1982; Brock 1977; Gordon and Hallauer 1976; Hart, Freel, and Crowell 1976; Holtzman, Beck, and Coggan 1978; Murphy-Russell, Die, and Walker 1986; Tobiason, Knudsen, Stengel, and Giss 1979). It is important to note that in these programs the students' initial contacts were with elderly people who were functioning relatively well in the community. This was intended to provide a more balanced perspective and realistic view of aging and the aged before the students were assigned to the frail and sick elderly.

The timing of these educational experiences was also an issue. Based on these studies and other findings, it has been recommended that the earlier in the training/academic experience the employee/student has gerontological content and the opportunity to interact with the well elderly, the greater the effect on positive attitudinal change (Benson 1982; Gordon and Hallauer 1976; Seltzer 1977; Wilson and Hafferty 1983). Also, it has been suggested that inservice orientations and periodic staff attitudinal development programs for health care providers would promote and maintain positive attitudes toward the elderly (Brower 1981; Hart, Freel, and Crowell 1976).

In summary, there is a need for creative gerontological teaching/learning activities to modify ageist attitudes beginning as early as possible in either the students' academic experience or in the health care and service providers' employment. Also, for reinforcement of learning, these activities should be continued at regular intervals.

Development of Experiential Activities

Given the findings, it is timely to develop experiential activities for use in the classroom as an integral part of a gerontological curriculum, as an orientation, or as an inservice training session. Ideally, these initial awareness-building, sensitizing activities would be used before the students had clinical or field work experience with the elderly.

The experiential activities in this handbook provide both gerontological information and the opportunity to interact with peers and the teacher in group discussions and general debriefing (two of the ways previously suggested to encourage students to examine and modify their attitudes). However, rather than arrange for direct interactions with the elderly, the students are asked to use their *own* experience with aging either in their past or in the age-related educational activities.

There are two reasons for this approach. First, it helps learners recognize that aging is not something that "happens" in the later years, rather it is a lifelong process in which *everyone* participates. This helps "aging" become more personalized and more relevant. This, in turn, helps break down the barrier between "we who are studying aging" and "they who are aged."

Secondly, in keeping with a principle of adult education, this approach recognizes the value of students' experiences. Webster's dictionary has defined experience as the knowledge, skill, or practice derived from direct observation of or participation in events that make up an individual's life. Experience involves the total person, including thoughts, sensations, feelings, and actions. As individuals mature, they accumulate an expanding reservoir of experience that can make them rich resources for other's learning as well as provide them a foundation on which to build new learning (Knowles 1978). The educator's challenge is to facilitate the students' optimum integration of their past experiences and current educational activities, thus maximizing their learning experience. This book uses three interrelated approaches to meet this challenge: the establishment of a supportive learning environment, experiential activities through which learning can take place, and group discussions and debriefing to reinforce that learning.

1. Establishment of a Supportive Learning Environment

As Brown (1971) has stated, for learning to take place at all, the learner must open up to new experiences, which always involves some risk that one will change. This ambivalence is always present, either to learn and grow or to maintain the security of the status quo. The learner ultimately makes two choices: whether to participate and at what level to participate. Because learning takes place through active involvement, the student's quality of participation is an important factor. It is not enough to be physically present; the learners must also engage their cognitive and affective processes.

Thus, it is the challenge for the instructor to create a learning environment in which the students will choose to involve themselves. Two areas for instructors to consider in establishing a supportive environment are the physical environment, and the instructor's roles as facilitator and role model.

a. Physical Setting

Most classroom environments are less than ideal. However, factors to consider include adequate lighting, avoidance of glare, comfortable temperature, a minimum of extraneous noises and distractions, and a seating arrangement that facilitates discussion. To the extent that these conditions are met, the learning environment is enhanced.

b. Instructor as Facilitator and Role Model

The instructor sets the tone for a climate that facilitates learning. The students should feel supported and accepted as well as challenged so that they will want to participate. However, they also need to feel secure in having the choice to decide their level of participation without fear of ridicule.

Throughout an activity, the teacher facilitates not only the learners' linking their past experiences with the activity at hand, but also their beginning to identify with it intellectually and emotionally as "their" experience. As part of this process, learners are supported in their participation, analysis, and discussion of their thoughts and feelings regarding the experience. Pullias and Young (1977) have said a teacher gives life and meaning to an activity so that it can become a meaningful part of the student's life and thought rather than remain separate and inapplicable to the problems of life.

Setting the stage for an experiential activity using mental imagery is important. This includes the teacher's verbal instructions, the learner's nonverbal responses, and the pacing of the activity. The teacher needs to use a quiet, well-modulated tone, speaking slowly and clearly. This initiates a feeling of tranquility and relaxation in the environment. The verbal directions should be paced according to the nonverbal responses of the participants. These initial directions, which include closing their eyes and slowly taking in and letting out a few deep breaths, are aimed at relaxing the learners and quieting and clearing their minds. This process facilitates their ability to focus their "mind's eye" on the subject of the activity and get involved in a real rather than detached way.

The instructor also serves as a role model by acknowledging each learner as a unique individual with experiences of value and by demonstrating good communication skills. Such skills include active listening, appropriate feedback, and empathy. In addition, it is vital that anyone who teaches gerontological content have expertise in the field, have positive attitudes toward aging, and be able to communicate genuine liking, interest, and concern for older people.

2. Experiential Activities

Experiential learning is a participative approach to education. It emphasizes a process of learning in which the participants become personally involved in the activities. Such learning involves the total person, including cognitive (intellectual processing of information, application of knowledge) and affective (feelings, emotional aspects of learning) domains of learning. Brown (1975) has defined this as confluent education, which means the flowing together of these two domains of learning, resulting in their interacting and influencing each other. This results in more holistic behavior on the part of the student because, as Brown says, it is impossible to have cognitive experience without an accompanying affective component and vice versa. Towle (1954) and Steinaker and Bell (1979) support the importance of the student's emotional involvement in the learning experience if it is to effect change in attitudes and behavior.

Tyler (1949) has said there is no way persons can be forced to change their attitudes. Shifts in attitudes develop as individuals process new knowledge and experiences with resulting insights and changes in perceptions toward the attitudinal target. Thus, the challenge in the educative process is not only to facilitate new attitudes and behaviors but also to develop learning activities that will motivate individuals to scrutinize the old attitudes and behaviors they brought with them into the classroom. These require self-evaluation to see if they are compatible with the learners' new knowledge, enhanced self-awareness, and insights.

a. Types of Experiential Activities

In the summary of their findings from learning process research, Darkenwald and Merriam (1982) report that active rather than passive participation in the learning activity brings about more permanent and meaningful learning. However, because learners control their level of participation, the activities must be of sufficient quality to capture their interest and motivate them to their optimum level of involvement. This requires a novel approach to the learning situation because, as Steinaker and Bell (1979) have reported, people become accustomed to routine stimuli (for example, lectures). Any unusual occurrence causes a re-alerting reaction that raises students' interest. These new experiences can help them relate to the issues and concepts that will be discussed and debriefed later in the activity, thus making learning relevant and meaningful.

The types of activities developed for this handbook are representative of a creative variety that can be developed to meet the growing need for educational activities that increase the awareness, sensitivity, and understanding of those who work with the elderly to help them promote and maintain the quality of their lives. The activities have been divided into four major categories and are listed by their chapter titles.

i. Mental Imagery: Future Self, Home Assessment, Relocation, Recognition Day, Family Interactions, An Unexpected Role, Reminiscing.

This teaching/learning approach involves having the students visualize in their mind's eye a place, situation, or event they either have experienced, are experiencing, or could experience. Experiences in the past and present evoke more affective responses than those visualized in the future because even though participants can "visualize" the situation or event, they have not yet "felt" it.

ii. Case Study: Needs and Services: Optimum Fit.

This teaching/learning method gives participants a written account of a particular situation and asks them to analyze the case, discuss the issues of the situation in a group, and decide on a problem-solving approach.

iii. Simulation: Pacing and Patience, Developing Trust, A Surprise Snack, Maintaining Mobility.

This educational approach puts learners in a situation that approximates a physical condition elderly people might have to face and requires the participants to handle the situation. It provides learners with an opportunity to cope with the physical and interrelated psychosocial aspects of aging.

iv. Analogies: First Impressions, Skin Sensitivity.

This teaching/learning approach uses one object to represent another, implying similarity between the two. The learners must be able to recognize the similarity so they will be able to interpret new information in light of prior knowledge. Thus, the analogy needs to be described at the beginning of the activity and references to it should be made throughout the lesson. This method can deepen the understanding of the information related to the subject.

b. Group Discussion and Debriefing Process

Group discussions and/or debriefing immediately following each activity are integral parts of the experiential learning process. These interactions with group members and the teacher provide an opportunity for participants to share and examine their experiences and discuss observations, ideas, feelings, and insights. Also, because group discussion promotes interaction among the members, it can be an effective setting to facilitate examination of attitudes and perceptions, receiving feedback, different points of view, and reinforcement for change. Steinaker and Bell (1979) have reported that interaction results in a pooling of resources, which provides for a greater understanding of the total experience.

Large groups are not as effective as small ones because interaction is limited and the more verbal participants usually try to dominate. If possible, break up a large class into smaller groups. Also, arrange the seats in a circle so that everyone can see the others. This promotes participation and enhances communication. Though the level of participation varies among group members, almost everyone becomes involved because they have just actively participated in a learning activity and want to discuss it.

Proper sequencing of the debriefing process encourages participation. The learners should complete individual worksheets first, then discuss the activity in small groups, and finally debrief as a class. This process gives them an opportunity to focus privately on their thoughts and feelings first, then decide what they want to share with the group and finally with the class.

Teachers have a facilitating role in this group process. If small groups are used, they can circulate as a resource person. It is usually better not to actually participate in any group as it changes the dynamics. When the participants regroup as a class, the teacher conducts a debriefing of the highlights of the participants' experiences. During this process, the teacher can enhance the participants' learning experiences by asking clarifying questions, giving empathetic feedback, promoting the merger of affective-cognitive learning, and integrating appropriate information to augment the participants' understanding of themselves, their class members, and older adults in relation to the processes of aging.

c. The Development of Empathy

White (1981) has said we can come closer to experiencing another individual's feelings when we have had similar feelings of our own. These experiential activities provide stimuli for students to actively engage in a learning process that focuses on their own experiences to increase their awareness and sensitivity to the universal experience of aging. This, then, can promote the development of empathy, the skill in communicating to others that they are truly understood.

Empathy is a skill that is learned. It is an active interpersonal process that includes identifying, acknowledging, accepting, and responding to another person's feelings. It involves an individual's ability to accurately understand the perceptions and feelings of another person and then convey that understanding back to the person. It is the foundation on which caregivers and service providers can build a helping relationship with older people. This relationship, in turn, can be the catalyst for promoting the elderly's optimal functioning.

Summary

The elderly population's growing need for care and services has been well-documented. An essential factor in meeting this need is the availability of caregivers and service providers who can interact effectively with older people and assist them in maintaining their quality of life. To do this optimally, these professional and nonprofessional caregivers and service providers need knowledge, positive attitudes, understanding, and skills. One barrier to acquiring these attributes is ageism, which is a reflection of American society's negative attitudes toward aging and the aged. Ageism predisposes individuals to avoid older people, perceive them unrealistically, and negate their individuality. This, in turn, prevents the elderly from receiving appropriate care and services. The need for creative gerontological teaching/learning experiences is evident.

An educational approach that has been successful in changing students' attitudes in a positive way toward older people includes three interrelated components: gerontological content; selected, supervised direct contact with the relatively well elderly; and an opportunity for debriefings with peers and the instructor. It has been suggested that this approach will be most effective in changing attitudes if it is used early in the learner's gerontological academic/work experience.

The experiential activities developed for this book build on these findings. Each activity includes gerontological content and is structured to promote teacher-facilitated discussion of the learners' experience. However, instead of having the students participate in a field work/clinical setting directly with older people, these activities are designed for classroom settings and involve the students' use of their own experiences. Ideally, these activities, which focus on enhancing understanding of older adults through awareness building and sensitization, would be used before the learner's clinical or work experience. This could promote the beginning of a positive shift in attitudes toward the elderly, which can then be continued through selected, direct experiences with older people. However, using the activities at any point in the teaching/learning continuum can enhance the participants' understanding of the aging process as it relates to themselves and older adults.

PART 1

PERCEPTIONS OF AGING

2 Anticipating Your Future Self

Rationale for Activity

Most people have been socialized, in varying degrees, to negative notions about aging: their own, their relatives', and the aging population's in general. Butler and Lewis (1982) have called this ageism, or the prejudices and stereotypes applied to older people strictly on the basis of their age. This stereotyping can be a major obstacle in health care and service providers' ability to work optimally with older people because it negates individuality, creates biases, and reduces objectivity. This, in turn, can result in inappropriate assessments of and delivery of services to the elderly. Therefore, it is important that those who work with older people examine their attitudes and feelings about aging and the aged which can influence their interactions with older adults. This two-part activity focuses on normal aging and its variations for different individuals as a means to sensitize participants to their perceptions of self and of older adults.

Participants: These activities are appropriate for graduate and undergraduate students, professionals, and paraprofessionals in mental health, social work, health care, gerontology, and adult education, other service providers, and volunteers.

Objectives

Upon completion of these activities participants will:

1. Be able to identify four general facts about elderly people.
2. Have an enhanced appreciation of the growing diversity among older individuals.

3. Have a heightened awareness of how past experiences with elderly people can influence their current and future expectations of aging and the aged.
4. Be able to give at least one example of how this activity will affect their interactions with older adults.

Class Size: Open. If a large class, it can be broken up into small groups (five to seven) so participants can compare and contrast their own "future" selves.

Time: Sixty to seventy-five minutes.
Activity #1, Future Self: Forty to fifty-five minutes (depending on size of class and debriefing format).

Ten minutes: introduction and activity
Thirty to forty-five minutes: debriefing (if break up into small discussion groups, allow fifteen minutes for compare and contrast, then spend the rest of the time debriefing as a class)

Activity #2, Experiences with Elderly People: Twenty minutes.

Five minutes: introduction and activity
Ten minutes: debriefing
Five minutes: evaluation

Materials:

Activity #1, Future Self: Future Self Worksheets or blank 8-1/2 × 11-inch papers.
Activity #2, Experiences with Elderly People: Experiences with Elderly People Worksheets, Evaluation Sheets.

Teaching Notes

1. This activity is based on one in which I participated and was led by Helen Monea (1976).
2. This exercise focuses on the person first, his or her environment second, social supports third, and activities fourth. The intent of the sequence is to get the participant to project into the future and to note spontaneous thoughts about aging and its many dimensions. In discussing these dimensions, the participants can increase their understanding of normal aging and its variations for different individuals.
3. Encourage participants to draw themselves with stick figures or any graphic interpretation, as well as draw their environment. Then they can be given the option of drawing or listing those in their social world and their activities. The act of drawing themselves helps them visualize and get in touch with the aging process.

The act of drawing their environment gets them in touch with their preference for geographic locations (open spaces versus city) and type of housing (one level versus high-rise).

4. As the participants share aspects of their "future selves:"
   a. Bring into focus the idea that though the aging process is inevitable throughout the life cycle, its impact is very individualized. Thus, everyone can optimize physical and psychosocial functioning by taking the responsibility to minimize the effect of age-related changes through developing good health practices and a supportive environment.
   b. Point out similarities and differences among the participants' expectations of their physical health, environment, social world, and activities and how this will make them even more individualized when they are eighty years old.
   c. Discuss how either positive or negative stereotypes about aging can affect attitudes and expectations regarding:
      i. the projection of their own future selves.
      ii. the delivery of health care and services to the present elderly population.
5. This is a most effective icebreaker at the beginning of a semester or workshop. It serves to begin to break down the "we who are not old" and "they who are old" barrier because it brings into focus that aging is a lifelong process and everybody is doing it! For many younger participants it's the first time they have associated aging with themselves. One twenty-two-year-old student said in her evaluation:

> *I had never thought of myself older. I was really surprised at how I pictured myself. I imagined myself still working at the age of seventy-five; this is probably because I've always worked and not working or having some regularly scheduled events in my life would probably drive me nuts. I'm a busy person and I don't anticipate that to change as I get older. I pictured everything to be close and convenient. I also pictured myself with grandchildren, which surprised me because I don't anticipate having children of my own. All of this has real implications on me as a gerontologist. Having a perspective of my own aging process will better able me to handle others further along in the aging process.*

Another example from a thirty-two-year-old health care professional:

> *When I described myself in the future, I saw me as being relatively healthy with no debilitating illnesses, spry, participating in social activities, active in sports, and living with only my spouse in a suburban home near our children (who visit regularly!). This was my Utopian version of how I wanted to be in my later years. I did not envision myself to be widowed, living in a nursing home, suffering from dementia, or*

isolated from my family and friends. Now, when I look at older people who are in this state, I will remind myself that they, too, never chose these losses, infirmities, or inactivity. When they were my age, they shared the same dreams and could only view themselves as eternally youthful. This exercise has helped to make me more reality-based toward my own aging, how to prepare for age-related changes, and be more emphatic toward those who are having to cope with some of the uninvited losses associated with aging.

6. Overall, participants usually enjoy this activity and generally their projections of their own aging are quite positive. They discover they are planning on more continuities than changes in their lives, still wanting control and choices. One participant looked at her future self and exclaimed, "Why, I'm still me on the inside, just changed on the outside."

Here is a very brief summary of participants' responses over the years I've conducted this activity.

a. Physical aging: Most participants have drawn happy faces. They are usually wearing glasses, whereas hearing aids are more difficult to accept. Chronic diseases have been realistically represented, especially if family members currently are coping with them. Mental illness and the dementias are the most dreaded diseases.

b. Environmental projections: Most participants projected living in the same geographic area, though some planned on returning to their birthplace. The participants were very clear in their desire to have their "own space," even though it would likely be smaller. Many are expecting to "scale down" in order to have minimal upkeep but they still want room for family and friends to visit and have similar environments, such as lots of windows, ground floor, small garden, and everything close and convenient. Many expressed the need for a "peaceful" environment, as too many people or too much activities would make them "nervous."

c. Relationships: Many participants had difficulty in projecting the loss of a spouse. It was something they recognized intellectually, but did not want to process emotionally. They looked forward to having more time to spend with family and friends they hoped would be of all ages. Many could not imagine growing old without a pet.

d. Activities: Most participants have projected themselves as keeping busy with activities they like to do and when they want to do them. Most professionals who have a license plan to keep it valid by taking the necessary continuing education. Overall, participants want to continue to contribute to their professions, volunteer for interesting community projects, expand their hobbies, do some traveling, and, for those who are currently very physically active, expect to adjust the pacing of their exercise programs.

e. On rare occasions, some people have initially refused to participate, saying they don't expect to live until they are seventy-five or eighty. I respond by saying that of course we can't guarantee our future. However, we all have choices as to whether we take steps to prepare optimally for it. Then I let these individuals decide if and how much they want to participate. Usually they get involved, if not about their personal aging, then in the group discussion.

Introduction to Activity #1: Future Self

1. The process of aging is inevitable as we progress along the life cycle. We're all aging every second of our lives. As evidence, we are older now than when we entered this room! "Aging" is not something that "happens" just to old people. It is not a disease; rather, it is a lifelong process. The only difference between young people and elderly people is that the elderly have been aging longer.
2. Understanding this lifelong process of aging has importance for us as professionals in our interactions with older adults and in our personal lives with our families and for ourselves.
3. Some subjects—like statistics—can be learned on an intellectual basis. However, when we are preparing to work with older people we can benefit from learning about them and trying to get some idea of what it may be like to be older.
4. In our daily lives most of us are very busy dealing with the present, including maintaining our health, carrying out our activities of daily living, and trying to balance our education and/or work with other activities. So we hardly have the time or the interest to dwell on thoughts or feelings about our future selves . . . until today. Now you are being given the time to project into the future and think about your own expectations of aging as one way to increase your sensitivity to those who have preceded us in reaching the age of between seventy-five and eighty years old.

Instructions to Participants

1. Place your Future Self Worksheet in front of you.
2. Close your eyes, take a few deep breaths, and block out the people around you.
3. Begin to project yourself into the future and in your mind's eye visualize yourself as you imagine you will be when you are between seventy-five and eighty years old. Think about how you will look,

where you will be, who will be with you, and what you'll be doing. (Allow participants one to two minutes.)
4. Open your eyes and focus on your worksheet.
5. Please respond to the following questions.

Future Self Questions

1. In square 1, first draw *how* you visualize yourself *physically*. Taking into consideration your family's health history as well as your current physical state, do you anticipate:
   a. Wrinkles: Laugh lines? Frown lines?
   b. Hair color: Gray? Colored? Thinning?
   c. Teeth: Own? Dentures?
   d. Sensory decrements: Visual? Hearing?
   Now, consider if you will be:
   e. Coping with a chronic disease: Arthritis? Heart disease? High blood pressure? Diabetes?
   f. Able to function independently?
2. In square 2, draw *where* you visualize yourself *living*, geographically and in what type of housing:
   a. Geographical location:
      i. Where you are living now?
      ii. If you expect to live in another area, what would be different (city to country, cold to hot climate, desert to ocean, etc.)?
   b. Type of living arrangements:
      i. Your own house? Townhouse? Condo?
      ii. Rent an apartment?
      iii. Retirement community?
3. In square 3, draw or list *whom* you visualize will be in your *social world* and their proximity.
   a. Members of social world:
      i. Relatives: Spouse? Children? Grandchildren? Brothers? Sisters? Cousins?
      ii. Friends: Your age? Younger people? Old friends? New friends? Confidant?
      iii. Acquaintances: At work? Through volunteer work? Social organizations? Religious activities?
      iv. Pets: Dog? Cat? Bird? Fish? Rabbit?
   b. Considering all these members of your social world,
      i. With whom would you like to live?
      ii. Whom would you like close by?
      iii. How will you keep in touch with the others?
4. In square 4, list *what activities* you visualize would like to be doing:
   a. Work: Do you anticipate being employed? Full or part time? Regular or flexible scheduling?

b. Hobbies: Lifelong interests? New ventures?
c. Recreation: Active? Observer? Regular exercise program?
d. Travel?
e. Volunteer activities: Church? Community programs?
f. Educational seminars: More expertise in current field? New interests?
g. Transportation: Do you anticipate having your own car?

Transition to Debriefing

Now that you've met your future self, I would like you to share some of your anticipations so that you can become aware of your projected similarities and differences as well as compare yourselves to the current elderly population. Let's begin.

Debriefing

1. Physical Self (Square #1)

a. How many of you anticipate having wrinkles? Laugh lines? Frown lines?

Wrinkles, folds, and lines in the face and neck are a part of normal aging and result from a combination of factors: loss of supporting subcutaneous fat, diminished elasticity in the skin, and pull of gravity on the tissue (Ham and Marcy 1983; Ebersole and Hess 1985).

b. How many of you antipate having gray hair?

About 50 percent of people over fifty have gray or graying hair. Hair usually becomes thinner and more sparse. Race, sex, sex-linked genes and hormonal influences determine the amount of hair and the changes that occur throughout life (Ham and Marcy 1983; Ebersole and Hess 1985).

c. How many of you anticipate having your own teeth? Dentures?

There is some normal deterioration of the pulp that surrounds teeth and supplies the blood for their nutrition. The incidence of periodontal disease and prevalence of tooth loss steadily increases with age. Men have more periodontal disease than women. Currently, among older people between fifty-five and seventy-four years old, only 50 percent have any of their own teeth. However, regular dental care can deter periodontal disease and loss of teeth (Ham and Marcy 1983; Harris 1978). Thus, it is likely that more older people in the future will retain their own teeth.

d. How many of you anticipate having some sensory decrements? Visual? Hearing?

Visual changes do occur with age and after age forty-five, increasingly more people experience these changes. At sixty years old, 65 percent of people have some change, and at seventy-five years old, 85 percent have some change (Harris 1978). These changes include a reduction in the amount of light arriving on the retina and the eye taking longer to respond to changes in light (Ham and Marcy 1983). A supportive environment including increased lighting and allowing elderly people more time to adapt to changes in light can help them to compensate for these visual changes. In addition, the lens in the eye becomes less elastic, resulting in presbyopia or the inability to focus sharply on close objects (Ham and Marcy 1983). It is important to have yearly eye examinations so that changes can be monitored, corrective lens prescribed, and diseases such as cataracts and glaucoma detected early and treated.

Hearing changes are rare under thirty; then there is a marked increase in people who experience some hearing loss. In the forty-five–to–fifty-four age group, 19 percent have some impairment. In the sixty-five–to–seventy-four age group, 40 percent have some impairment. In the seventy-five–to–seventy-nine age group, 75 percent have some impairment (Harris 1978). Degeneration of nerve and hearing apparatus in the inner ear causes presbycusis, which affects the high tones and consonants (*f*'s, *j*'s, *th*'s). Vowels that have a lower pitch are more easily heard (Ham and Marcy 1983). As with vision, regular hearing examinations can evaluate changes and determine their causes, and corrective measures can be prescribed.

e. In addition to sensory impairments, how many of you anticipate having to cope with chronic disease conditions? Arthritis? Heart disease? High blood pressure? Diabetes?

Seventy-two percent of people between forty-five and sixty-four have one or more chronic conditions. This increases to 86 percent of people when they are over sixty-five. Though multiple chronic conditions are common among the elderly, most of these people still manage to carry out their activities of daily living (Harris 1978).

A prevalent chronic condition is arthritis, which affects 40 percent of people over sixty-five years old. Some older people have degenerative or osteoarthritic changes, particularly in the weight-bearing joints, but this doesn't significantly impair their functioning. Others have rheumatoid arthritis, an inflammatory condition of the joints that has a significant affect on joint function (Ham and Marcy 1983).

Three major cardiovascular diseases prevail in the older population. Twenty-seven percent of people over sixty-five have coronary heart disease; 39 percent have hypertension; and 12 percent have arteriosclerosis. However, it has been demonstrated that screening for high blood pressure, weight reduction, limited fat intake, and exercise are factors in the reduction of deaths from these diseases (Ham, Kerzner, and Smith 1983).

The incidence of diabetes rises with age. It prevails in 16 percent of people over sixty-five and 25 percent of people over eighty-five. These figures are steadily rising because people with diabetes are living longer, the increasing prevalence of obesity in middle and later years can promote the onset of diabetes, and there are more extensive efforts to detect diabetes (Williams 1983). However, once diagnosed, diabetes can be treated with diet and/or medication, weight control, and a regular exercise program.

f. Do you expect to be able to function independently?

In the community, over 80 percent of older Americans report no limitation of mobility (Harris 1978). Most elderly people live independent and active lives. However, with advanced age, the likelihood of illness does increase and at any point in time, approximately 5 percent of the elderly population over sixty-five require twenty-four-hour-care in a long-term care facility (Harris 1978).

2. Environment (Square #2)

a. Geographic location:
  i. How many of you plan to stay where you are now?
  ii. How many of you plan to move to another area? City to country or vice versa? Cold to hot climate or vice versa?

Except for a small number of highly visible persons who migrate to the sun belt, older people move at about 50 percent of the rate of young people. The "graying" of the suburbs is more than in the metropolitan areas. This increase of older people in outlying areas can present special problems for transportation, services, and facilities for less mobile people.

b. What type of living arrangement would you prefer?
  i. Own home? Townhouse? Condo?
  ii. Rent an apartment?
  iii. Retirement community?

Sixty-six percent of the elderly living in cities and 90 percent of those in rural areas own their homes. Most of these older Americans have lived in their present dwellings for more than twenty years (Atchley 1987). However, with increasing age, elderly people are more inclined to relinquish their homes. Congregate living and multilevel care retirement facilities are a growing alternative to support semi-independent lifestyles.

3. Social World (Square #3)

a. Whom do you project will be in your social world?
  i. Relatives: Spouse? Children? Grandchildren? Brothers or sisters? Cousins?
  ii. Friends: Your age? Younger people? Old friends? New friends? Confidant?
  iii. Acquaintances: At work? Through volunteer work? Social organizations? Religious activities?
  iv. Pets: Dog? Cat? Bird? Fish? Rabbit?

b. How do you project the proximity of these people in your social world:
   i. With whom would you like to live?
   ii. Whom would you like close by?
   iii. How will you keep in touch with the others?

In relation to marital status, most older women are widows while most older men are married. Contributing to this fact is the shorter life expectancy of males, the tendency for men to marry younger women, and the higher remarriage rate of widowers (Harris 1978). Relationships with adult children are very important to older people. However, the majority prefer to live near, rather than with their children and then interact with them frequently (Atchley 1987). Most elderly people promote and maintain their intergenerational relationships.

Friends provide important support. However, a confidant, a person in whom you can confide and talk about yourself or your problems is the most significant relationship, especially in the later years. It is usually a spouse, adult child, or friend. The maintenance of this stable, intimate relationship seems to serve as the single most important variable in protecting individuals' morale and mental stability against various social losses associated with aging and in promoting their effective coping (Kimmel 1980).

Pets offer social and sensory stimuli and are an important source of companionship. In addition, the responsibility of caring for a pet can give older people a sense of purpose and a reason for establishing a daily routine.

4. Activities (Square #4)

a. Work: Do you anticipate being employed? Full time? Part time? Regular or flexible scheduling?
b. What hobbies? Lifelong interest? New ventures?
c. What types of recreation? Active? Observer? Regular exercise program?
d. How many anticipate traveling?
e. What volunteer activities do you project yourself doing? Church? Community programs?
f. Do you anticipate attending educational seminars? More expertise in current field? New interests?

Labor force participation declines for men and women beginning in their early fifties. For men, there are significant drops occurring at age sixty-two and sixty-five, when people become eligible for social security benefits, and again at age seventy. The pattern for women dropping out of the labor force is not so clear yet (Atchley 1987). The percentage of part-time employment among older workers is high; however, overall, the positions are usually low-paying (Harris 1978).

Retirement from full-time work provides people with more options on how to spend their time. Most retirees appear to continue their preretiree patterns and levels of activity, but allocation of time for each activity is changed. More time is spent fulfilling obligations of daily living, such as shopping, banking, puttering around the house, writing letters, and visiting with friends (Robinson 1986). Thirty-five percent of older Americans' leisure is spent at home with activities such as watching television, visiting, reading, and handiwork. Gardening and walking are the only outdoor activities that increase with age. Travel is limited to those who can afford the expense (Atchley 1980).

In relation to community activities, church membership is the most common for older people, especially after seventy-five. However, the elderly's roles in the church and its response to their needs varies widely (Atchley 1987). Opportunities for community volunteerism are growing. Federally funded programs include Retired Senior Volunteer Program (RSVP), Foster Grandparent Program (FGP), Senior Companion Program (SCP), and Service Corps of Retired Executives (SCORE). Also, the American Association of Retired Persons (AARP) offers its members an extensive range of volunteer opportunities.

People who consider themselves lifelong learners continue to pursue educational activities in formal and informal settings (Peterson 1983). Educational resources include radio, television, videocassettes, community libraries, schools, churches, hospitals, and colleges. An excellent program designed specifically for senior citizens is Elderhostel. This program is held at various college and university campuses around the world and offers older people the opportunity to combine travel, education, and socialization at a low cost.

g. How many of you anticipate having your own car?

The automobile is the primary source of transportation for all age groups and becomes increasingly important as a person ages. However, forty percent of people over sixty-five do not own a car. This has a major effect on an older person's mobility as public transportation may not be available and taxis are too expensive (Harris 1978). In some cities, Dial-a-Ride services are available for the elderly. However, more needs to be done in this important area, as available transportation is a key factor in maintaining the elderly's independence.

Transition to Activity #2: Experiences with Older Adults

Now that you have met your future selves, I'd like you to consider for a moment the people in your lives who have influenced these projections.

Instructions to Participants

1. Look at your worksheet once again and review the components of your future self.

2. Now close your eyes for a moment and think about people over sixty-five years old with whom you have interacted or about whom you have knowledge:
   a. in your personal life: Relatives? Friends? Acquaintances?
   b. in your school or work life: Colleagues? Teachers? Employers?
   c. in public life: Local, national, world leaders? Artists? Entertainers?
3. Now, on your Experiences with Elderly People Worksheet list all of these people (allow two to three minutes).
4. Next, based on your experiences with these elderly people, did they represent for you a positive or negative image of old age? Indicate by writing a number from one to five opposite their names, one being a negative image and five being a positive image (allow one to two minutes).

Debriefing

1. Each of us has an individualized collection of experiences with older people. Some of those experiences have been positive and some negative.
   a. How many of you have more positive than negative experiences with older people in your life?
   b. How many of you have had more negative experiences?
   c. Would any of you like to share your experiences? (Allow five to ten minutes, depending on available time).
2. Thank you for sharing your experiences with older people. For each of you, your experiences have been unique, as have been your responses to them. For most of you, the recollections that you have shared have not been neutral ones. They have been either positive or negative and you expressed them with feeling. Such significant experiences influence your expectations of your future selves and your perceptions of current elderly people with whom you interact. It is important to stay aware of these dynamics so you can monitor them. This self-monitoring of your perceptions can promote the individualization of the elderly with whom you interact.

Summary

You've certainly expressed the uniqueness and commonalities of your expectations of aging. Also, as a group, you have demonstrated your current diversity and if you were to get together twenty years from now, you could expect to be even more so!

Though there are inevitable physical and social changes associated with aging, everyone can choose how they let those changes affect their lives. For example, now that you have "met" yourself in the future, you can begin today to take steps toward optimizing that future by:

1. Maintaining what you like about yourselves.
2. Changing what you don't like.
3. Exploring ways to promote and maintain your optimum health.
4. Starting to develop options and opportunities for your future environments, social relationships, and activities.
5. Keeping updated on the latest research and resources in the field of aging.

I hope that by participating in this activity you have increased your knowledge of facts on aging, enhanced your appreciation of the growing diversity among older people, and heightened your awareness of how your past experience with elderly people can influence your current and future expectations of aging and the aged.

Evaluation

Please take a few moments now to complete the evaluation.

Future Self, Worksheet	
I. Physical	II. Environmental
III. Relationships	IV. Social Activities

Experiences with Elderly People, Worksheet

Elderly person (over 65 years)	Number of years you've known person	Connection			Image of Old Age				
		Personal	Professional	Public Figure	Neg 1	2	Mixed 3	4	Pos 5

Future Self, Evaluation

1. Identify four general facts about elderly people.

   _____

   _____

   _____

   _____

2. Did this activity enhance your appreciation of how people become more diverse as they age?

Not much		Some		A lot
1	2	3	4	5

3. Did this activity heighten your awareness of how your past experiences with elderly people can influence both your current and future expectations of aging and the aged?

Not much		Some		A lot
1	2	3	4	5

4. Give one example of how this activity will affect your interactions with older adults.

3 Needs and Services: Optimum Fit

Rationale for Activity

Health care and human service providers for the elderly inevitably become involved at some level in decision-making processes regarding the provision of services to older persons. The goal of such decision making is to achieve an optimum fit between the elderly client's needs and available services. This is a multidimensional challenge that usually includes many interactions among the service providers and between them and the client. Because of their varying life experiences and education, service providers have different attitudes, perceptions, and biases. These dynamics need to be constantly monitored or they can unduly influence service providers' assessment of and care plan for their elderly clients.

This activity provides participants with an opportunity to enhance self-awareness of their "selective" perceptions. This in turn can increase their self-monitoring abilities during the process of assessing older adults and working with them to develop a supportive plan that will promote their optimum functioning.

Participants: This activity is appropriate for graduate and undergraduate students and professionals in mental health, social work, health care, and gerontology.

Objectives

Upon completion of this activity participants will:

1. Be able to identify five major categories of services that may be used to assist older adults.

2. Have an increased self-awareness of how their life experiences and education as helping professionals can influence their perceptions of client's need for services.
3. Have an increased appreciation of the value of group process in selecting services for elderly clients.
4. Have an increased understanding of why an older person may be ambivalent toward accepting services.
5. Be able to give at least one example of how this activity will affect their interactions with older adults.

Class Size: Open. During second part of exercise, divide class into groups of six to eight.

Time: Fifty to sixty minutes depending on size of class.

>   Five minutes: introduction
>   Fifteen minutes: individual assessment and recording
>   Fifteen minutes: group assessment and recording
>   Ten minutes: group reports and debriefing
>   Ten minutes: summary
>   Five minutes: evaluation

Materials: Case Study, Needs, and Services: Optimum Fit Worksheets for participants, group reporters, and teacher, Evaluation Sheets.

Teaching Notes

1. This activity uses a case-study approach to focus on the dynamics involved in a team decision-making process for the delivery of services to the elderly. It consists of three parts:
   a. Each participant reviews the case study on Mr. Smith and selects the services he is perceived to need.
   b. The participants divide into small groups and compare and contrast their individually selected services, negotiate the differences, and arrive at a consensus for the services they perceive Mr. Smith to need.
   c. Each group reports its perceptions to the class. If time permits, a class consensus of needed services for Mr. Smith is attempted.
2. This activity stimulates lively discussions. Most group participants are very articulate in defending their selection of prioritized services. Initially, they seem quite surprised that there can be strong, differing opinions from their colleagues. Then you can observe the varying responses of the members as the negotiating process proceeds to a consensus.
3. The selection of groups for the second part of this activity can vary according to the educational backgrounds of the participants. If

they are all students or graduates of one profession, they can self-select their own groups. If the participants represent several professions, you can either have a representative from each profession in each group or keep each profession in a group. Both methods of group selection will enhance class awareness regarding the influence of professional education on their perceptions. In the former, it will usually become apparent during the group assessment. In the latter it will usually become more evident as each group reporter gives a summary.

4. Though the case study for this activity provides only an overview of Mr. Smith's physical and psychosocial functioning, it provides enough information for the participants to get an understanding of and feeling for Mr. Smith. My purposes in keeping the case study brief were to promote a relatively fast-paced activity so some of the participants would likely experience some frustration because of the lack of time and information to do a "thorough and thoughtful" assessment and negotiate in a manner that would result in all the group members being satisfied with the prioritized services.

5. Inevitably, after reading the case study, some of the participants ask me for more information about Mr. Smith. I do not give them any further information. Rather, I write the questions down and discuss their relevance at an appropriate point in the debriefing.

Introduction to Activity

Regardless of which roles you may have in the fields of health or human services, you will likely become involved at some level in decision-making processes regarding the provision of services to the elderly. The goal of such decision making is to achieve an optimum fit between client's needs and available services. This is a multidimensional challenge involving many interactions among service providers and between them and the client.

Because of service providers' varying life experiences and education, they bring different perceptions, attitudes, and biases into the client assessment and care plan process. It is important to be aware of these factors and the possibility of them having an undue influence on decision making processes.

This activity offers you an opportunity to enhance your self-awareness. This in turn can increase your ability to monitor your perceptions so that your decision-making will be more objective and reflect your best professional self.

Instructions to Participants

1. Place your case study and Needs and Services Worksheet in front of you.

2. Let's review the major service categories on the worksheet before you begin your selection of services for Mr. Smith.

   Basic services: Include those needed by all persons in the community, including the elderly.

   Supportive services: Include services to help older people retain their established living arrangements when they can no longer do so through their own efforts.

   Adjustment and integrative services: Include services to help older people cope with legal problems, participate in community life, adjust to new social roles, and retain and use their capabilities.

   Congregate care services: Include services to provide elderly people with impaired functioning a therapeutic, supportive environment.

   Protective services: Include services to protect the civil rights and personal welfare of older persons who are subject to neglect and exploitation by relatives, friends, the community, or themselves.

3. Now review Mr. Smith's case and select all the services you think he needs. Base your selections on the premise that all the services listed are available. Mark your selections on your worksheet in the "client needs" column (allow ten to twelve minutes).

4. Now, unfortunately, you have just been notified that because of new budgetary constraints, any client is only eligible for five services, regardless of need. So from "client needs" column, select five and prioritize them (one being the most needed and five being the least) in "priority" column (allow three minutes).

5. Now you have been told that the final decision for services to this client will be decided at a multidisciplinary staff meeting. You are to go to the staff meeting now.

6. Divide up into groups of six to eight and do the following:
   a. Compare and contrast the services you have selected for Mr. Smith.
   b. Negotiate and arrive at a consensus regarding the five services. Then prioritize them (one being highest priority and five being lowest priority) on your Group Reporter's Worksheet.
   c. Select a reporter to report to the class on your group's selection of priority services.
   d. You have fifteen minutes to reach a consensus.

Debriefing

Call on each group's reporter to give a two-to-three-minute summary, which you can record on your teacher's worksheet.

Suggestions for the Debriefing Process

1. As the group reporters take their turns to summarize their groups' recommendations for services for Mr. Smith, encourage their comments regarding their groups' process of arriving at a consensus. Sample questions include:
   a. How did the personal and professional experiences of the group members influence their prioritization of services?
   b. How were the differences resolved?

   Responses to these questions helps increase both the participants' self-awareness and their appreciation of group process.

2. As the group reporters present their selection of services, you can record them on the teacher's Needs and Services Worksheet to facilitate your summary of the prioritized services. If time permits, you may wish to try and achieve a class consensus for services for Mr. Smith.

3. After you have finished your discussion on the class' selection of services, ask if any participants have ambivalent feelings about their group's selection of services and, if given the opportunity, would like to reconsider their choices.

   > Responses may include: *Yes, I was too rushed to think it through. I just went along with the group. I was the least experienced in the group and didn't feel I had an equal voice. I got caught up in the process of reaching a consensus. I should have asked more questions.*

   Such responses can be used to illustrate and discuss the point that clients frequently have similar feelings of ambivalence after they have accepted a plan developed to enhance their physical and psychosocial functioning. Their ambivalence, frequently expressed by either active or passive resistance, can be the result of many interrelated factors, including:

   a. Not wanting to change their lifestyle. Erikson (1963) has said that the possessor of ego integrity is willing to defend his lifestyle against all physical and economic threats. People become emotionally vested in the behavior patterns they have developed to enable them to survive and are resistant to change (Brill 1985).
   b. Having had negative experiences with "helping" persons in the past but not wanting to voice them to a perceived "authority figure" (Nelsen 1975).
   c. Not wanting to ask questions and appear stupid.
   d. Having a cultural background that makes accepting help very difficult.

To minimize retrospective resistance, it is important that the helping person acknowledge that ambivalent feelings are normal, provide an opportunity for the client to express doubt, ask questions, and discuss the limitations as well as the benefits of the offered services (Perlman 1957). The issue is not whether clients will have questions; rather, it is will they feel free to voice them (Nelsen 1975).

Remember your experience today and your acknowledged ambivalence, yet a consensus was reached. Such a consensus may not hold up tomorrow. So it may be with plans you help develop for clients unless you acknowledge their feelings and discuss them as an integral part of the planning process.

Summary

We have discussed five major categories of services that can be used to assist older adults. They are basic services, supportive services, adjustment and integrative services, congregate care services, and protective services.

You have demonstrated in your individual and group selection of services for Mr. Smith how different backgrounds and experiences can contribute in a major way both to perceptions of clients' needs and to subsequent selection of services to meet those needs. We need to be aware of these influences so we can monitor them during our assessments of older people.

As you recognized, your information on Mr. Smith was quite brief. Some of you asked for additional input. In a real-life situation you would indeed need much more information. It is most important that a careful, comprehensive medical, nursing, and psychosocial evaluation be carried out before any care plan is made and services recommended. The information must be organized in a systematic way that would be helpful in identifying specific long-term care services (Williams 1983). A comprehensive review of assessment guides for the elderly has been published by the Kanes (1981), who are recognized leaders in the field.

Any services we initiate for our clients will have a ripple effect in their lives, even a relatively simple service.

For example: Initiation of Dial-a-Ride to take a client to the doctor:

Positive ripple effect—the person no longer has to rely on friends, so feels more independent.

Negative ripple effects—the person no longer has a regular reason to contact friends, thus has reduced socialization, and also has less flexibility because Dial-a-Ride is on tight time schedule.

Thus, the effect of intervention in an elderly person's life must be comprehensively assessed because, as we discussed before, there are limitations and benefits.

As you experienced today, participating in a group made you rethink your prioritized services and increased your objectivity. The use of case management is one group approach that promotes the filtering out of perceptual biases, a careful and comprehensive evaluation, and the assessment of implications of a service intervention. It involves a group decision process involving a multidisciplinary team. This team develops an individualized care plan based on clients' needs, personal and community resources, *and* the client's approval. It emphasizes coordination of services to ensure the most comprehensive program to meet client needs (Austin 1983). An excellent handbook on planning and administering case management programs for the elderly has been published by Steinberg and Carter (1982), recognized experts in this field. Case management programs are supported because this interdisciplinary group approach meets the complex interrelated physical and psychosocial needs of the elderly (Grau 1984).

Finally, yet certainly important, we have experienced and discussed how ambivalent feelings regarding the introduction of change into older people's lives needs to be acknowledged and discussed. Such a discussion should occur among professionals and between professionals and their elderly clients in order to have a plan with an "optimum fit" between the clients' needs and available services. Such a plan will be more acceptable and used by the clients. Thus, they will be helped to maintain their highest level of physical and psychosocial functioning in their appropriate environment.

Evaluation

Please take a few moments now to complete the evaluation.

Needs and Services: Optimum Fit
Case Study

Mr. Smith is a sixty-seven-year-old retired army sergeant. He is still living in the apartment he and his wife occupied at the time of her death five months ago. The apartment has deteriorated steadily. The landlord has raised the rent in an attempt to get Mr. Smith to move, but he chose to pay the increase.

Mr. Smith is able to care for himself but shows little motivation to do so. His mobility is somewhat limited because of a shattered ankle bone incurred during World War II. He is quite deaf and does not have a hearing aid. Mr. Smith has a hernia that is bothering him, but he procrastinates going to the hospital to have surgery. Mr. Smith appears to do minimum eating and maximum drinking. His main activity of the day is walking down to the corner liquor store.

Apparently he and his wife were heavy drinkers, but since her death his drinking has steadily increased. He says all their friends "shoved me aside when Millie died. I have nobody who cares about me now. Oh, I have fair-weather friends who come and eat my food, then they're on their way leaving a mess behind." He has alienated his neighbors because of his temper when he is drunk. Recently he has been jailed for being drunk on the street.

Mr. Smith's dog, Sam, died last month. The neighbors say Mr. Smith did not care for the dog as well as his wife had. Mr. Smith has no children or known relatives.

Mr. Smith said he would love to leave the area and "get on a boat and travel like I used to do in the service—like going to China. There's nothing for me here. But then, I have so much stuff here. Millie bought it all years ago. It's all I have left." "We used to go out and dance. I'd like to be with people more."

Needs and Services: Optimum Fit, Participant's Worksheet

Services and Programs for Older Adults Living in the Community	Individual Professional Assessment	
	Client Needs	Priority
Basic Services		
1. *Housing* a. Home assessment for safety/psychosocial dynamics		
b. Subsidized by Dept. of Housing and Urban Development (HUD)		
c. Board and Care: Twenty-four-hr. supervision for ambulatory elderly		
2. *Financial Assistance:* SSI (Supplemental Security Income), MediCal		
3. *Out-patient Medical Care:* including dental care, eye examination, hearing test, regular physical examination, diagnostic screening tests		
4. *Mental Health Services:* evaluation and counseling		
5. *Nutrition* a. Food stamps		
b. Congregate meal sites in community		
c. Public Health Dept.—nutrition counseling		
Other:		
Supportive Services		
1. *Home-Help Services* a. Homemaker Service: light housekeeping, cooking, run errands, do shopping, provide escort service		
b. Household Handyman: household repair, seasonal tasks including changing screens, yard work, moving furniture		
2. *Home calls by doctor for evaluation and diagnosis*		
3. *Visiting Nurse Service*		
4. *Rehabilitation Support Groups* a. Alcoholics Anonymous		
b. American Cancer Society		
c. Arthritis Foundation		
d. Heart Association		
Other		
5. *Friendly Visitor*		
6. *Daily Telephone Reassurance Service*		
7. *Meals on Wheels*		
8. *Home Delivery:* groceries, medicines		
9. *Transportation*		
10. *Respite Care*		
Other:		

Needs and Services: Optimum Fit, Participant's Worksheet (Continued)

Services and Programs for Older Adults Living in the Community	Individual Professional Assessment	
	Client Needs	Priority
Adjustment and Integrative Services/Programs		
1. Consumer Protection		
a. State Dept. of Consumer Affairs: investigates violation of laws; education		
b. Public Health Dept.: investigates environmental health hazards		
2. Legal Aid		
a. Lawyer's Referral Service: legal advice, low fee		
b. Legal Aid Foundation: civil law only (housing, estate planning)		
c. U.S. Dept. of Labor: protects against age discrimination		
3. Information and Referral to available services and programs		
4. Retirement Counseling		
5. Senior Citizen Center		
6. RSVP (Retired Senior Volunteer Program)		
7. Gray Panthers (advocates for older people as national resource)		
8. AARP (American Association of Retired Persons)		
9. Foster Grandparents		
10. Mobile Library Unit		
Other:		
Congregate Care Services		
1. Adult Foster Care: elderly live with surrogate family		
2. Adult Day Care Center: discussion groups, congregate meals, podiatrist, barber, beautician, library, classes, day trips		
3. Adult Day Hospital: day care plus physical therapy, treatment for chronic illnesses, skilled nursing care, dental services		
Other:		
Protective Services		
1. Power of Attorney (regular/durable; property/health care)		
2. Adult Protective Services: elder abuse		
3. Public Guardianship/Conservatorship: when person declared incompetent		

Needs and Services: Optimum Fit, Group Reporter's Worksheet

Services and Programs for Older Adults Living in the Community	Team Professional Assessment	
	Client Needs	Priority
Basic Services		
1. *Housing* a. Home assessment for safety/psychosocial dynamics		
b. Subsidized by Dept. of Housing and Urban Development (HUD)		
c. Board and Care: Twenty-four-hr. supervision for ambulatory elderly		
2. *Financial Assistance:* SSI (Supplemental Security Income), MediCal		
3. *Out-patient Medical Care:* including dental care, eye examination, hearing test, regular physical examination, diagnostic screening tests		
4. *Mental Health Services:* evaluation and counseling		
5. *Nutrition* a. Food stamps		
b. Congregate meal sites in community		
c. Public Health Dept.—nutrition counseling		
Other:		
Supportive Services		
1. *Home-Help Services* a. Homemaker Service: light housekeeping, cooking, run errands, do shopping, provide escort service		
b. Household Handyman: household repair, seasonal tasks including changing screens, yard work, moving furniture		
2. *Home calls by doctor for evaluation and diagnosis*		
3. *Visiting Nurse Service*		
4. *Rehabilitation Support Groups* a. Alcoholics Anonymous		
b. American Cancer Society		
c. Arthritis Foundation		
d. Heart Association		
Other		
5. *Friendly Visitor*		
6. *Daily Telephone Reassurance Service*		
7. *Meals on Wheels*		
8. *Home Delivery:* groceries, medicines		
9. *Transportation*		
10. *Respite Care*		
Other:		

Needs and Services: Optimum Fit, Group Reporter's Worksheet (Continued)

Services and Programs for Older Adults Living in the Community	Team Professional Assessment	
	Client Needs	Priority
Adjustment and Integrative Services/Programs		
1. *Consumer Protection* a. State Dept. of Consumer Affairs: investigates violation of laws; education		
b. Public Health Dept.: investigates environmental health hazards		
2. *Legal Aid*		
a. Lawyer's Referral Service: legal advice, low fee		
b. Legal Aid Foundation: civil law only (housing, estate planning)		
c. U.S. Dept. of Labor: protects against age discrimination		
3. *Information and Referral to available services and programs*		
4. *Retirement Counseling*		
5. *Senior Citizen Center*		
6. *RSVP (Retired Senior Volunteer Program)*		
7. *Gray Panthers* (advocates for older people as national resource)		
8. *AARP* (American Association of Retired Persons)		
9. *Foster Grandparents*		
10. *Mobile Library Unit*		
Other:		
Congregate Care Services		
1. *Adult Foster Care:* elderly live with surrogate family		
2. *Adult Day Care Center:* discussion groups, congregate meals, podiatrist, barber, beautician, library, classes, day trips		
3. *Adult Day Hospital:* day care plus physical therapy, treatment for chronic illnesses, skilled nursing care, dental services		
Other:		
Protective Services		
1. *Power of Attorney* (regular/durable; property/health care)		
2. *Adult Protective Services:* elder abuse		
3. *Public Guardianship/Conservatorship:* when person declared incompetent		

Needs and Services: Optimum Fit, Teacher's Debriefing Sheet

Services and Programs for Older Adults Living in the Community	Teams' Professional Assessment & Priorities			
	1	2	3	4
Basic Services				
1. Housing a. Home assessment for safety/psychosocial dynamics				
b. Subsidized by Dept. of Housing and Urban Development (HUD)				
c. Board and Care: Twenty-four-hr. supervision for ambulatory elderly				
2. *Financial Assistance:* SSI (Supplemental Security Income), MediCal				
3. *Out-patient Medical Care:* including dental care, eye examination, hearing test, regular physical examination, diagnostic screening tests				
4. *Mental Health Services:* evaluation and counseling				
5. Nutrition a. Food stamps				
b. Congregate meal sites in community				
c. Public Health Dept.—nutrition counseling				
Other:				
Supportive Services				
1. *Home-Help Services* a. Homemaker Service: light housekeeping, cooking, run errands, do shopping, provide escort service				
b. Household Handyman: household repair, seasonal tasks including changing screens, yard work, moving furniture				
2. *Home calls by doctor for evaluation and diagnosis*				
3. *Visiting Nurse Service*				
4. *Rehabilitation Support Groups* a. Alcoholics Anonymous				
b. American Cancer Society				
c. Arthritis Foundation				
d. Heart Association				
Other				
5. *Friendly Visitor*				
6. *Daily Telephone Reassurance Service*				
7. *Meals on Wheels*				
8. *Home Delivery:* groceries, medicines				
9. *Transportation*				
10. *Respite Care*				
Other:				

Needs and Services: Optimum Fit, Teacher's Debriefing Sheet (Continued)

Services and Programs for Older Adults Living in the Community	Teams' Professional Assessments & Priorities			
	1	2	3	4
Adjustment and Integrative Services/Programs				
1. *Consumer Protection* a. State Dept. of Consumer Affairs: investigates violation of laws; education				
b. Public Health Dept.: investigates environmental health hazards				
2. *Legal Aid*				
a. Lawyer's Referral Service: legal advice, low fee				
b. Legal Aid Foundation: civil law only (housing, estate planning)				
c. U.S. Dept. of Labor: protects against age discrimination				
3. *Information and Referral to available services and programs*				
4. *Retirement Counseling*				
5. *Senior Citizen Center*				
6. *RSVP (Retired Senior Volunteer Program)*				
7. *Gray Panthers* (advocates for older people as national resource)				
8. *AARP* (American Association of Retired Persons)				
9. *Foster Grandparents*				
10. *Mobile Library Unit*				
Other:				
Congregate Care Services				
1. *Adult Foster Care:* elderly live with surrogate family				
2. *Adult Day Care Center:* discussion groups, congregate meals, podiatrist, barber, beautician, library, classes, day trips				
3. *Adult Day Hospital:* day care plus physical therapy, treatment for chronic illnesses, skilled nursing care, dental services				
Other:				
Protective Services				
1. *Power of Attorney* (regular/durable; property/health care)				
2. *Adult Protective Services:* elder abuse				
3. *Public Guardianship/Conservatorship:* when person declared incompetent				

Needs and Services: Optimum Fit, Evaluation

1. Identify five major categories of services that may be used to assist older adults.

   _____
   _____
   _____
   _____
   _____

2. Has this activity increased your awareness of how your life experiences and education as helping professionals can influence your perceptions of clients' needs for services?

Not much		Some		A lot
1	2	3	4	5

3. Has this activity increased your appreciation of the value of group process in selecting services for elderly clients?

Not much		Some		A lot
1	2	3	4	5

4. Has this activity increased your understanding of why an older person may be ambivalent toward accepting services?

Not much		Some		A lot
1	2	3	4	5

5. Give at least one example of how this activity will affect your interactions with older adults.

4 First Impressions

Rationale for Activity

People's first impressions of others can have an important and lasting effect on their subsequent relationship. First impressions are influenced by multiple and interrelated factors including the perceiver's past experiences, socioeconomic status, educational background, employment, and societal attitudes. These influences can frequently produce biases and unrealistic expectations.

It is important that providers of care and services to the elderly be aware of and understand how these factors can influence their helping relationship. This awareness can motivate them to consciously monitor their perceptions to reduce their biases, enhance their ability to remain more objective, and respond optimally to the needs of the elderly.

This activity provides participants with an opportunity to enhance their awareness and understanding of the importance of monitoring their perceptions of older people, thereby reducing biases and increasing objectivity in their helping relationships.

Participants: This activity is appropriate for graduate and undergraduate students, professionals and paraprofessionals in mental health, social work, health care, gerontology, and adult education, other service providers, and volunteers.

Objectives

Upon completion of this activity the participants will:

1. Have an increased awareness of how their life experiences can influence their perceptions and responses to older adults.

2. Have an increased understanding of the importance of monitoring their initial perceptions of older people.
3. Have an increased appreciation of the uniqueness of each person.
4. Be able to give at least one example of how this activity will affect their interactions with elderly people.

Class Size: Fifteen or fewer, as students need to be able to walk around a table to observe each plant representing an older person. If class is larger and logistics permit, a separate observation table with eight plants can be set up for each group of fifteen students.

Time: Forty minutes.

> Twenty minutes: introduction and activity
> Fifteen minutes: debriefing
> Five minutes: evaluation

Materials: Eight coleus plants in two-inch plastic pots, name tags for plants, display table or desks, First Impressions Worksheets, Teacher's Debriefing Outline, Evaluation Sheets.

Teaching Notes

1. This activity uses plants to represent elderly people. It focuses on how a person's perceptions are influenced by preconceived attitudes regarding an individual's physical appearance, age, and name. If suitable plants are difficult to obtain, fruits, vegetables, flowers, or leaves can be used effectively. The essential point is the need to provide significant variations in appearance including color, size, and health. I have usually elected to use variations of one species. However, this activity lends itself to using your creativity.
    a. I frequently select the coleus because of its varied colors, formation, and size. In order to assure this variation, I either:
        i. Buy "Punch and Grow" Kits two months in advance, grow my own plants, and repot them into individual containers, or
        ii. Go to a plant nursery and purchase the required number of plants in two-inch pots (they usually cost about sixty cents each, but then don't require repotting for the activity).
        iii. In either case, I usually do some pruning to assure a variation in each plant's appearance.
    b. I select various names and ages for the plants to represent people from our multicultural society and the participants "tune into" this right away. Examples of names I have used include: Mrs. Ramirez, Mrs. Sanchez, Mrs. Oto, Mrs. Washington, Mrs. Levine, Mr. Gold, Mrs. Mehta, Mrs. McCoy, Mr. Smith, Mr.

Sorenson, Mrs. Webber, Miss Brown. The ages range from seventy-five to 101 years. I stick the names and ages on the plastic pots using gummed labels. The "health status" of each plant varies. Some are healthy, bushy, tall, or short. Others have sparse leaves, brown leaves, or appear wilted. In one case, a plant's main branch became broken in the process of bringing it to class. I used it anyway. Some of the participants immediately perceived this as a "broken back."

   c. The appearance of plants in a classroom usually surprises the participants and their interest is immediately aroused and maintained.

2. The setting and work role for this analogous situation can be varied according to the occupations of the participants and their work settings (for example, senior center, nutrition site, church, nursing home, hospital). I assign the participants to chair a new planning committee and their first duty is to select members for this committee. I give this assignment because most participants, regardless of their work role, have served on committees and can relate to the role of chairperson.

3. I am always impressed at how quickly the participants personify the plants and how they take very seriously the task of selecting the four members for their planning committee.

4. To heighten their understanding of how their own unique experiences influence their perceptions, I ask the participants to refrain from comparing notes as they each make their selections for the committee.

5. During the debriefing period, participants look at each other in amazement as they share their different perceptions of each elderly person. The "ah-ha's" that occur as they each tune in to their own preconceived expectations makes for a lively discussion.

6. This activity is usually evaluated very highly. The participants say they gain valuable insights into both their positive and negative biases and expectations.

   a. A Hispanic student related the following to me on an individual basis after class:

> *I learned something that was most interesting to me. I realized that I, too, can discriminate against others. When I looked at my committee, I hadn't picked one Caucasian! I have experienced discrimination at times but I never thought I could do it too!*

   b. Another student said:

> *I didn't realize how I had selected those who looked the healthiest with the assumption that they would know the most and contribute the best, after this debriefing I'll never forget that a strong mind can be housed in a frail body.*

7. At the end of the exercise participants may take the plants home or give them to an older person. If more than one participant wants the same plant we draw numbers. If the participants are members of an ongoing class I frequently get updates on how "Mr. Levine" or "Mrs. Oto" is doing! This informal dialogue serves to spontaneously reinforce the participants' "first impression" experience.

Preparation for Activity: Arrange the plants on a table so that each plant and its name can be viewed easily.

Introduction to Activity

Our first impression of others is based on our selective perceptions. Ashburn and Schuster (1986) have said individuals perceive selectively, choosing to complete the perceptual process by interpreting some input and disregarding other input. This selective process differs according to biological inheritance, past experiences, self-concept, socioeconomic group, and educational background. Interrelated factors that contribute to these initial perceptions include the observed person's general appearance, ethnicity, age, sex, health status, verbal, and nonverbal cues. Specifically in relation to older adults, people's perceptions can be further influenced by the additional factor of society's negative stereotypes of the elderly.

It is important that those who interact with older adults be aware of and understand how these multiple and interrelated factors can influence their helping relationship. As a means to increase your awareness and understanding of these factors, I would like you to participate in the following activity.

Instructions to Participants

1. Place your First Impressions Worksheet in front of you.
2. Close your eyes and take a few deep breaths.
3. Now, I'd like you to imagine that you have just started a new position as the director of social services for a large residential and geriatric center. This is a new role for you and you want to be successful in it. The administrator has told you just this morning that the center has received special funding to develop a model therapeutic community and she wants you to be the chairperson of the planning committee. She suggests that you select four residents to work with you on the planning committee and has given you the names of eight potential residents. She wants to meet with you and your committee this afternoon.
4. Obviously, on such short notice you will not have time to interview each resident. However, at least you will be able to observe them before you make your selections.

5. On the table before you are the eight "residents" (represented by coleus plants). Observe each "resident." As you do so, please refrain from "comparing notes" with the other participants. We will do that after each of you has completed your selection of the four residents to serve on your committee.
6. After your observations, please list on your worksheet the four committee members you selected and the reasons for their selection.
7. Now list the four residents you rejected and your reasons.

Suggestions for Debriefing

1. Recording the participants' responses on a blackboard or flip chart can facilitate the debriefing process. See the Teacher's Debriefing Sheet, which can be used as a guide. If you choose to do this while the participants are selecting their committee members, you can put the outline on the board and include the names and ages of the potential members.
2. As you observe the participants finishing their selection process, remind them not to compare notes until everyone is done.
3. Make a transition by saying, "Now that you've made your selections for your planning committee, let's share some of your selections and the reasons for them. In this way we can enhance our awareness of both the similarities and differences in your perceptions."

Debriefing

1. What were the reasons for your selection?

    Responses may include: *Minority representation. A man. Looks strong and healthy, well enough to visit other residents and find out their needs. Need diversity of ethnicity, age, sex, marital status. Disabled, thus could represent views of those who need help the most. Tall and vibrant-looking and is probably well-liked. Had positive, healthy attitude. Was both a minority and a man. Single woman who will understand needs of that group. Small but a dynamic character. Cheery personality.*

2. What were the reasons for your rejection?

    Responses may include: *Had a broken back so couldn't come to meetings. Because of age (one hundred years old) may not be around long enough to serve even if she has valuable input. Didn't look as good as the other residents I selected. Needed diversity. Looked too frail and had a quiet person-*

ality. Was Asian so wouldn't be as verbal. Looked like he was dying. Seemed uninterested, too feeble to put forth enough energy.

As you have discovered during this debriefing, each of you perceived the potential committee members differently. In some cases you selected or rejected the same member but for different reasons. In other cases, some of you selected a member for the same reason others of you rejected the person. This certainly demonstrates how each of you perceived these potential committee members differently based on your unique selective perception.

Also, it is important to note that though, in reality, there was only the residents' physical appearances on which to base your selections (they were certainly nonverbal), some of you also gave reasons based on their psychosocial characteristics (pleasant personality, poor verbal skills, seemed uninterested, etc.). This certainly gives evidence as to how people use their frame of reference, usually without conscious awareness, to "fill in" the missing perceptual pieces in order to complete their "first impression." The need to monitor this process is obvious.

3. Let's spend a few moments now reviewing the process of our selective perceptions, as seen in figure 4–1.

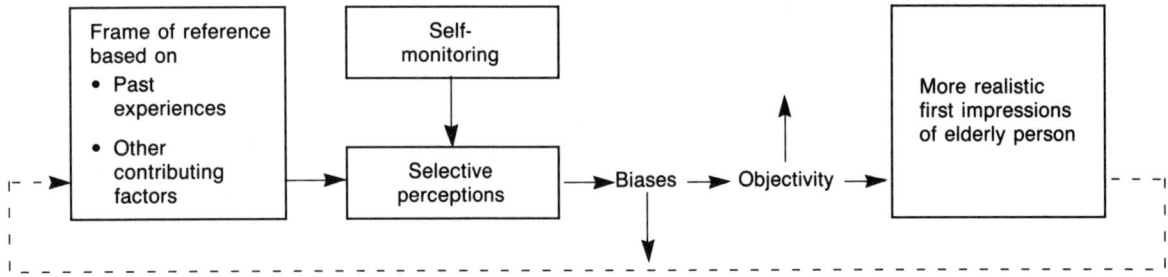

Figure 4–1. Self-Monitoring of First Impressions

a. Our frame of reference is formed by multiple and interrelated factors including biological inheritance, past experiences, self-concept, socioeconomic group, education, and employment. In addition, in relation to the elderly, our perceptions can be influenced further by negative societal attitudes, and our feelings of helplessness because we as providers of care and services are unable "to turn back the clock" and restore the elderly person's health and youth. This can result in a syndrome that has been described as "the innocent victim," a tendency to inbue negative characteristics to persons in need whom we feel impotent to help (Kane and Kane 1981). This frame of reference has a major influence in our actual perceptions. It acts like a filter, screening out some things and selecting others. The resultant selective perception is the basis for our first impressions.

b. This complex and interrelated selective screening process usually takes place without our conscious awareness. This can be detrimental to our relationships with the elderly because it can contribute to our either over- or underassessing their strengths and impairments. The wide variations in your rationales for selection and rejection of the "people" to serve on your committee are relevant examples of this screening process.

4. Thus, it is vital that those who interact with the elderly become aware of the factors that can influence their perceptions and make a conscious effort to monitor them. This monitoring can serve to reduce biases and promote more objective assessments and expectations of the elderly.

Summary

You've certainly demonstrated how each person's perceptions are unique. We've also observed how these selective perceptions can influence the decision-making process in relation to selecting older people for social roles or activities. These perceptions can also influence the process of determining the provision of services and health care for the elderly.

I hope that by participating in this activity you have enhanced your awareness and understanding of the importance of monitoring your perceptions of older people. This can result in the fulfilling of a unique requirement in the delivery of human services, which is a knowledgeable and disciplined use of the helping person's self (Brill 1985). Such self-awareness can reduce biases and increase objectivity in our helping relationships.

Evaluation

Please take a few moments now to complete the evaluation.

First Impressions, Worksheet

List the names of your four committee members and why you selected them.

Name	Reason for Selection
1.	
2.	
2.	
4.	

List the names of the four potential members you rejected and state why.

Name	Reason for Rejection
1.	
2.	
3.	
4.	

Name	Age	Select	Reasons	Reject	Reasons

First Impressions, Debriefing Outline: Teacher

First Impressions, Evaluation

1. Did this activity increase your awareness of how your life experiences can influence your perceptions and responses to older adults?

Not much		Some		A lot
1	2	3	4	5

2. Did this activity increase your understanding of the importance of monitoring your initial perceptions of older people?

Not much		Some		A lot
1	2	3	4	

3. Did this activity increase your appreciation of the uniqueness of each person?

Not much		Some		A lot
1	2	3	4	5

4. Give at least one example of how this activity will affect your interactions with elderly people.

PART 2

PHYSICAL AGING

5 Pacing and Patience

Rationale for Activity

Pacing and patience are two important techniques to enhance interactions with older adults and promote the maintenance of their independence. These techniques are significant because they can be used to compensate for the elderly person's slowed reaction time. Reaction time is defined as the period between the perception of a signal and the beginning of a responding movement (Greenberg 1973). If sensory deficits or a chronic disease that impairs dexterity are present, it will take the older person even longer to respond.

If the elderly are not allowed the time to compensate for this lengthened reaction time, their resultant behavior can contribute to what Bengtson describes as the social breakdown syndrome. This is a cycle that involves the gradual breakdown of older people's perception of their competence because of negative labeling by society (Bengtson 1973). This labeling can occur with increasing frequency in our advanced, high-technology society. In all modern life, the habit of speed has accelerated. This encourages greater impatience with those who cannot keep up (Moody 1986). Older people are clearly at a disadvantage.

It is vital that people who interact with the elderly develop an understanding of ways to help them compensate for their slowed reaction time. In this way, older adults will be supported in their efforts to maintain their optimum level of psychosocial functioning.

This activity provides the participants with an opportunity to increase their appreciation of the importance of pacing and patience in working with the elderly and to enhance their understanding of ways to help older adults compensate for their slower reaction time.

Participants: This activity is appropriate for graduate and undergraduate students and professional and paraprofessionals in mental health, social work, health care, gerontology and adult education, other service providers, volunteers, and family caregivers.

Objectives

Upon completion of this activity, participants will:

1. Have an increased appreciation of the importance of allowing the elderly person more time to perform a task.
2. Be able to identify two ways to help older people learn a new task.
3. Be able to give at least one example of how this activity will affect their interactions with older adults.

Class Size: Open

Time: Twenty minutes.

>Five minutes: introduction and activity
>Ten minutes: debriefing
>Five minutes: evaluation

Materials: One three-by-five-inch card or a sheet of plain white paper for each participant, Pacing and Patience Worksheets, Evaluation Sheets.

Teaching Notes

1. This activity works well when it is interjected at the appropriate place in a lecture or discussion topic where you want to make a point regarding the implications of an elderly person's reaction time. Topics could include: communications with the elderly, teaching older adults, or physical changes with aging.
2. It works best if you have established:
   a. A good reciprocal relationship with the participants and
   b. A supportive, well-paced learning environment
3. To set up a stressed, competitive situation give a brief description of reaction time and then suddenly:
   a. Change pace as you give them an unexpected assignment with unrealistic expectations.
   b. Become authoritarian.
   c. Set unrealistic limits.
   d. Deliver instructions fast in a barely audible voice.
   e. Get irritated when asked to repeat them.
4. As the participants struggle to complete the task, you continually:
   a. Pace the floor among them and look at their work.
   b. Look at your watch and make comments like "I really expected

you'd be done by now;" "I expected that you would set a record;" "You're really slower than any other group who has participated in this simple activity."
5. This short activity consistently "makes the point" of the importance of individualized pacing and patience. The element of surprise increases its effectiveness as the participants try to cope with an unexpected challenge involving performance, timing, and evaluation.

Introduction to Activity

As people age, their reaction time lengthens gradually after age sixty. Reaction time is defined as the period between the perception of a signal and the beginning of a responding movement (Greenberg 1973). If sensory deficits or a chronic disease that impairs dexterity are present, it will take the older person even more time to respond. It is vital that those who interact with the elderly be sensitive to these changes and pace themselves accordingly.

Instructions to Participants

1. I've just remembered that I wanted to *test* you on a *timed* but simple activity (start handing out three-by-five-inch cards as you continue to give your instructions).
2. I've done it many times before with other groups and the average time to complete it is only thirty to forty-five seconds. You're such an exceptionally good group, you'll likely set a record time.
3. Switch your pen or pencil into your opposite hand and write the following information down as quickly as possible on the card I've just given you:
    a. Name.
    b. Address.
    c. Phone number—either home or work or both.
    d. Social security number.
    e. Driver's license number.
    f. Place and date of birth.
4. I'll be collecting them after you're finished for comparative purposes.
5. Please hurry!

Suggestions for Debriefing

1. Stop the activity before everyone has finished.
2. Ask the participants to take a few moments to respond to the questions on their worksheets before debriefing as a class.

Debriefing

1. How did you feel about my abruptly changed pace, style, and expectations?

    Possible responses: *I was distraught. I felt stressed. I was irritated at myself and you. I was very anxious. I felt inadequate. I was frustrated. I was angry at not being given time to do my best. I felt discouraged. I was feeling great, then I became insecure. I was nervous.*

2. How did it affect your behavior?

    Possible responses: *I felt tense. I had to write slowly so the response was legible. I really had to concentrate. I looked over to see how the people next to me were doing.*

3. How many of you were tempted to stop participating? Did any of you stop and say to yourself "forget it?"

    Possible responses: *I'm not a quitter. I like a challenge. I would have quit if I'd been by myself.*

4. What is your assessment of your information card?

    Possible responses: *Pride, because I'm ambidextrous. I am ashamed. It is sloppy. It is very hard to read. I felt competent "inside" but couldn't express it for the "outside." I'd give myself an F and I'm used to A's.*

5. How do you expect your family/friends/colleagues would react if you sent them your card?

    Possible response: *They'd think I had a stroke or Parkinson's. They'd wonder if I was on drugs or drunk. They'd worry that I may be sick. I wouldn't send it. They'd phone me to see what was going on.*

Thank you for sharing your feelings. You have certainly expressed how irritated you were with me. Your irritation was appropriate because I changed pace on you abruptly, gave you a task for which you were unprepared, and made it both timed and competitive. Because you were secure enough in your identity and self-esteem you were fine in letting me know your feelings about my behavior.

In addition, you also were frustrated with yourselves. Yet, given the reality of the situation it was unrealistic for you to expect yourselves to perform up to your usual standards. However, you had these expectations and berated yourselves when you fell short.

As we move into pointers to help the elderly compensate for their slower reaction time, remember the feelings you had about me and yourselves. In my experience, older people have similar feelings but they are less likely to say anything to the helping person and much more likely to blame themselves. In the process their feelings of competence and self-esteem deteriorate. This is why it is so important that people who interact with older adults understand the changes in their reaction time and ways to compensate for them.

Pointers to Compensate for Changes in Reaction Time

1. When we are working with the elderly we may unintentionally quicken our pace and expectations as we get pressed for time and lose our patience. We need to guard against this for it can be very detrimental to older people's ability to learn a new procedure, perform a task, or maintain their motivation to complete an activity.
2. Older people tend to be more cautious and less willing to respond quickly in situations where they perceive the risk of failure or loss to be high (Schaie 1980). Some older adults may choose not to even try to perform a task because of fear of failure. Eisdorfer (1977) has said we cannot ignore the possibility that "the fear of failure" may supercede "the need to achieve" as a motivating force in older persons. This possibility may be reduced if people who interact with older adults create a supportive environment and let them set their own pace.
3. Factors that may affect reaction time and need to be considered in working with older people include:
    a. Complexity of stimulus.
    b. Familiarity with stimulus.
    c. Preparation for or expectancy of stimulus.
    d. Complexity of response.
    e. Age and general condition of the person who is responding.
    f. Reaction time lengthens gradually after sixty and is more evident when:
        i. A choice must be made between two or more alternatives.
        ii. It involves changing movement from one direction to another (Greenberg 1973).
4. To help the older person compensate for changes in reaction time:
    a. Preferably prepare the person in advance for the scheduled task.
    b. Give instructions that are:
        i. Concisely and clearly stated in small, understandable units and preferably based on what the person already knows.
        ii. In a vocabulary the person understands.
5. If an older person is to learn a new procedure or task, develop the steps from the concrete to the abstract:
    a. Initially, give older people time to get their attention *focused* on the task. For example, if a procedure is to be learned, let them *examine* the equipment.
    b. *Demonstrate* the procedure/task to be accomplished.
    c. Let the person *practice.*

d. *Review* and *discuss* clearly printed and concise instructions.
e. Leave instructions with the person to be reviewed as needed.
6. At *each* step toward the completion of a task:
   a. Ask for feedback as a means to assess what the older person has understood.
   b. Give positive feedback regarding the successful completion of that step.

Summary

1. Remember that changes in reaction time vary from person to person as do all normal age-related changes. However, one of the best-documented psychological changes that occur with age is a slowing of behavioral functioning. Older people consistently perform more slowly in tasks requiring response speed such as reaction-time and movement-time tasks (MacRae 1986).
2. If the elderly are not allowed the time to compensate for this lengthened reaction time, their resultant behavior can contribute to what Bengtson describes as the social breakdown syndrome. This is a cycle that involves the gradual breakdown of older people's perception of their competence because of negative labeling by society (Bengtson 1973). This labeling can occur with increasing frequency in our advanced, high-technology society. Older people are clearly at a disadvantage.
3. The importance of pacing cannot be overemphasized. Laboratory learning studies, research on adult intelligence, and practical classroom experience clearly indicate the need for slowly paced or self-paced instruction for older people (Peterson 1983). These findings can be applied to all interactions with older adults. Pacing and patience are essential for optimum performance.
4. When given the opportunity to monitor and inspect signals for as long as they wish, older people are slower but more accurate than younger people (Welford 1977). Thus, when allowed their individualized pacing, the elderly can have the time to perceive, process the information, mobilize their more limited physical and psychological resources, and respond to the best of their ability. This in turn reinforces their feelings of competence and control.
5. Your participation in this activity has certainly demonstrated your feelings associated with an unexpected challenge. Most of you would have preferred more preparation time, more time to perform the task, or both. You all wanted to do well. Also, you expected me to be more patient. Please remember these feelings when you interact with the elderly. As we've discussed, they have even more reason to want and need more time, yet they also may be more reluctant to ask for it. So it is our challenge to see that our pacing and patience are appro-

priate to support the optimum functioning of older adults with whom we interact.

I hope that by participating in this activity you have increased your appreciation of the importance of appropriate pacing and patience when you interact with older adults and enhanced your understanding of ways to help the elderly compensate for their slower reaction time.

Evaluation

Please take a few moments now to complete an evaluation.

Pacing and Patience, Worksheet

1. How did you *feel* about my abruptly changed pace, style, and expectations?

2. How did it affect your behavior?

3. How tempted were you to stop participating?

Not at all		Somewhat		A lot
1	2	3	4	5

4. What is your assessment of your information card?

5. How do you expect your family/friends/colleagues would react if you sent them your card?

Pacing and Patience, Evaluation

1. Did this activity increase your appreciation of the importance of allowing older people more time to perform a task?

Not much		Some		A lot
1	2	3	4	5

2. Identify two ways to help older people learn a new task.

   _____
   _____
   _____
   _____

3. Give at least one example of how this activity will affect your interactions with older adults.

6 Developing Trust

Rationale for Activity

People talk about trust and its importance in a relationship. A common expression today is "trust me." Yet trust is usually not instantaneous. It takes time to develop feelings of confidence and belief in other people.

Unfortunately, that time is not always available when individuals find themselves unexpectedly in a dependency state because of sudden changes in their psychosocial or physical status. Being in a dependency state is difficult because our society places such a high value on independent functioning. So a major task for older people is to learn how to accept appropriate assistance from others.

Butler and Lewis (1982) have coined the term "responsible dependency" to describe the process by which an older person recognizes the need for help, does a realistic self-evaluation, and then accepts needed assistance with dignity and cooperativeness. However, to accept help from family and friends with whom one has a trusting and reciprocal relationship is one thing, but to accept help from an unknown service provider can arouse anxiety, vulnerability, insecurity, and loss of control. When an elderly person is confronted with a stressful situation, success in handling it will depend upon his or her adaptive capacity. Conditions underlying adaptive capacity include physical and cognitive states, energy potential, and social resources (Lieberman and Tobin 1983).

It is important that individuals who work with older adults acquire an understanding of how to reduce these stress-producing feelings in the elderly and promote their adaptive capacities. This can be facilitated by developing a trusting relationship with them. The relationship is essential to the helping process. This two-part activity provides participants with an opportunity to enhance their understanding of some of the dynamics of a trusting relationship.

Participants: This activity is appropriate for graduate and undergraduate students and professionals and paraprofessionals in mental health, social work, health care and gerontology, other service providers, and volunteers.

Objectives

Upon completion of this two-part activity, participants will:

1. Be able to identify four ways to earn elderly person's trust.
2. Have an increased awareness of the elderly person's feelings of dependency.
3. Have an increased appreciation of a person's adaptive capabilities.
4. Have an increased awareness of a caregiver's mixed feelings related to the responsibility of providing care.
5. Be able to give at least one example of how this activity will affect their interactions with older adults.

Class Size: Open. If there are more than sixteen participants, an assistant is needed to help put on the blindfolds.

Time: Fifty minutes.
    Activity #1: Trusting Relationships: fifteen minutes

        Five minutes: introduction and activity.
        Ten minutes: debriefing

    Activity #2: Trust Walk: thirty-five minutes.

        Five minutes: preparation
        Ten minutes: activity
        Fifteen minutes: debriefing
        Five minutes: evaluation

Materials:
    Activity #1: Trusting Relationships Worksheets.
    Activity #2: For every two students—one blindfold, one Dependent Person Worksheet, one Helping Person Worksheet; cellophane tape in dispenser, Evaluation Sheets.

Teaching Notes

Activity #1: Trusting Relationships

I have found this activity helps to set the stage for the Trust Walk because it helps focus participants on their own experiences with trust. As a result, they are more tuned in to the similarities and differences in their feelings of trust when they are put in an unexpected position of dependency on a stranger.

Activity #2: Trust Walk

1. Exercises to simulate visual changes have been developed by numerous researchers, including Ernst and Shore (1976). This activity, adapted from them, focuses on a sudden loss of vision and its impact on a person. This rarely happens as sensory changes in the elderly usually come on very gradually. However, the dramatization for this simulated activity enhances its effectiveness in increasing the participants' sensitivity to the psychosocial implications of unexpected dependency.

2. Prepare blindfolds ahead of time. I use either three paper towels or three pieces of tissues joined together with cellophane tape. I also carry the tape in a dispenser to get the participants blindfolded quickly. If you plan on having an assistant or colleague help you, have an extra dispenser for them.

3. Stay in the classroom as the participants take their Trust Walk, for two reasons:
   a. The participants know their belongings are safe while they are gone.
   b. If any participants decide to terminate the activity for any reason, you are immediately available for supportive debriefing. A case example was a nurse attendant in her fifties. Her helper had just guided her out of the room and down the hall when she panicked and said, "I feel the walls are closing in on me, I can't go on," and took her blindfold off. They came back in the room, she sat down and we discussed what had happened. She was startled by the intensity of her feelings. She had always worn glasses and acknowledged her dependency on them. However, her fear of going blind and being totally dependent on another person had not surfaced until this activity. Also, she said if she had known her helper beforehand, she might have been able to go through with it. She said she would never forget those feelings and always be more sensitive and supportive with her patients who were newly admitted and had sensory impairments.

4. Allow enough time to debrief the Trust Walk. The participants are full of feelings needing to be expressed. I request that they write their feelings down before discussing them because:
   a. It helps them tune into and acknowledge their feelings to themselves. If they choose not to share their feelings with the group, that's their privilege.
   b. It gives them time to get out of their "impaired" or "helper" role.

5. As participants share their experiences, point out how multiple feelings and thinking of adaptive processes can be occurring simul-

taneously. Both can produce stress and drain energy. So it is with the older person who has a more limited energy reserve. Thus, when faced with a new challenge, the older adult will benefit from empathetic physical and psychosocial support.
6. If you find yourself running short of time, ask participants to hand in their worksheets for your review and summarization for the next session of the class. In this way everyone has an opportunity to contribute to the debriefing and receive a summary of the commonalities and uniqueness of this activity for the participants.

Introduction to Activities

The ability to function as an independent person is highly valued in our society. Few individuals want to be in a dependent position of having to rely on others for help. However, most of us, at various times throughout our lives, have found ourselves in a dependent position. As we all know, this probability increases with age.

An important task for the older person is to learn how to accept appropriate assistance from others. Help is usually much easier to accept from family and friends than it is from unknown service providers. When the elderly are put in such a dependent position, they often experience feelings of anxiety, vulnerability, insecurity, and loss of control with resultant stress.

However, those stress-producing feelings associated with dependency can be reduced when elderly people develop feelings of trust toward those who assist them. We have the challenge of developing a trusting relationship with them.

How can we achieve this? Let us start by discussing the word "trust."

Activity #1: Trusting Relationships

1. What does the word "trust" mean to you? (Write participants' suggestions on board). Descriptors can include: Can always be counted on. Has integrity. Will always watch out for me. Feelings of security. She will do what she says she will do. Can keep a secret. Really listens to me. I can "dump" on her and she'll understand. I believe in him. Is dependable. Is honest. I have confidence in her. Dependable.
2. You've certainly covered the meanings of the word "trust."
3. Now, place your Trusting Relationships Worksheet in front of you.
4. I'd like you to close your eyes and think for a few moments of the people in your life whom you trust and why you trust them.
5. Open your eyes and list those people on your Trusting Relationship Worksheet (allow two or three minutes).

Debriefing Activity #1

Would you share a few of your trusting relationships by describing them and the length of time you've known the person? (Categories can include family, friends, co-workers, helping professionals, minister, doctor).

Thank you for giving examples of your trusting relationships. It is evident that these relationships are very special to you and you value them highly. It is also clear that for most of you, these trusting relationships have developed over a long time. For some of you, they began the day you were born! Usually, the longer we have known someone, the deeper the trust.

Transition to Activity #2: Trust Walk

Now that you are in touch with your own trusting relationships, I would like you to participate in an activity that will give you an opportunity to experience an unusual case of unexpected dependency brought on by a sudden change in your ability to function.

You will temporarily lose your eyesight. Though sudden blindness doesn't happen often, it's a valuable simulation because it dramatically demonstrates sudden dependency, a person's adaptive capabilities, and the importance of trust.

Instructions to Participants

1. Divide yourselves into pairs, preferably with someone you don't know.
2. One of you will experience a sensory loss and the other will be the helper.
3. Partner #1: Once you become impaired, tune into your *feelings* associated with dependency and *think* about how you're going to adapt to this situation.

   Partner #2: When your partner becomes impaired, begin to tune into your *feelings* associated with the responsibility for the well-being of another person and your *thoughts* on how you're going to be an effective helper.
4. When everyone is ready, you will be instructed to begin your "Trust Walk."
5. You are to take approximately *ten minutes* to do the following:
   a. Walk around the room.
   b. Get a drink of water.
   c. Go outside and explore your environment (but do *not* use the stairs).
   d. Return to the room and your seats.

6. If at any time you wish to discontinue the exercise, you may do so but please return to the room right away. I will be here waiting for all of you to return.
7. Once you are back in your seats, those of you who experienced a sensory loss can remove your impairment.
8. *Before* talking to anyone, write down your feelings about the experience on your Trust Walk Worksheets.
9. We will debrief as a group when everyone is finished.

Preparation of Participants

1. Go to each couple and apply a blindfold to partner #1.
2. During this procedure, remind them to get "tuned in" to the experience.
3. When all partner #1's have an impairment, instruct the participants to begin their "Trust Walk."

Transition to Debriefing

1. As participants return to the room, remind those with impairments that once they are seated they can take off their blindfolds. Then, before talking, all participants are to write down their feelings associated with the activity. (Allow about five minutes.)
2. "Now that you've written down your feelings associated with this activity, let's share some of them as a group. In this way we can all learn from each other and once again appreciate both the commonalities and uniqueness of an experience for each of us."

Debriefing Activity #2

1. *Dependent persons:* What were your feelings regarding your dependency as a result of your visual impairment?

    Responses may include: *I was not recognized as a person. I felt clumsy, inadequate, and helpless. I was cautious and frustrated. I was afraid of bumping into things. I felt I'd lost control and was angry. I felt insecure. I was impatient with myself. I felt my partner would become impatient with me unless I moved fast. I was tired from concentrating so hard. I felt off balance. I felt isolated. I felt more insecure outside of building. I didn't like it, but doggone it, I was going to learn to cope.*

    It can be very threatening to be thrust into a dependency state at any time of our lives. We feel the helplessness of being out of control and angry that this happened to us.

2. *Dependent persons:* What were some of the ways you adapted to your impairments?

> Responses may include: *I started walking slower. I put my arms out in front, moving them from left to right to avoid hitting anything. I took tiny steps. I walked with my hands touching the wall. I was more aware of breezes and temperature changes. I could feel the sunshine. I wanted to touch everything, it gave me more time to get oriented. I heard more noises like birds, planes.*

Please "process" how all of you who were put in a dependent situation immediately started to adapt and gain some control over your environment. Every one of you began to tune in more to your other senses for environmental input. You used touch more to reach out to people, touch walls and doors, take smaller steps to give you more input from the ground, and feel the elements when you were outside. You adapted well in a short period of time. If you had had longer, you would have been even more effective.

3. *Helping persons:* What were your feelings regarding the helping role?

> Responses may include: *I felt good being able to help a person. I felt very responsible. I wanted to do everything right. I was impatient. I appreciated my own health. I got progressively more irritated. I felt a sense of both power and responsibility. I was scared as I wasn't sure what to do. I was overprotective. I didn't want the responsibility. I felt guilty because I was impatient. I had to be her eyes and plan ahead so she wouldn't get hurt.*

Thank you for sharing these responses. Your caring and commitment for the well being of others is evident as is your honesty in relating your ambivalence in the caregiving roles. Having the responsibility to assist another person is a heavy assignment, even with adequate preparation, and in many cases, there is not time to be prepared, as you experienced today!

4. *Helping persons:* What were some things you did to develop trust?

> Responses my include: *I used the person's name frequently. I offered as many choices as possible. I encouraged her to set her own pace. I praised his efforts to do things for himself. I encouraged my partner to use all senses: to listen, touch, smell. I described the surroundings. I told her what to expect so she could be prepared for what changes were coming in the environment. I identified noises and voices. I was empathetic. I was always there when he needed me.*

Your suggestions are excellent. You reinforced the individuals' sense of identity and importance by calling them by name and by being trustworthy and empathetic. You also encouraged the people's maintenance of control by providing choices, letting them set their own pace, and praising their efforts on their own behalf. In addition, you helped the participants compensate for their sensory loss by supporting their efforts to use their other senses to the maximum. Well done!

Transition to Pointers

Your participation in this exercise has clearly demonstrated the multiple and interrelated factors involved in the helping process and in the establishment of trust.

In your debriefing, two key factors emerged in relation to the establishment of trust. They were how and what you communicated, and ways you tried to help your partners compensate for their impairments. So, let's spend the next few minutes discussing some ways to enhance communication skills and to help elderly people compensate for their sensory impairments.

Pointers in Communication and Compensation

Communication Pointers

1. Individualize.

    The older people are the more *individual* they become because they've had a lifetime to establish patterns of activities of daily living and socialization that fits their needs and life style, so:

    a. Recognize their individuality by calling them by name (by surname unless given permission otherwise) and use it frequently.
    b. Enhance the elderly person's feelings of self-esteem by encouraging their maximum participation and acknowledging their being an authority on their own aging. When assessing their situation, remember, they are the product of their total life's experiences, and they are the only ones who know what these experiences have been. The past plays a significant part in their current functioning.

2. Reduce excessive background noises such as the radio and television. They take energy to screen out. However, ask permission first!

3. Tune in to "present state."

    a. If the person is ill, he or she is more prone to poor oral hygiene and a dry mouth. If indicated, offer to get the person a drink of water or juice before you start your conversation.

b. Regardless of what your "agenda" is, relate to what the person is focusing on at that moment. Then take time to find out what has been going on in the life of the person since you last saw him an hour, a day, or a week ago. If there is a current problem, find out and deal with it accordingly, then shift to your agenda. It takes a person time to "switch gears" and get "tuned in."
c. *Pace* the conversation and length of interaction according to the person's variable energy level and physical condition. You may need to put more of *your energy* into the interaction to compensate for the older person's *reduced supply*.
d. Pay attention to nonverbal cues such as pain, needing to go to the bathroom, or tiredness.
4. Sit close to the person, no more than one-half to two-and-one-half feet away. A foot stool can give the proper perspective, as the older person is an "authority figure" on his/her own aging and thus is seated in the "higher position" and you are looking up to him or her.
5. Face the person directly, be in a good light, do not have your hands around your face.
6. Use touch as a meaningful communication bridge. It conveys concern and caring.
7. Avoid information overload by:
    a. Speaking clearly and using a moderate pace.
    b. Using short sentences.
    c. Asking for *feedback* to be certain that *meaningful* communication has taken place. On the average it takes 15 percent more time for the elderly person to process information and respond to it (Greenberg 1973).
8. As much as possible, work together on alleviation or solution of problems by:
    a. Finding out the person's perception of or experiences with the problem.
    b. Exploring alternatives.
    c. Providing choices:
        i. Gives people the opportunity to maintain some control over their lives.
        ii. Lets people decide priorities on which they want to spend their limited energies.
        iii. Demonstrates your confidence in their ability to make choices and follow through.
    d. Setting realistic goals with the aim of restoring or achieving what is possible given the older person's physical status and psychosocial supports.

Ways to Compensate for Sensory Changes

1. Visual Impairments
    a. As you approach, announce yourself by name and greet the person appropriately.

b. If you want to shake hands, give a verbal cue such as "I'd like to shake your hand." Depending on the degree of impairment, the person may not be able to see your nonverbal cues.
c. Be certain there is enough nonglare lighting. Elderly people require about three times as much light as young people.
d. If offering a drink, do not fill the cup too full.
e. If you need to touch or move anything in the room, obtain permission first. Then, when finished using the article, put it back in exactly the same place.
f. If you have to take visually impaired people anywhere:
   i. Give detailed instructions. Tell them where they are going, why, and how long they will be gone.
   ii. Allow *them* to take your arm and set the pace.
   iii. As you go from one place to another, *describe* the environment, the people in it, and what to expect next.
   iv. Ask if they would like help with activities along the way (opening doors, getting a drink, etc.). If they prefer to do things themselves, let them. Visually impaired people orient themselves by touch (feeling a door before finding a handle); allow them time. The elderly know their impairments and have developed strategies to compensate, including asking for help when they need it.
   v. If going from light to dark or the reverse, allow extra time for the older person's eyes to adjust.
g. Environmental supports can include:
   i. Large clocks and calendars to facilitate orientation.
   ii. Contrasting bright colors where possible (between light switches and walls, tablecloth and dishes, etc.)
   iii. A small transistor radio to keep elderly person updated on current events and to provide music.

2. Hearing Impairments
   a. Watch for signs of hearing loss: failure to respond when people speak, inattention, frequently requesting repetition, turning one ear toward you.
   b. As hearing loss progresses:
      i. Some people may not realize the extent of their hearing loss and respond incorrectly or not at all.
      ii. Relatedness to others can become negative because people react to the deaf with frustration and anger because of inability to communicate.
      iii. Feelings of identity can be threatened because feedback from others is reduced and withdrawal, suspicions, and paranoia can result.
   c. If hearing loss is sudden, have the person's ears checked for possible blockage by ear wax.
   d. Approach the person from the front to avoid startling and get the individual's attention before starting to speak.

e. If person is wearing a hearing aid, be certain it is working and turned on.
f. Facilitate lip reading by:
   i. Being face to face with the person and at eye level.
   ii. Keeping your hands away from your face and not chewing gum.
   iii. Facing a light.
g. Don't raise your voice; speak only slightly louder, clearly, and at a moderate rate.
h. Make the change to a new subject, a new name, or an unusual word at a slower rate.
i. Watch the listener's facial expressions for clues that you are not understood. Ask for feedback to determine if you have communicated clearly.
j. If the person does not understand what you have said, repeat the whole sentence once. If the person still does not understand, try a different way of saying the same thing. Some sounds are easier to hear or to see on the lips than others.
k. Provide a black pen and paper for written communication and use large, clear print.
l. Remember that group situations are particularly difficult for the hard-of-hearing as they may be unable to distinguish between speakers in a group. This can lead to frustration and stress.

Summary

This activity has focused on the challenge of earning the trust of the elderly with whom we work. You have shared your experiences about your own trusting relationships, how it feels to be thrust into unexpected dependency on others, and how you and your helping person adapted to it.

We have also discussed ways to enhance general communication skills as well as specific ways to help elderly people compensate for their sensory impairments. The goal in enhancing these skills was to become more effective in your ability to develop a trusting relationship between yourselves and the elderly with whom you work.

I hope that by participating in this activity you have:

1. Increased your understanding of the elderly person's feelings of dependency associated with decreased ability to function, less control over life, and reduced self-esteem.
2. Increased your appreciation of how older people will strive to maintain as much independence as possible by adapting to and compensating for their physical impairments and that these strivings should be praised.
3. Increased your awareness of how caregivers may have mixed feel-

ings in providing help to the elderly, such as on one hand, feeling good in being able to help the older person, yet on the other hand, feeling inadequate, stressed, and not wanting so much responsibility. Such mixed feelings are normal and being aware of negative feelings can help a caregiver keep them under control and try to practice patience and pacing.
4. Helped you identify ways to earn the trust of elderly individuals so that you can work effectively with them to maintain their optimum level of functioning. Based on our previous discussion on suggested ways to develop this trusting relationship, two key factors emerged. These factors were the importance of the service provider's ability to communicate, verbally and nonverbally, care and concern for the older person and compensate appropriately for his or her sensory impairments. Your suggestions can be summarized in a "pen tip":

P *Praise* the elderly person's efforts to do things for himself or herself.
E Tell the person what to *expect:* what you expect them to do and what you're going to do, and what changes are coming up in the environment.
N Help the person when he or she *needs* you.
T Use *touch* to express caring and concern and to give support and security.
I *Identify* person by name, identify surroundings by describing them.
P *Practice* patience and pacing.

Every time you pick up your pen and write with the tip, think of these six suggestions to help you develop a trusting relationship with the elderly.

Evaluation

Please take a few moments now to complete the evaluation.

Trusting Relationships, Worksheet

Whom do you trust?	Why?	How long have you known this person?

Trust Walk, Worksheet: Dependent person

1. How did you feel in the dependent role?

2. What did you do to adapt to your impairment?

3. What did your helper do to develop your sense of trust?

Trust Walk, Worksheet: Helping person

1. What were your feelings regarding your helping role?

2. What did the dependent person do on his or her own behalf to adapt to the impairment?

3. What did you do to develop a sense of trust in the dependent person?

Developing Trust, Evaluation

1. Identify four ways to earn an older person's trust.

   _____

   _____

   _____

   _____

2. Did this activity increase your awareness of an older peson's feelings of dependency?

Not much		Some		A lot
1	2	3	4	5

3. Did this activity increase your appreciation of how an older person tries to adapt in order to maintain as much control as possible?

Not much		Some		A lot
1	2	3	4	5

4. Did this activity increase your awareness of how a caregiver can have mixed feelings regarding the responsibility of providing care?

Not much		Some		A lot
1	2	3	4	5

5. Give at least one example of how this activity will affect your interactions with older adults.

7   A Surprise Snack

Rationale for Activity

Eating is associated with health and socialization. As such it plays a vital role in the maintenance of every individual's physical and psychosocial well-being. However, the quality of this eating experience is affected by many interrelated factors. Beattie and Louie (1983) have defined eating as a complex reaction determined by the physiological, psychological, biochemical, social, educational, and sensory reactions of the individual, which move in a framework of race, religion, tradition, economic status, and environmental conditions. It is important to be aware of these multiple factors because they will remind us of how individualized people are in their approach to food and they become more so as they age!

Also, in the later years, other activities may be reduced or eliminated, but the importance of eating remains central to the maintenance of physical and psychosocial well being. However, as people grow older, physiological and social changes can create barriers to the enjoyment of eating. It is important for those who work with the elderly to be aware of these barriers, and ways to compensate for them so that they can help older adults continue to make mealtimes a quality experience, both nutritionally and socially.

This activity provides the participants with an opportunity to increase their appreciation of the effects of reduced sensory input on people's enjoyment of eating and to enhance their understanding of ways to compensate for these changes.

Participants: This activity is appropriate for graduate and undergraduate students and professionals and paraprofessionals in health care and gerontology, other service providers, and family caregivers.

Objectives

Upon completion of this activity participants will:

1. Have an increased awareness of how reduced sensory input affects the enjoyment of eating.
2. Have an increased appreciation of an older person's adaptive efforts to maintain as much independence as possible.
3. Have an increased appreciation of the importance of socialization during eating.
4. Be able to identify three ways to promote an enjoyable eating experience for an older adult.
5. Be able to give at least one example of how this activity will affect their interactions with older adults.

Class Size: Open. If there are more than sixteen participants, an assistant is needed to help put on the blindfolds.

Time: Thirty-five minutes.

>Ten minutes: introduction and preparation
>Five minutes: activity
>Fifteen minutes: debriefing
>Five minutes: evaluation

Materials: For every two students—a blindfold, a four- or six-ounce paper cup with fruit cocktail, two salt-free crackers, a plastic spoon, a napkin, Dependent Person Worksheet, Helping Person Worksheet. Other supplies—cellophane tape in dispenser, can opener, serving tray, Evaluation Sheets.

Teaching Notes

1. Exercises to simulate sensory changes have been developed by numerous researchers, including Ernst and Shore (1976). This activity, adapted from them, uses sensory deprivation to focus on feeling associated with dependency, control, and self-image.
2. Prepare blindfolds ahead of time. I use either three paper towels or three pieces of tissue joined together with cellophane tape. I also carry the cellophane tape in a dispenser to facilitate getting the participants blindfolded quickly. If you plan on having an assistant or colleague help you, have an extra dispenser for them.
3. Use water-packed fruit cocktail. If time allows, rinse and drain it. This reduces the flavor of the fruit even more. Allow time to put fruit cocktail into paper cups before class. Place cups on tray and cover with towel before entering classroom so that participants won't be able to identify their "surprise snack."

4. If this activity is conducted in conjunction with the Developing Trust Activity (chapter 6), instruct the participants to keep the same partners but switch roles. In this way, both will have the opportunity to experience visual loss with the resultant feelings of dependency and adaptability.
5. In relation to the role of helper, I'm not directive. When the participants have all been prepared, I just say, "You may begin the activity now." Inevitably, one of the helpers will ask, "Do I feed my partner?" I reply, "Handle it any way you think is best." This open-ended approach allows more opportunity for the paticipants to get in touch with their feelings related to control, dependency, power, self-esteem, frustration, isolation, and accepting or rejecting help. I have found that this enhances the learning experience.

Introduction to Activity

Everyone has to eat to survive. Even though many older adults need fewer calories because they lead more sedentary lives and less energy is required to maintain body processes, they still need a daily nutritionally balanced diet (Alfin-Slater and Friedman 1978). The challenge for older people is to get the same amount of nutrients in a lesser amount of food. *Quantity* of food doesn't necessarily equate to *quality* nutrients. We need to do all we can to make meals for older adults a quality experience—both nutritionally and socially. This becomes more challenging with age because of physiological changes in the mouth involving the taste buds, saliva, and teeth.

The sense of taste changes with age. There is a reduction in taste buds that identify sweet and salty, while sour and bitter tastes are less affected (Beattie and Louie 1983). These changes can contribute to an older person's using more sugar and salt in an effort to make foods "taste like they used to." This adaptation can have a negative effect on the person's health, especially for those individuals who are on a restricted diet. A diminished sense of smell can compound the problem.

With advancing years, the saliva glands produce a thicker and less watery substance. This contributes to older people having dry mouths, regardless of their states of hydration (Ham and Marcy 1983). This condition makes chewing and swallowing more difficult.

Normal aging of teeth and surrounding tissues makes them more vulnerable to deterioration, cavities, and chipping. However, the major factor leading to loss of teeth is periodontal disease (Ham and Marcy 1983). Poorly fitting dentures and lack of oral hygiene can further deter the older person's interest in eating. This can progressively lead to malnutrition and social withdrawal.

Thus, the importance of being aware of age-related physiological changes in the mouth is evident. Without awareness, it is unlikely that those who interact with older people will help them initiate interventions to enhance their enjoyment of eating.

Transition to Activity

To enhance your awareness, I would like you to participate in an activity that will give you an opportunity to experience reduced sensory input in relation to eating.

Instructions to Participants

1. Divide yourselves into pairs, preferably with someone you don't know.
2. One of you will experience a sensory loss and the other will be the helper.
3. Partner #1: Once you become impaired, tune into your *feelings* associated with dependency and your *thoughts* on how you're going to cope with this situation.
   Partner #2: When your partner becomes impaired, tune into your *feelings* associated with the responsibility for the well-being of another person and your *thoughts* on how you're going to be an effective helper.
4. When everyone is ready you will be instructed to begin your "surprise snack."
5. It will take about five minutes for you to complete your snack. When you have finished, please leave your blindfold on until everyone has finished eating.
6. Then, *before* talking to anyone, write down your feelings about the experience on your worksheet.
7. We will debrief as a group when everyone is finished.

Preparation of Participants

1. Go around to each couple and apply a blindfold to one partner. During this procedure, remind them to "tune in" to the experience.
2. After the blindfolds have been applied, distribute to each pair: a cup of fruit cocktail, a spoon, two crackers, and a napkin. Remind helpers not to begin until everyone has been served. Suggest again that they use the few minutes to really "get into" the feelings associated with sensory deprivation.
3. When everyone has been served, instruct helpers to begin serving their "surprise snack."

Transition to Debriefing

1. As you observe participants finishing their snack, remind them to leave their blindfolds on until everyone has finished.
2. Once everyone is finished, instruct participants to take off their blindfolds and write down their feelings about the experience on their worksheet.
3. Then make transition by saying: "Now that you've written down your feelings associated with this activity, let's share some of them as a group. In this way we can all learn from each other and once again appreciate both the commonalities and uniqueness of an experience for each of us."

Debriefing

1. *Dependent persons:* How did your sensory impairments affect your enjoyment of eating your surprise snack?

    > Responses may include: *I was embarrassed when I spilled some. I lost my appetite as I didn't know what I was eating. I never knew where the spoon was. I felt foolish so I just said I wasn't hungry. I was too tense to enjoy it. I felt out of control when I needed help to eat. I felt helpless when I spilled my food and couldn't see to clean it up. The food didn't have any flavor or smell, so I started to concentrate on the different textures. I felt degraded being fed so I insisted I'd do it myself, and it still wasn't enjoyable as I couldn't see, taste, or smell the snack. I didn't like eating food I didn't select for myself. I ate too fast because I didn't want to seem slow. I felt like a baby when I was told "open your mouth wide."*

    It's very difficult to carry out the task of eating when sensory input has been markedly reduced. If the challenge becomes too great, the elderly person may withdraw from the task and deny hunger. If this pattern persists it can have a major impact on the individual's physiological state.

2. *Helping persons:* What were some of the ways the dependent participants adapted to their sensory impairments?

    > Responses may include: *She made efforts to feed herself by asking for the spoon and food. He asked for a description of the food before eating. She gave up the struggle by saying she was not hungry. She told me she would indicate when she was ready to eat by a nod of her head. She asked what the food was and what it was in, then held it up to her mouth*

and "spooned it in" herself. He asked to hold the cracker himself. He wanted to smell the food before he ate it. She asked if I was eating a snack too. I was surprised to see how well she did by helping herself. When she changed my role from a helper (I was feeding her) to a facilitator (I gave her directions so she could help herself) we both felt pleased at her progress.

The difficulty of trying to enjoy a meal is further compounded when people have to be helped to eat, thus putting them in a dependent position with a potential threat to self-esteem. This threat is diminished when people are supported in their efforts to maintain as much control as possible over the situation through appropriate adaptive strategies.

3. a. *Dependent persons:* How did your sensory impairment affect the social aspects of this experience?

   Responses may include: *Eating wasn't social; I was just being fed. My helper didn't seem like a real person because I couldn't see her and didn't know her. I felt like a child trying to please a grown-up by not spilling anything. I didn't feel like small talk. I had to concentrate on eating so didn't want to talk. My helper gave me the choice to feed myself or she'd help me, that made me feel more equal and social. I felt lonely and isolated even though I knew my helper and other participants were present; I couldn't see them. I appreciated praise when I tried to feed myself. I was relieved and pleased my helper didn't use the spoon to clean my lips as one does with a baby; she gave me a napkin to wipe my own mouth as needed. Eating was a chore, not a pleasure. I felt left out when I heard laughter in the room and I couldn't see why.*

   b. *Helping persons:* What did you do to help make it a social experience?

   Responses may include: *I described the food and gave directions on where it was and how to eat it but I was very task-oriented and not social. I'm embarrassed to say I found myself talking to her like a child, saying, "Open wide, that's a good girl." I was so busy helping her I didn't think about making conversation. All I asked her was, "Are you ready for the next bite?" That wasn't very social but how else was I to know when she'd had time to empty her mouth? I made it an educational experience by teaching her how to do it herself, we both felt good. Initially I forgot to offer her a napkin to wipe her mouth between spoonfuls—using it did make the experience a bit more social.*

Traditionally, eating is most enjoyable when the occasion includes socializing with others. It provides a medium for conversation as well as a sense of belonging. However, when the helper and the elderly person become so focused on the task of "feeding and eating" that conversation is forgotten, the nutrients *if* ingested will still be beneficial to the body, but the person's sense of identity and self-esteem will be reduced.

4. *Helping persons:* What were your feelings regarding the helping role?

> Responses may include: *I didn't like the responsibility because I didn't know how much or how fast to feed her. It's a good feeling to help someone but it's draining. I was afraid I'd spill food on her. I didn't realize how "visual" food is. I found myself being patronizing and felt like a parent; I didn't like it. I had to slow my pace and it was irritating. I needed to think ahead to prepare her. I struggled with independent-dependent balance; if I knew her before it would have been easier.*

Being thrust into the role of helper is not easy, especially without preparation. However, it does happen professionally and personally. It is useful to remember that a helping relationship is a dynamic relationship between two or more people and is a reciprocal process (Brill 1985). Both the person and the helper have a shared responsibility to successfully complete a given task. This involves interdependency and ongoing communication.

Pointers to Promote and Maintain Optimum Nutrition

1. In General
   a. Encourage regular dental checkups to help to prevent periodontal disease and loss of teeth. If the person has dentures, they should be checked regularly for proper fit.
   b. Excellent oral hygiene is essential to help compensate for declining taste buds. Thus encourage older adults to brush their teeth both *before and after* meals.
   c. Before any dietary change is initiated, verify its necessity (Yen 1981). Older adults' nutritional requirements need to be individually assessed. People should eat the food they like as long as their diet is reasonably balanced and addresses any specific health problem (Kalish 1982).
   d. Dassenko (1981) says that by age fifty-five eating habits are more established than in younger age groups. Thus, if there are some inadequacies in an older person's diet that need to be corrected, just changing to new and unusual foods without an explanation may not correct the problem. The elderly adult needs informa-

tion on *why* the change is important, *how* it will be beneficial, and *what* may happen if it's ignored (Yen 1981). Allow the person time to assimilate the new knowledge and if conditions permit, introduce the change gradually.

2. Creating a Positive Dining Environment
   As circumstances permit, compensate for other sensory changes to enhance the enjoyment of the meal:
   a. Have adequate lighting in order to visually enjoy the food.
   b. Prepare foods where the aromas can be enjoyed.
   c. Fresh flowers add both to visual and smelling pleasures.
   d. Music adds a hearing dimension.
   e. Bright cloths and serving dishes add further visual stimulation.

3. Preparing an Appealing Meal
   a. Enhance the moisture of foods with low-calorie sauces, gravies, salad dressings.
   b. Enhance the flavor of foods with herbs and spices, or fruit juices.
   c. Serve small, attractive portions of foods consisting of a variety of colors, textures, and sizes. Temperatures can be varied, but neither too hot nor too cold, because either will diminish the effectiveness of the taste buds.
   d. A larger meal served at noon is more easily digested, followed by a smaller meal in the evening.

4. Facilitating the Eating Process
   a. Diet permitting, start the meal with a refreshing appetizer to stimulate the taste buds.
   b. Offer a warm liquid before starting to eat a meal as it relaxes the esophagus, promotes swallowing, and helps to compensate for changes in saliva. In addition, offer an older person the opportunity to have a few swallows of liquid frequently throughout the meal. Thirst responses tend to be impaired in the later years. This increases the potential for dehydration because many older people habitually don't drink enough (Beattie and Louie 1983). Thus *every* opportunity should be used to encourage fluid intake.
   c. If vision is severely impaired, describe the position of the food on plate in relation to hands on a clock: for example, potatoes at twelve, carrots at three, meat at six, and beans at nine.
   d. Encourage and support the elderly in their efforts to do as much as possible on their own behalf. Everyone needs to maintain as much control over their lives as possible because it helps them maintain competence and self-esteem.
   e. However, if assistance in eating is required, identify each bite of food and say when you are going to switch to a drink so that the person will be prepared to respond appropriately. For example, we prepare differently for chewing meat, munching a potato

chip, or taking a sip of coffee. Also, ask the person if he or she prefers to eat all of one kind of food at once or would prefer to switch from food to food.
5. Promoting Socialization
   a. Encourage individuals to make eating a social event whenever possible. They could either invite people to join them or go out. Another alternative is to participate in nutrition programs available in their communities. These include Meals on Wheels and federally funded congregate meal programs. In addition to the nutritional benefits, these programs can extend people's social support systems and decrease feelings of isolation and loneliness.
   b. Regardless of the setting, encourage older adults to eat at a pace that will allow time for conversation to take place. Every mealtime should be arranged for the fullest benefit of the person. It is one of the few occasions that offer the opportunity for both physical and emotional nurturance. The interaction of both enhances the effect of each. On this basis, mealtimes can still be legitimized as opportunities for vital socialization, even in our fast-paced society with time-ruled lifestyles.
   c. Those who interact with the elderly at mealtimes may need to initiate the conversation. Topics can include the latest news, personal anecdotes, reminiscing, the older person's food preferences, or family traditions. Such personalized recognition can enhance the elderly individual's self esteem and diffuse the focus on the need for assistance. Such conversations can also contribute to the helper's understanding of the person's uniqueness.

Summary

Adequate diet and sound nutritional practices remain key factors in the deterrence of disease and maintenance of the quality of life of elderly people. However, there is increasing evidence of the apparent existence of widespread subclinical malnutrition among persons fifty-five and over (Weg 1980). It is imperative that people who interact with older adults do all they can to change this situation.

Everyone usually has some degree of control over what, when, how, and whether to eat. Such interrelated factors as motivation, health status, culture, lifelong habits, availability of food, economics, and education influence a person's ultimate decision. To the extent that we can work together *with* older people to assess their nutritional status and modify their diet if indicated, we have contributed to the correction of malnutrition among the elderly and promoted the achievement and maintenance of their optimum physical and psychosocial well-being. As an initial step, I hope that by participating in this activity you have increased your appreciation of the effects of reduced sensory input on people's enjoyment of eating and enhanced your understanding of ways to compensate for these changes.

Evaluation

Please take a few moments now to complete the evaluation.

Surprise Snack, Worksheet: Dependent Person

1. What were your feelings regarding eating with reduced sensory input?

2. What did you do to adapt to your impairment?

3. How did your reduced sensory input affect the social aspects of this experience?

Surprise Snack, Worksheet: Helping Person

1. What were your feelings regarding your helping role?

2. What did the dependent person do on his or her own behalf to adapt to the impairment?

3. What did you do to help make it a "social experience"?

Surprise Snack, Evaluation

1. Did this activity increase your awareness of how reduced sensory input affects the enjoyment of eating?

Not much		Some		A lot
1	2	3	4	5

2. Did this activity increase your appreciation of an older person's adaptive efforts to maintain as much independence as possible?

Not much		Some		A lot
1	2	3	4	5

3. Did this activity increase your appreciation of the importance of socialization during eating?

Not much		Some		A lot
1	2	3	4	5

4. Identify three ways to promote an enjoyable eating experience for an older adult.

   _____

   _____

   _____

5. Give at least one example of how this activity will affect your interactions with older adults.

8 Maintaining Mobility

Rationale for Activity

Independence is highly valued in our society. Studies have shown that elderly people list fear of dependency as very high among their concerns about growing older (Saxon and Etten 1978). Mobility is the key factor in maintaining independence and the musculoskeletal system (muscles and bones of the body) is the key to this mobility. This system allows for an extensive range of body motions, from those that move the entire body to those that carry out precise actions. This system also provides the mechanisms for differing rates of movement. Such versatility of movements are necessary for a person to function independently in today's complex society.

Progressive age-related changes in the musculoskeletal system affect its ability to continue to function at levels of peak performance. However, individuals' ability to continue to function independently can be promoted if they have an understanding of age-related changes that occur in this system and strategies to minimize the effect of these changes. It is important that those working with older adults be aware of these physiological changes and ways to minimize their effect so they can be more sensitive in their interactions with the elderly and try to motivate them to take appropriate responsibility to promote and maintain their own mobility. This exercise provides participants with an opportunity to gain both an increased awareness of the effects of musculoskeletal changes on people's mobility and an increased understanding of ways to minimize the effects of these changes.

Participants: This activity is appropriate for graduate and undergraduate students and professional and paraprofessionals in health care and gerontology, and family caregivers.

Objectives

Upon completion of this activity participants will:

1. Be able to identify four changes in the musculoskeletal system.
2. Have an increased awareness of the effect of musculoskeletal changes on an elderly person's mobility.
3. Be able to identify four strategies to promote the maintenance of strength and mobility.
4. Be able to give at least one example of how this activity will affect their interactions with older adults.

Class Size: Open. Enough space is required for participants to walk around the room.

Time: Thirty minutes.

> Fifteen minutes: introduction and activity
> Ten minutes: debriefing
> Five minutes: evaluation

Materials: Maintaining Mobility Worksheets, Evaluation Sheets.

Teaching Notes

1. This activity is based on one initially conducted by Dr. Robert Wiswell, who was a guest lecturer in one of my classes.
2. I have found it to be very useful in helping participants become aware of the effect of postural changes on individuals' mobility, "view of the world," and communication. Never has any participant expressed positive feelings regarding this experience. They don't like being "put in that position." When we move on to the debriefing, which includes pointers on how to delay the aging process and minimize its effect on the musculoskeletal system, I usually have their full attention.
3. This activity can be used with a variety of topics including: physiological changes, exercise, and health promotion.

Introduction to Activity

1. People's mobility is the key to their independent functioning and such independence is highly prized in our society. To the degree that mobility is lost, so is a person's control over life threatened, lifestyle altered and negotiation with the environment made more hazardous.

2. We perform a variety of movements in every activity of our daily lives. Some are complex, some are relatively simple; some are gross, some are refined; some are fast, some are slow. However, regardless of their type or rate, all these movements depend on our musculoskeletal system, which is comprised of the muscles and bones of our bodies. Our posturing is also dependent on this system.
3. Normal age-related changes in the musculoskeletal system progressively affect its ability to function at peak performance. It is important for those who work with older adults to be aware of these physiological changes and ways to minize their impact. This awareness can increase their sensitivity toward the elderly and their interest in motivating them to take appropriate responsibility to promote and maintain their own mobility.
4. Age-related changes in the musculoskeletal system include the following:
    a. The chief aging change in bone is osteopenia, or a decrease in skeletal bone mass, resulting in bones that are lighter and more porous. Mild osteopenic change is common, occurring in approximately 25 percent of women and 6 percent of men over sixty-five. Many authorities would now reserve the term "osteoporosis" for the more marked degrees of osteopenia. These changes predispose older people to skeletal fractures (Ham and Marcy 1983).
    b. Degenerative or osteoarthritic changes in joints could be regarded as part of normal aging, as such changes are found in the majority of older people (Ham and Marcy 1983). This noninflammatory disorder of movable joints is characterized by deterioration and abrasion of articular cartilage. It affects mainly the weight-bearing joints (knees, hips, and lumbar spine), cervical spine, and distal finger joints. The main symptom is aching joint pain that occurs on motion and weight-bearing like a "friction effect." It is relieved by rest. Stiffness after sitting or on arising (articular gelling) may occur but persists only for a few minutes. The course of the disease is usually slowly progressive (Grob 1983a).
    c. There is a decrease in height caused by the thinning and flattening of the vertebral discs (Ebersole and Hess 1985).
    d. The reduction in the size of muscles has been estimated to be as much as 30 percent from ages thirty to eighty. This decrease reduces muscle strength. It has been noted that these changes are more evident in the muscles of the lower extremities because these muscles are used less in later life, in contrast to the upper extremity muscles which are used more often for daily activities such as preparing meals and eating (Sullivan 1987).
    e. As muscle mass and strength decrease, so does endurance. Muscles are less able to sustain activity without fatiguing.

100 • *Understanding Older Adults*

    f. Arms, hands, legs, and feet are thinner and bones become more prominent because of the reduction in muscle mass.
    g. Normal gait changes with aging include:
        i. For women: waddling gait, narrow walking and standing base.
        ii. For men: small-stepped gait, wide walking and standing base (Ham and Marcy 1983).
    h. Flexibility of joint movement is affected by the length of muscle fibers and the composition of the surrounding connective tissue. With aging, the decrease in muscle fibers and changes in collagen impede joint flexibility. Flexor and extensor muscles are affected, but the greater loss occurs in the extensor muscles (Milde 1988). Thus, older people are more prone to flexion or bending of their joints. Grob (1983b) concurs and further says that in old age the posture tends to become one of *general* flexion. This is caused in part by changes in the vertebral column, intervertebral discs, ligaments, joints, tendons, and muscles. Changes in posture can include:
        i. Head and neck bent forward.
        ii. Dorsal spine gently kyphotic (hump back).
        iii. Upper limbs bent at elbows and wrists.
        iv. Hips and knees slightly flexed.

Transition to Activity

To increase your awareness of the effect of some of these changes on an older person's posture, mobility, and communication patterns, I would like you to participate in the following activity.

Instruction to Participants

1. Place your Maintaining Mobility Worksheet in front of you.
2. Please stand up as straight as you can and do the following:
    a. Raise up on your toes and down again.
    b. Raise your arms over your head and reach up as far as you can.
    c. Rotate your arms in their sockets, now rotate your legs.
    d. Now, just shake all over to loosen up.
3. Now, I'd like you to focus on your muscles and connective tissues. You are beginning to feel their accelerated aging. They are beginning to feel tighter, and you feel your joints beginning to bend, so "go with the flexions."
    a. Bend you head and neck forward.
    b. Bend your shoulders forward.
    c. Bend slightly at the waist.
    d. Bend your elbows, wrists, and knees.

4. Maintain this flexed position as you walk around the room and talk to each other (allow three to four minutes).
   a. Observe changes in yourself.
   b. Observe changes in the other participants.
5. Now find a partner and one of you sit down and the other remain standing. Carry on a conversation after a few minutes (allow two to three minutes).
6. Now return to your seats and answer the questions on your worksheet (allow three to five minutes).

Transition to Debriefing

Now that you've recorded your experiences and observations on mobility in the later years, let's discuss them.

Debriefing

1. Describe your feelings about this experience.

   Responses may include: *Frustrating; looking down made me unhappy. I like to hold my head up and see people. I felt deformed. I felt miserable and wanted to let people know. I felt sad and isolated. I felt abnormal. I lost my self-esteem. I'll be more sensitive to anyone's postural changes. I felt tired and tense. I felt I looked humble but know I was angry inside. I felt less in control of my environment. I wasn't different inside but I knew people saw me differently.*

   Thank you for sharing. You've certainly expressed feelings that indicate your sensitivity to these postural changes.

2. What changes did you observe about yourself?

   Responses may include: *My neck hurt. I walked slower and shuffled. My knees hurt. I couldn't see anything but the floor unless I tilted my head back. It was harder to breath. I got tired quickly. I was very self-conscious. I took smaller steps. I couldn't move very fast.*

3. What changes did you observe about the other participants?

   Responses may include: *They looked "crooked." We couldn't look at each other. We had less to talk about. It was too much of an effort to talk. They looked old and ill. They were self-absorbed. They walked carefully as if they were afraid of falling.*

You've certainly demonstrated how "experience is the best teacher." You've reported on some of the major implications related to postural and mobility changes in the elderly: negative feelings associated with a changed body image, less in control of life, communication was more difficult, and movement took more effort. Thank you for sharing these insights.

Transition to Pointers

Now that you've experienced and observed some of the effects of impaired mobility on the elderly, let's discuss some pointers that can help delay the aging process and minimize its effect on the musculoskeletal system.

Pointers to Promote and Maintain Mobility

1. The extent of many musculoskeletal changes in older people is mistakenly attributed to the aging process, when much of the deterioration is caused by their poor physical fitness and disuse of their muscles. These changes include shortened flexor muscles, weak antigravity muscles supporting the head and body joints, deteriorated back and joint muscles that produce poor posture and kyphosis. Such postural changes restrict expansion of the chest and diaphragm and curtail ventilation, which further limits physical activity and mobility (Harris 1983). There is strong evidence that aging muscles' atrophy is a result of such factors as disuse, poor nutrition, and chronic disease (Sullivan 1987).
2. The combination of normal aging changes and immobility in the elderly often results in major complications that can result in discomfort, pain, and even death. Keeping the body active through a specific exercise program will help prevent these complications and result in an improved quality of life for older adults (Benison and Hogstel 1986). Even though the intensity of exercise and maximum potential decreases with age, the need for exercise does not (Wiswell 1980).
3. Appropriate exercise can develop, maintain, and improve muscular strength, flexibility, endurance, range of motion, and balance. For example, ordinary calisthenics and light weightlifting can improve muscle strength and restore lean muscle mass even in persons beyond age seventy, unless hypertension or cardiac problems limit such activity (Harris 1983).
4. Activities and exercise programs vary in complexity, duration, and intensity. Everyone needs to be individually assessed because of the great variations in people's functional losses associated with aging.

Harris (1983) suggests that before exercise is prescribed, a thorough history and physical examination should be performed to assess a person's health.
5. Regardless of a person's age and level of fitness, it is never too late to begin an exercise program (Sullivan 1987). Almost every older person, even those confined to wheelchairs and beds, can tolerate and will benefit from a modified form of movement therapy (Benison and Hogstel 1986). For example, a 102-year-old wheelchair-bound lady who squeezes a soft ball or small bean bag while watching her favorite television program is maintaining her grip strength and the flexibility of her fingers.
6. The functioning of all body systems is directly or indirectly enhanced by periodic changes in body position. Thus, it is important for people to establish their own individualized daily routine which provides frequent change of body position and pacing of activities. This will:
   a. Minimize stress on any body system.
   b. Promote circulation and maintenance of functioning.
   c. Maintain capabilities to carry out activities of daily living.
   d. Provide a balance of rest and activities.
7. In addition to the contribution of exercises to the improvement of physiological performance, there is substantial literature that suggests exercise plays an additional role in the maintenance and improvement in cognitive functioning, psychomotor performance, and, possibly, positive personality characteristics. These changes may improve elderly individuals' self-care potential, increase their desire for maintenance of vitality, and assist them in coping with physical and emotional stress (Wiswell 1980).
8. In conjuction with a regular program of exercise and activities, other pointers to promote and maintain optimum mobility include:
   a. Practicing good nutrition by:
      i. Eating a well-balanced diet containing adequate vitamins, minerals, fiber, and fluids.
      ii. Not smoking or using excessive alcohol.
   b. Coping with normal joint stiffness by:
      i. Keeping room temperatures around seventy degrees at night, as coldness tends to aggravate stiff joints.
      ii. Before getting out of bed, "stretching like a cat," slowly and thoroughly, gradually flexing, extending, and rotating all joints.
      iii. Taking a warm bath to help loosen stiff joints.
      iv. Walking, which is perhaps the best exercise for loosening up stiff joints in the legs.
   c. Maintaining good posture, proper weight, and good body mechanics to minimize joint stress and strain.
   d. Wearing shoes that provide good support and have nonskid soles.

e. Safeguarding the environment to reduce risk of falls by:
   i. Removing scatter rugs.
   ii. Keeping indoor and outdoor pathways clear of extension cords and clutter.
   iii. Putting grab bars in bathroom and nonskid strips in bathtubs and showers.
   iv. Putting contrasting colored strips on the edge of stairs to increase visibility.

Summary

This activity has focused on age-related changes in the musculoskeletal system. Though these changes are progressive, this process can be delayed and its results minimized if older adults will build into their lives an appropriate activity and exercise program and make it an integral and valued part of their daily lives. Benison and Hogstel (1986) have said it is important to emphasize the benefits of physical activity in slowing the rate of the aging process.

The overall goal is to promote and maintain older people's muscular strength, endurance, flexibility, joint mobility, and posture. Proper maintenance of the musculoskeletal system is the key to achieving this goal. It can provide the aging person with continued independence and a positive self-concept by minimizing the debilitating effects of disuse and impaired mobility (Sullivan 1987).

I hope that by participating in this exercise you have increased your awareness of the effect of musculoskeletal changes on an elderly person's mobility and your knowledge of the musculoskeletal system and of ways to promote and maintain its optimum functioning in the elderly.

Evaluation

Please take a few moments now to complete an evaluation.

Maintaining Mobility, Worksheet

1. Describe your feelings about this experience.

2. What changes did you observe
   a. about yourself?

   b. about the other participants?

Maintaining Mobility, Evaluation

1. Identify four changes in the musculoskeletal system.

   _____

   _____

   _____

   _____

2. Did this activity increase your awareness of the effect of musculoskeletal changes on mobility?

Not much		Some		A lot
1	2	3	4	5

3. Identify four strategies to promote maintenance of strength and mobility.

   _____

   _____

   _____

   _____

4. Give at least one example of how this activity will affect your interactions with older adults.

9 Skin Sensitivity

Rationale for Activity

An individual's skin, as the most visible part of the body, is a general indicator of health and aging. Tindall (1983) says it serves as a witness to the long-term effects of a person's inheritance, environment, biochemistry, diet, emotions, activity, and longevity. As such, it would seem to merit the best care we can give it. Yet, as with other systems of our body, we frequently take it for granted and many times abuse it. We sun-bake it, bang it, sit on it for prolonged periods and decorate it as it suits our fancy.

In the earlier stages of the life cycle, the skin has its reserve capacity and recuperative powers to help compensate for such insults. However, in the later stages of life, normal age-related changes in the skin and surrounding tissues not only deter its ability to recuperate from such abuse but also predisposes it to new kinds of problems. As people age, appropriate care of their skin becomes increasingly important. This care may be undertaken by older people themselves, provided by caregivers, or a combination of the two. It is important that people who interact with the elderly be aware of age-related skin changes and ways to compensate for them so that in direct caregiving or in opportunities for informal health teaching they can promote good skin care for older adults. This activity provides the participants with an opportunity to gain an increased awareness of the importance of good skin care for the elderly.

Participants: This activity is appropriate for graduate and undergraduate students and professionals and paraprofessionals in health care and gerontology, and family caregivers.

Objectives

Upon completion of this activity participants will:

1. Have an increased awareness of the negative effects of too much pressure or prolonged pressure on an older person's skin.
2. Be able to identify four ways to promote good care for elderly persons' skin.
3. Have an increased understanding of the importance of good skin care for the elderly.
4. Be able to give at least one example of how this activity will affect their interactions with older adults.

Class size: Open

    Activity #1: Divide class into pairs.
    Activity #2: Divide into groups of six to eight.

Time: Forty-five minutes.
    Activity #1: Thirty minutes

        Ten minutes: introduction and observations
        Ten minutes: recordings
        Ten minutes: debriefing

    Activity #2: Fifteen minutes (if done following Activity #1; if done separately, allow five extra minutes for introduction).

        Five minutes: observation and recording
        Five minutes: debriefing
        Five minutes: evaluation

Materials: Activity #1: For every two students—two bananas: (one fairly green and one ripe with brown spots), two paper plates and napkins, two Activity #1 Worksheets.
    Activity #2: For every six to eight students—two peaches (one firm and unblemished and one with a large bruise, discolored, and skin broken); two paper plates and napkins, Activity #2 Worksheets and Evaluation Sheets.

Teaching Notes

1. This activity uses fruit to represent the skin of elderly people and to bring into focus how age-related changes increase the skin's fragility.
2. I selected bananas for the first activity because they clearly demonstrate the differences between young and old skin and also, when very ripe, they are easily and visibly damaged by even moderate pressure. Also, they are easy to peel so the underlying tissue can be

examined. If obtaining two bananas for each pair of students is a problem, you could ask for two volunteers to carry out the action steps of the activity, then pass the two bananas around the class so that they can be assessed by all the students. I selected peaches for the second activity because of their thinner skins and also because they can be considered to have a "sitting posture" and thus be able to illustrate the problem of prolonged pressure on the body. However, depending on your location, the season, and your imagination, other fruits or vegetables could probably be used as effectively.

3. In the process of developing this activity I tested it out with a few close colleagues. Initially, they could only see the humor but soon began to personify the bananas and really got into the examination of their skins. The following responses have been typical of subsequent participants: It was a fascinating comparison. I never thought I could "get into" bananas but I did. It was very impressive to make a point. I'll never forget that poor peach with that horrible-looking pressure sore!

4. In preparation for this activity, I start shopping at least a week ahead for the fruit. Invariably I have to go to several stores to get the right "greenness" and "ripeness" needed. One year I had to put some of the peaches outside in a baggie under the sun in order to speed up the aging process!

5. I bring into the classroom the bananas, peaches, and other materials on one or more covered trays. This has always aroused the interest of the participants. I respond to their questions by saying, "You're going to learn about an important part of the body." This helps to set the stage for a novel and positive learning experience.

6. It is especially important to practice this activity with family, friends, or colleagues. Its success is enhanced if you are comfortable with the blending of humor and insights.

Introduction to Activities

1. Age-related changes in the skin and surrounding tissues predispose it to special kinds of problems as well as reduce its ability to heal. Interrelated changes include the following:
    a. Reduction of subcutaneous fat on the extremities causes loss of insulation on bony prominences which promotes skin breakdown, increased susceptibility to cold temperatures, and less support for blood vessels that have become more fragile and more prone to bruises.
    b. Collagen becomes more fibrous so there is a loss of elasticity and strength, and the skin is more fragile and susceptible to breakdown.
    c. Decreased activity of oil glands results in increased dryness and fragility of the skin. This makes it particularly susceptible to the destructive effects of moderate pressure.

d. Cell regeneration is slower; skin breakdown or a wound take longer to heal.
e. Sweat glands atrophy so there is less ability to respond to changes in temperature.
f. Deterioration of peripheral nerves, by reducing sensation and slowing reflexes, contributes to the increased tendency to skin injury, particularly of hands and feet. Also, there is an impaired ability to feel sensations of heat, cold, pressure, and pain, so pathology is more easily ignored (Ham and Marcy 1983).
2. It is important to be aware of these changes as we interact with the elderly so that we can prevent injury and promote good skin care.
3. To help you appreciate the significance of these age-related skin changes and the skin's resultant vulnerability, I would like you to participate in two activities.

Preparation for Participants: Activity #1

1. Divide class into pairs.
2. Pass out to each pair: one green banana, one very ripe banana, two paper plates, two napkins.

Instructions to Participants

1. Place your Activity #1 Worksheet in front of you.
2. As you receive your young and old bananas begin to examine:
    a. the similarities between banana skin and human skin (texture, blemishes, etc.).
    b. the differences between the "young" and "old" skin.
3. Record these differences under Findings #1 on your Worksheets (allow one to two minutes).
4. Now I'd like you to do a familiar activity that we do everyday as a way of greeting each other. It involves touch, which is very important to all of us.
    a. Give your partner a *firm* "I'm glad to know you" handshake; now turn to the next closest person to you and give that individual a *firm* "Hello" handshake.
    b. Next, I'd like you to shake hands "across the generations." Since I couldn't arrange for actual people to be here today, I'm going to ask you to be imaginative and simulate shaking a younger, then an older person's hand by utilizing two bananas as follows:
        i. One of you hold the green banana as if supporting a person's arm to receive a handshake (demonstrate).
        ii. Now have your partner give the simulated "young hand" a firm "glad to know you" handshake.
        iii. Repeat the procedure with the simulated "old hand."

5. Now, once again examine your bananas and observe any outward changes resulting from the pressure of the handshake.
6. Record the changes under Findings #2 on your worksheets (allow one to two minutes).
7. Now carefully peel the skin off both your bananas and place one on each plate.
8. Examine:
   a. the differences in the underlying tissues of your young and old bananas.
   b. the similarities between banana tissue and human tissue.
9. Record your findings under Findings #3 on your worksheet (allow one to two minutes).
10. Now complete the last question on your worksheet (allow one to two minutes).

Transition to Debriefing: Activity #1

Now that you've recorded your observations on the differences between younger and older skin in response to pressure, let's discuss them.

Debriefing

1. Findings #1: What initial differences did you find in your bananas?
   Responses may include:
   a. Young banana.
      i. Visual: Nice-looking. Pretty. Looked fresh and appealing. Clear skin. Unblemished. "Uptight."
      ii. Touch: Nice to touch. Well-supported. Easier to "shake hands with." "Tough skinned." Resilient. Smooth.
      iii. Smell: Not much smell.
   b. Old banana.
      i. Visual: Unattractive. Ugly. Shriveled. Dull skin. Looked smaller even though actual size was the same. Dehydrated. "Brown spots." Wrinkled. Fragile. More mellow.
      ii. Touch: Soft and flabby. Thin skin. Kind of mushy. Hard to really get a firm grip. Less response. Felt weak and vulnerable.
      iii. Smell: Sweet smell. Smells better than the young banana.

You've certainly examined your young and old bananas well and drawn some insightful conclusions. It is interesting how skin can come to represent a total person! We look at a person and certain characteristics remind us of youth while other characteristics remind us of old age.

2. Findings #2: What differences did you find in the young and old skin after the handshake?
   Responses may include:
   a. Young banana.
      i. Visual: Kept shape. Still looked good. No observable changes.
   b. Old banana.
      i. Visual: More bruises. I didn't mean to squash it. The skin broke. Mashed where I grabbed it. I left an indentation.

   Again, your observations are very good and sensitively shared.

3. Findings #3: Once you peeled the skin off, what differences did you find in the underlying tissues of your young and old bananas?
   Responses may include:
   a. Young banana.
      i. Visual: Seemed okay. Tissue looked unblemished. Same color all over.
      ii. Touch: Was firm and smooth. No mushy areas.
   b. Old banana.
      i. Visual: Skin broke as I tried to peel it off. Tissue looked mashed and discolored. Didn't hold its shape. Looked ulcerated.
      ii. Touch: I didn't want to touch it. Felt "yucky." Liquid seeping out.

   You've certainly demonstrated your examination skills and sensitivity.

4. Would some of you like to share your thoughts and feelings about this experience?

   > Responses may include: *I am more aware that you can't always see if you've hurt someone unintentionally. I never thought of the differences between young and old skin. When I rub lotion on my grandmother, I will be more gentle and take more time. I will handle older people with more care.*

   Thank you for sharing. Remember, it's not just a handshake that requires gentleness, it's any contact we have with an older person's skin. For example: helping them get up from a chair, holding their arm when crossing a street, helping them on with their clothes, rubbing lotion on their arms. The overall point I want to make is "reach out and touch someone" but "handle with care."

Transition to Activity #2

Now that you've completed an activity that focused on increasing your awareness of the results of too much immediate pressure on an elderly person's skin, I'd like you to observe the potential result of prolonged pressure on the skin caused by immobility.

Once again I am going to simulate human skin by using fruit. This time, I am using peaches.

Preparation for Participants

1. Place each peach on a separate plate. Place the old peach on the plate so that the large bruise is resting directly on the plate. This helps the students visualize an example of pressure on the skin.
2. Divide up participants into groups of six to eight.
3. Give a young peach and an old peach to each group. Also give each person a napkin.

Introduction to Activity #2

When purchased from the store one week ago these peaches were clearly from different "generations." One was golden, mellow, and soft. The other was a lighter yellow and firm. However, neither had any bruises or breaks in the skin. Since that time, they have been "sitting together," experiencing the same environmental conditions, but their skin has responded quite differently.

Instructions to Participants

1. Place your Activity #2 Worksheet in front of you.
2. Pass both peaches around so each of you can pick them up and examine the differences between the two.
3. Record your observations on your worksheets.

Transition to Debriefing

1. What differences did you observe between your peaches?
   Responses may include:
   a. Young peach.
      i. Visual: Good color all over. No marks on bottom.
      ii. Touch: Firm. Good support.
      iii. Smell: Not much odor.
   b. Old peach.
      i. Visual: Good color on top and sides but very discolored on bottom It looked awful. It looked sore. It was brownish and yucky. It looked infected.
      ii. Touch: Soft but looked okay on top and sides; however,

114 • *Understanding Older Adults*

        when I picked it up it was squishy on bottom, fluid was oozing out from the broken skin on the bottom. I didn't want to touch it.
     iii. Smell: Pungent. Not healthy.
  2. Would some of you like to share your thoughts and feelings about this experience?

> Responses may include: *I'm going to keep better track of time when my patients are up in their wheelchairs. What you see on the top doesn't mean everything's okay underneath. Every time I see an older person in a chair I'm going to wonder how long they've been sitting there and what their skin looks like. It made me feel kind of sick to see a person's skin look so awful. I didn't realize how important changing position was for older people.*

Thank you for sharing your thoughts and feelings.

Transition to Pointers

Now that you've experienced and observed the effect of too much pressure and prolonged pressure on an older person's skin, let's discuss some pointers to promote the maintenance of healthy skin.

Pointers to Promote Healthy Skin

1. Be sensitive whenever you have a physical contact with older adults. For example, use a gentle, prolonged handshake using your free hand to cover the older person's hand rather than a "skin crusher" quick handshake (demonstrate). This provides a longer "caring connection" and maximizes touch.
2. Be considerate of older people's skin when assisting them to change positions in a bed or chair. Lift rather than slide them in order to avoid a friction rub, which can cause a breakdown of their skin.
3. Keep an older adult's extremities covered to compensate for the loss of subcutaneous fat and less efficient temperature control.
4. Prevent sudden changes or extremes in temperature.
5. Promote skin health by avoiding overuse of soaps, astringents, and perfumes, which promote dry skin; using tepid rather than hot baths; patting rather than rubbing skin to dry it; using emolients frequently, including after a bath or shower when the skin is still moist; protecting from sun by avoiding direct exposure as much as possible and using maximum sunscreen thirty minutes before exposure to sun.
6. Encourage good personal hygiene and frequent self-examination of skin for any changes in appearance.

7. Encourage the maintenance of optimum nutritional and fluid intake and body weight. This will promote the health of all body systems, including the skin.
8. Iverson-Carpenter (1988) has reported that anyone, regardless of age, who stays in one position without the relief of pressure on bony prominences (elbows, sacrum, ankles, etc.) can develop a pressure sore. A pressure sore is caused when external pressure causes blood vessels to collapse and interferes with blood and fluid flow to and from the cells resulting in ischemia (local anemia). If prolonged, death of tissue will result. To help prevent pressure sores, discourage people from sitting in a chair any longer than one hour at a time. If they do, they should shift their body position at least every thirty minutes and move their arms and legs frequently. It is best if they can get up every hour and walk around for a few moments. This stimulates circulation and deters the development of pressure sores.
9. Encourage a physician-approved regular exercise program to maintain endurance, strength, flexibility, and mobility. This in turn will promote optimum functioning.

These pointers are valid for everyone at any age but become increasingly important in later years.

Summary

This activity has focused on the importance of being aware of and sensitive to age-related changes in the skin and the need to know ways to compensate for these changes to promote the maintenance of healthy skin. I hope that by participating in this activity you have increased your awareness of the negative effects of too much or prolonged pressure on an older person's skin and increased your knowledge of ways to promote the maintenance of healthy skin in later years. A one-line summary: *Don't* be thrifty with touch; *do* be gentle!

Evaluation

Please take a few moments now to complete an evaluation.

Skin Sensitivity, Activity #1 Worksheet

1. *Findings #1* What differences do you find in your bananas?
   a. Young banana

   b. Old banana

2. *Findings #2* What differences do you find in your bananas now?
   a. Young banana

   b. Old banana

3. *Findings #3* What differences do you find in your bananas now?
   a. Young banana

   b. Old banana

4. Describe your feelings about this experience.

Skin Sensitivity, Activity #2 Worksheet

1. What differences did you find in the peaches?
   a. Young peach

   b. Old peach

2. Describe your feelings about this experience

Skin Sensitivity, Evaluation

1. Did this activity increase your awareness of the negative effects of immobility of an older person's skin?

Not much		Some		A lot
1	2	3	4	5

2. Did this activity increase your understanding of the importance of good skin care for the elderly?

Not much		Some		A lot
1	2	3	4	5

3. Identify four ways to promote good care for an elderly person's skin.

   _____

   _____

   _____

   _____

4. Give at least one example of how this activity will affect your interactions with older adults.

PART 3

ENVIRONMENTAL CHANGES

10 Home Assessment

Rationale for Activity

Being a homeowner is highly valued in our nation. As a reflection of this value, 66 percent of the elderly living in cities and 90 percent of those in rural areas own their own homes (Atchley 1987). A home can represent status, achievement, independence, competence, control, and self-esteem. Home is also "where the heart is," holding treasured memories of the past, providing a familiar environment in the present and a source of continuity in the future. However, ironically, it is because the environment is so familiar that it can present a hazard to the functioning of elderly people. They don't observe either the changes that have happened gradually over the years and/or the toll of deferred maintenance. Atchley (1987) has said the majority of older Americans have lived in their present dwellings for more than twenty years, that these homes tend to be more than forty years old, and are more likely to be dilapidated than homes of younger people.

At just the time when the elderly are spending more hours in their homes, and coping with sensory and mobility changes that can make functioning in any environment more difficult, their homes are also showing the decrements of age and therefore putting the aging resident in double jeopardy. This can result in reduced safety and increased vulnerability to accidents.

It is important that those who interact with the elderly help them look at the familiar with a new perspective, that of assessing their environment for potential hazards that can place them in jeopardy. The home assessment visit is one way to begin this important educative process.

In addition, the home visit can provide insights into the older person's past and present lifestyles, activities, and social support system.

122 • *Understanding Older Adults*

The ultimate goal is to work with elderly people to help them create a supportive home environment that will promote their optimum physical and psychosocial functioning. This in turn will enhance the probability of their being able to remain in their own homes until they decide to move.

This activity provides the participants with an opportunity to practice using a framework designed to facilitate their assessment of an elderly person's home environment. This in turn will prepare them to do an actual home assessment.

Participants: This activity is appropriate for graduate and undergraduate students and professionals and paraprofessionals in mental health, social work, health care, and gerontology.

Objectives

Upon completion of this activity participants will:

1. Have an increased appreciation of the value of a home environmental assessment visit.
2. Be able to identify four things to assess for home safety.
3. Be able to identify four interventions to provide a more supportive environment.
4. Be able to identify four indicators of an elderly person's lifestyle, activities, and psychosocial supports.
5. Be able to assess a home environment.
6. Be able to give at least one example of how this activity will affect their interactions with older adults.

Class Size: Open. If a large class, it can be broken up into small groups of five to seven so participants can compare and contrast their own "visualized" home.

Time: Forty-five to sixty minutes (depending on class size)

> Five minutes: introduction
> Thirty-five to fifty minutes: exercise and discussion (if break up into small discussion groups, allow the additional 15 minutes)
> Five minutes: evaluation

Materials: Home Assessment Worksheets, Debriefing Sheets, Evaluation Sheets.

Teaching Notes

1. Everyone lives in a home, so it is "a given," a familiar environment. In such an environment, we tend not to be objectively observant

because we know what's there. This exercise helps the participant "look at the familiar in a different way," focusing on the multiple and varied structural and psychosocial details that can significantly affect an older person's functioning. Encourage participants to share their recollections about their homes, but be supportive if they can't "remember the obvious." A point to be made during the activity is that because of the familiarity of the environment, we don't recognize potential hazards.

2. When the participants visualize in their mind's eye a home in which they have a personal interest, assessment of safety, security, and psychosocial resources becomes more significant because the home involves people about whom they care. This personalization enhances the learning experience and its transferability to doing home assessments in a professional capacity.

3. Participants' selected homes can vary widely depending on their ages and socioeconomic status. If the group is homogeneous, point out similarities regarding their homes and then contrast with other homes at different economic levels.

4. Follow-Up assignment for participants:
   a. If the home assessment activity is part of an ongoing class, I follow it up with an assignment that requires the student to carry out an assessment of an elderly person's home.
   b. I usually let the students make their own selection of a home to visit. Some choose a home of an elderly relative (and are usually amazed at the things they "see for the first time"). If they don't know an elderly person, I help them find one.
   c. Before the visit, I discuss with them that a home assessment is only done at the invitation of the person. My experience has indicated that most people are proud to act as host or hostess and show the interviewer through the home (Remnet 1981). However, the extent of the tour and questions need to be in accordance with the purpose of the visit and the stage of the relationship between the visitor and the older person.
   d. When the students go out on their visit, they use the worksheet from this activity as a guideline for their assessment. Also, I suggest that they make an extra copy to give to the host/hostess so that they can actively participate in the assessment as they "walk through" their home. This "team approach" helps to keep the interview focused.
   e. Any assessment of a home environment, favorable or unfavorable, is somewhat subjective. Students need to be cautioned to remember that there is no "ideal" environment, per se. The optimum environment is one that has been individualized to provide its occupants the physical and psychosocial supports necessary to promote their maximum functioning.
   f. Depending on the objectives for the class, I have expanded this activity to include the additional assignment of having the students use their home assessment data as one guideline for

determining the older person's need for services from the community. The activity, Needs and Services: Optimum Fit, in chapter 3 provides more information on this topic.

g. Students enjoy this assignment. It gives them an opportunity to get out into the community, visit the well elderly, and in the process sharpen their observation skills and enhance their appreciation of the strengths and coping strategies of older people. Their comments have included:

> *It gives me a chance to put everything I've learned about old people together and use it effectively. I have never 'tuned into' a home environment before; it tells you so much. I was amazed at how a ninety-year-old lady can do so much for herself; she only has a homemaker help her three hours a week. My grandfather is installing a smoke alarm because of my visit. My eighty-two-year-old neighbor is legally blind, yet you should see how she cooks and keeps her home; she taught me how important it is to keep everything in its place.*

Introduction to Activity

1. We have all lived in a family home. For some of us, it's been only one home; for others it's been many, depending on lifestyles, occupations, and stage in the life cycle.
2. As people grow older, their homes not only may be their major financial asset, but also may represent psychosocial ties with the past and the comfort and convenience of a familiar environment in the present. Most elderly want to remain in their own homes as long as possible.
3. However, many older people are not aware of how an environment that was safe in their younger years may now contain potential safety hazards because of:
   a. changes in the neighborhood.
   b. the normal wear and tear on a home and its deferred maintenance.
   c. their unsafe habits in carrying out activities of daily living.
   d. their decreased sensory input.
4. An assessment of the home, when conducted with the elderly person, can be the beginning step in creating a more supportive environment.
5. A home assessment has advantages for the elderly person and the visitor:
   a. it is on the older person's "home ground," so he or she is in a familiar environment and you are the visitor.
   b. because it is his or her "home ground" you have a unique opportunity to assess:

i. the surrounding neighborhood and its visible resources.
ii. the physical environment of the home with its supports and barriers.
iii. objects and pictures that provide insights into important events in the person's past.
iv. current crafts, hobbies, cards, books, journals, or bulletins that provide insights into present interests and activities, interpersonal relationships, and potential social resources in the person's life.

6. In order to help you gain a renewed appreciation of the significance of a home, I would like you to do an environmental assessment of a home in which you have lived. You will be assessing it in terms of safety and for insights into the occupant's past and present lifestyle, interests, and social supports. Also, we will discuss possible interventions that can provide a more supportive environment to maximize an older person's safety.

Instructions to Participants

1. Place your Home Assessment Worksheet in front of you.
2. Now close your eyes and take a few deep breaths.
3. Picture in your mind's eye the family home in which you spent most of your growing-up years or another home that is emotionally significant to you. Picture the neighborhood, the type of home, the yards, the front door. Now visualize each room and what is in it (allow one to two minutes).
4. Open your eyes and as we discuss a home assessment framework, keep in your mind's eye the home you have chosen and respond to the following questions. If you can't respond, indicate why not. For example, you may have never noticed, forgotten, or the question may not apply to your home.
5. As we "walk through" the assessment, mark the boxes beside the descriptors that apply to your home. At the end of each section, we'll discuss similarities and differences among your homes, as well as interventions for a more supportive home environment.

Questions for Participants

Let's start with some background information about the home you've chosen to assess.

Background Information on Home

1. Style: Early American? Modern? Other?
2. Type: Single dwelling? Duplex? Townhouse? Condo? Apartment? Mobile Home? Other?

3. Structure: One story? Two story? Other?
4. Age:
5. Location: City? Suburb? Rural? Other?
6. Length of time resident has lived in home:

It is important to consider some basic information about a person's home because it provides insights into the overall type and meaning of an individual's environment. Some people are accustomed to living in a multistory apartment that provides a distant view or looking out on nearby buildings. Others are used to stepping out onto the ground and feel imprisoned in high places or apartment buildings. They want a porch, patio, and yard. Some like to live in close proximity to people, be able to look out on activity, and hear others nearby. Others prefer to have open spaces around them and a more private environment (Hartford 1985).

The location and structure of the home also needs to be assessed in relation to its suitability to the provision of in-home services, should they be needed. The type of home, size of dwelling, cooking facilities and plumbing are structural features that can promote, impede, or preclude the delivery of long-term care services (Newman 1985).

In addition to the structural characteristics of the home, the number of years spent in the home is also significant. Most elderly owners have lived in their current place more than twenty years. The home and the neighborhood is the location in which they have built their adult identities and represent emotional investments in people and events (Howell 1985). The longer the years, the more the investment. This concurs with O'Bryant (1982), who has reported on four subjective factors that contribute significantly to older homeowners' satisfaction and preference to remain in their own homes rather than relocate. These are: competence in a familiar environment; traditional family orientation and memories; status value in home ownership; and a cost-versus-comfort trade-off factor. Thus, any visitor to an elderly person's home needs to be aware and appreciative of the multiple dynamics that make it so meaningful.

Assessment of the Physical Environment

1. Neighborhood
   a. Safety: Routine police patrols? Neighborhood watch? Buddy system for outings?

Fear of crime is pervasive in the lives of millions of older Americans, both the victimized and nonvictimized. Threat of assault restricts the lifestyle and mobility of older people. Above all else, older people suggest that safety is the one essential feature of a community environment (Toseland 1979). Though national crime statistics report lower victimization rates for older people than for the population as a whole, local studies often show a higher and growing incidence of certain crimes, particularly personal larceny against older, more physically vulnerable victims (Harris 1978). Crime prevention measures can include increased police patrols, police seminars on self protection, development of neighborhood watches, and buddy systems.

    b. Demographic changes:
        i. Generational: Mostly older people? Mixed generations? Mostly young families?
        ii. Ethnic: Predominant culture? Diverse cultures?

Generational and ethnic neighborhood changes can create psychosocial barriers for the elderly because these changes were initiated by long-standing neighbors either dying or moving away. The remaining residents can be coping with feelings of loss, isolation, and uselessness. Connections can be made with new neighbors through informal block parties, garage sales, neigborhood watch programs or through community center or religious activities. A structured meeting may be needed to formally introduce newcomers, as some older people are reluctant to do the initial reaching out because of their conservative upbringing, fear of victimization, or both.

    c. Services within walking distance (four to six blocks): Grocery store? Liquor store? Drug store? Bank? Post office? Beauty shop? Barber shop? Laundromat? Restaurants? Fast foods? Cleaners? Library? Educational institutions?

As mobility declines, the older person becomes more dependent on the local community to meet the needs of daily living (Toseland 1979). Therefore, it facilitates the maintenance of an elderly individual's independence if the basic services necessary to carry out activities of daily living are nearby. Also, daily socialization patterns can develop en route and inside these facilities.

    d. Activities: Multipurpose community center? Storefronts? Religious institutions? Civic programs? Parks?

Role losses associated with retirement, widowhood, death of friends, and the empty nest decrease an elderly person's opportunities for meaningful social interaction. Community activities can offer a supportive environment to develop new roles and relationships.

    e. Public transportation accessible: Bus? Dial-a-Ride? Minibus for seniors?

Public transportation is essential for older persons who cannot drive for financial or health reasons. For those who are not on a regular bus line, minibuses and Dial-a-Ride are vital.

    f. Terrain: Hilly? Flat?
    g. Traffic: Heavy? Light?

When assessing availability of services and community activities, distance is not the only criterion to consider. The surrounding environment can facilitate or impede an older person's ability to walk to a given destination. For example, a distance of six city blocks up a steep hill, across traffic-congested streets, and through a high-crime area is much more difficult for an elderly person to navigate than the same distance on level ground, with no traffic, through a safe neighborhood with several benches on the route (Regnier 1975).

Research comparing housing with neighborhood concerns often shows neighborhood issues to be a more critical consideration than housing satisfactions (Regnier 1983). It is important to improve neighborhoods that are potential settings for increased social interaction as well as a convenient location for needed goods and services.

2. Exterior of Home
   a. In good repair. Paint? Stucco? Roof?

Outside maintenance can indicate financial status, support systems, and physical functioning.

   b. Describe yards and include: Size: small? large? Fruit trees? Flowers? Shrubs? Dog house? Bird feeder? Patio? Pool? Fences: High? Low? None?
      i. Front yard:
      ii. Back yard:

A yard can provide many clues about an elderly person's functioning. If the yards are well kept up, either the person is tending to them or someone else is. In the former case, the person may be doing the yard work for exercise. In the latter case, someone else has been assigned to the job which is an indication that the older person may not be physically able to take care of the home. The presence of fruit trees and flowers can indicate an opportunity to share with neighbors, friends, and relatives, as well as enjoy the produce personally. Evidence of pets can provide a clue to psychosocial functioning, because it is evidence of a person's responsibility for the care of another. A patio or pool indicates the potential for social gatherings and health maintenance through exercise. Fences can promote or deter neighborhood connections.

   c. Describe garage: For car? Workshop? Game room? Storage? Clutter? Well lit? Automatic door opener? Open directly into the home?

A garage can provide information about a person's lifestyle, interests, and social activities. It also can promote or deter the safety of the home.

   d. Is a car present? More than one? Model? Year?

The automobile is the primary source of transportation for all age groups and becomes increasingly important as a person ages. However, 40 percent of people over sixty-five years old do not own a car. This has a major impact on an older person's mobility, as public transportation may not be available and taxis are too expensive (Harris 1978).

    e. Safety
        i. Sidewalk: Is there one? Uneven? Raised? Cluttered? Overhanging bushes, trees?
        ii. Stairs: Nonskid treads? Edge of tread painted white? Top and bottom steps painted in bright, contrasting color? Handrails?
        iii. Windows: Usually open? Locked when no one home? Screens? Blinds? Drapes?
        iv. Porch: Outdoor carpeting? Nonskid doormats?
        v. Mail box: Slot in door? Close to door? At curb?
        vi. Screens? Doors? Windows?
        vii. Front door: Working doorbell? Door locked or open? Deadbolt? Peephole?
        viii. Outdoor lighting: Street lights? Yard? Stairs? Porch? Carport or garage?
        ix. Alternate exit from home?

Safety can be defined as freedom from injury or danger. Accidental injuries become more frequent and serious in later life and for people over sixty-five; falls lead the causes of such injuries and death. Falls are the most frequently occurring accident among aged living in their own homes (Rodstein 1983). The number of falls increases dramatically with age (Butler and Lewis 1982). Also, living alone has been identified as a risk factor for falls (Craven and Bruno 1986).

Older people are more vulnerable to severe injury, especially women who have osteoporosis. Physical impairments resulting from falls include bruises, hematomas, lacerations, and fractures. Also, if the elderly person is confined to bed, there are hazards associated with immobility. In addition to the physical aspects, psychosocial trauma may cause the individual to lose confidence, courage, and control. In turn, the family experiencing guilt and fear may limit the person's independence to prevent further injury (Gray-Vickrey 1984).

Since falls seldom "just happen," preventive measures can be taken. These include establishing a safe environment and being aware of physical and mental conditions that increase an older person's potential risk of falling. It is estimated that two-thirds of falls by the elderly can be prevented (Ebersole and Hess 1985).

It is important to maintain sidewalks in good repair, free from cracks, raised parts, holes, and overhanging trees or bushes. If these conditions exist, request an assessment from the city or county maintenance department. Sidewalks should be free of clutter such as garden hoses and toys.

Stairs present a particular hazard to older people, especially if they are unfamiliar. The most frequent cause of falls on stairs is missing the last step or group of steps in the mistaken belief that the bottom has been reached. Unlike younger people, older people usually cannot regain their balance once they start to fall. Contributing to falls on stairs is poor visibility caused by impaired vision and poor lighting (Rodstein 1983). Ideally, stairs should have nonskid treads with edges painted white and the top and bottom stair painted in bright contrasting colors. Handrails should be installed on both sides of stairs and far enough from the wall so a person can grasp them; should have extra support at the top and bottom so they can support the user's weight; should extend beyond the last step; and should have special shaping at the ends to let the person know he or she is off the stairs. All stairways should be well lighted twenty-four hours a day.

To avert danger, older people need to take precautionary measures at and away from their home (as previously discussed). Antunes, Cook, Cook, and Skogan (1977) reported on a national survey of reported and nonreported crime against the public, including the elderly. They found that although older people are less likely than the general public to experience violent crimes such as assault or rape, when they did it was most likely to occur in their homes. It is critical that the elderly use available measures to safeguard their homes, such as adequate outdoor lighting, deadbolts on doors, peepholes or other means of identifying the visitor before opening the door, locks on windows and patio doors, and if indicated, a general alarm system. However, the best safeguards will be useless unless they are consistently used.

3. Interior of Home
   a. Assessment of safety
      i. General

      Flooring: Wood? Tile? Linoleum? Waxed? Carpet?
      Scatter rugs: Loose? Firmly anchored? Rubber-backed?
      Electrical cords: In good repair (especially heating pads)? Across walk areas? Outlets overloaded?
      Clutter? Low-lying objects? Low-hanging ceiling lights?

With old age, a person's gait changes and one walks with the feet farther apart and lifts them less off the ground. This contributes to tripping and falls (Rodstein 1983). It is important that all carpeting, mats, and tile be well-attached and small rugs removed or equipped with nonskid backing. Also, pathways need to be kept clear of extension cords, clutter, and unexpected objects.

      Storage spaces: Easily accessible? Too high? Too low?
      Furniture: Sturdy enough to give support? Arms to facilitate ambulation? Sharp corners?
      Doors: Open and close easily? Have locks? Safety release? Door knobs or levers?
      Smoke detectors?

Alarm system?
Weatherizing: Storm windows? Weather stripping?
Location of washer and dryer: Kitchen? Laundry room? Garage? None?
Water heater: Temperature set no higher than 120°F.?

In later years, an individual's skin becomes more fragile and less capable of assessing temperatures. To safeguard against scalding, hot water needs to be set no higher than 120°F.

ii. Heat and ventilation

Heater properly ventilated?
Temperature regulated at 70°–75°F.?
Cross ventilation?

The maintenance of an optimal environmental temperature becomes more critical with elderly people. Physiological thermoregulators such as the skin, peripheral blood vessels, and muscles become less efficient with age (Thatcher 1983). The older adult becomes more vulnerable to both hypothermia and hyperthermia. As a means to prevent these conditions, it is recommended that environmental temperatures be maintained at a minimum of 70°F. (Hayter 1980; Heymann 1977). Some studies have reported that the aged prefer a temperature of about 75°F. (Kolanowski and Gunter 1983). Older people need to be informed of their vulnerability to hypothermia and hyperthermia and ways they can protect themselves from these hazards.

iii. Lighting

Adequate in each room?
Wall switches that glow in dark?
Night lights in each room?
Lighted path between bedroom and bathroom?
On stairways? Halls? Always on?

With increasing age, the older person's visual acuity begins to decline. One finding is that the average sixty-year-old has one-third as much light arriving on the retina as the average twenty-year-old (Ham and Marcy 1983). Thus, the older person needs three times as much light to see. This need of increased light becomes critical in the area of safety. Night lights in halls, stairs, bedrooms, and bathroom are essential. In addition, more time is needed for the aging eye to adjust to changes from light to dark and vice versa. So the person needs to be cautioned to pace his movements accordingly.

iv. Phone

Location: Kitchen? Bedroom? Living room? Answering machine?
Emergency numbers: 911 posted? Doctor? Relatives? Neighbor?

The telephone is a person's lifeline to the outside world. It is essential that it is always accessible and usable. Having phone jacks in every room is one approach, though it may be difficult to detach and reattach the phone, depending on the location of the jack. An answering machine is a convenience and offers the assurance that calls will not be missed. However, returning calls can be expensive. Cordless phones offer many obvious advantages. If none of the above options are possible, the older person can request callers to always let the phone ring ten times to allow enough time to reach it without rushing.

    v. Kitchen

> Stove: Type? Clean? Well-functioning? Pilot light? Light above stove?
> In case of fire: Baking soda? Fire extinguisher?
> Refrigerator: Clean? Working well?

Price (1978) reports that such factors as defective wiring and gas leaks probably cause about 14 percent of home fires, faulty equipment, 36 percent, and human carelessness, 60 percent. Interventions to reduce the probability of fire include calling the gas or electric company to check appliances, repairing any frayed electrical cords, avoiding overloading outlets, having baking soda or a fire extinguisher handy, and not wearing loose-hanging sleeves around the stove. Smoke detectors are especially needed by the elderly because of their diminished sense of smell.

> Sink: Draining well? Garbage disposal? Nonskid mat?
> Food: Stored properly? Adequate for nutritional needs?
> Trash: Taken out regularly?
> Cupboards: Easily accessible?
> Sturdy step stool?

Many elderly have difficulty reaching into high or low cabinets. Physical conditions that contribute to this include decreasing muscle strength and agility, less efficient balance, and arthritis (Ham and Marcy 1983). Interventions include rearrangement of items used often and/or heavy objects onto shelves between waist and shoulder height, use of pegboards and revolving shelves, use of a reacher stick for other hard-to-reach items (Clark and Gaide 1986). If possible, avoid using even a sturdy step stool.

    vi. Bathroom

> Faucets easy to turn off?
> Electrical outlets: Properly placed? Grounded?
> Medicine cabinet: Good lighting? Drugs clearly labeled? Magnifying glass close by?

It is imperative that older people be able to see *what* medication they are taking, *when* and *how* they should take it, and be able to reach it. A strategy to facilitate this process is to ask the pharmacist to put the medication in a larger bottle with a screw cap and use capital letters on the label.

> Grab bars: Beside toilet? Tub?
> Nonskid strips: In bathtub? Shower?
> Skid-proof mats on floor?

Getting on and off the toilet and in and out of the bathtub becomes progressively more difficult for the aged because of decreased agility, muscle strength, and balance. Arthritis can make the problem even more difficult. Grab bars can ease safe movement from one bodily position to another. Also, a damp washcloth on the edge of the bathtub can provide traction. Nonskid strips in the bathtub and shower are imperative for safety.

Home maintenance is the number one force that impels retirees to move. Most commonly needed repairs include interior of home, plumbing, doors, windows, weatherization, grab bars, smoke detectors, and deadbolts (Greenstein 1985). Overall, these are minor home maintenance tasks. It would seem to be an appropriate challenge for local service organizations to develop a volunteer plan to tend to these tasks for older people in their community. Such organizations could also disseminate information on devices and helpful hints to facilitate the creation of an optimal environment for the elderly in their homes (Andrus Volunteers 1985; La Buda 1985).

It is important to notice if the person has prepared for an emergency or disaster. Let's discuss some basic considerations.

4. Preparedness for Emergency/Disaster
    a. Location of shutoffs for gas, water, electricity.
    b. Pipe and crescent wrenches for shutoffs.
    c. Portable radio with extra batteries.
    d. Two flashlights with extra batteries.
    e. Extra batteries for wheelchair, hearing aid.
    f. Whistle.
    g. First aid box.
    h. List of current medications.
    i. Cloth or paper bag for medications.
    j. Pencil and paper.
    k. Emergency canned food and water for two days (two quarts of fluid *minimum* per person per day for drinking only; extra water is needed for cooking and washing).
    l. Water purification tablets.
    m. Mechanical can opener.
    n. Plastic bags for toilets.

Preparedness for an emergency or disaster is widely recommended (American Red Cross 1984; Lafferty 1986). It can prevent unnecessary stress and injuries for everyone, but particularly for elderly people, who are more frail and vulnerable.

Transition to Psychosocial Aspects

In addition to assessing the home for safety, the tour can provide information about the person's lifestyle including relationships, activities, and interests. Let's discuss them.

Evidence of Relationships/Activities/Interests

1. Family, friends, neighbors: pictures, albums, scrapbooks, children's handicrafts, greeting cards, etc.

    This informal support system can be crucial in maintaining older people at home and helping them adjust to psychosocial changes in later years (Atchley 1987).

2. Past and present activities: newspapers, magazines, journals, church bulletins, awards, certificates of recognition, art work, collections, musical instruments, audio and video tapes, sports equipment, travel brochures, etc.

    These items provide insights into areas of expertise, talents, and memberships in professional, religious, and social organizations. This can be helpful in assessing the older adult's wider social network.

3. Clocks, calendars, and mirrors.

    The presence of running and accurate clocks, current calendars, and mirrors provides clues that the older person is aware of the present as well as the passage of time. This relates to their ability and interest in making and keeping appointments, taking medications as prescribed, and generally keeping connected with our "time-oriented" society.

4. Pets: food dishes, pet toys and bones, aquarium, bird feeder.

    Many older people who have no close fulfilling personal relationships lavish their affection and attention on pets. Based on his review of the literature, Brickel (1980–81) reports that in addition to their utilitarian functions, pets can be unquestioning sources of affection and comfort and can provide companionship, entertainment, and a sense of purpose.

5. Plants and flowers.

    The presence of plants and flowers is another indicator of a person's being "connected" to the world and taking responsibility for the care of a living thing. Atchley (1987) reports that there is no research on the elderly's attachment to plants, but it is clear from the data on gardening that working with plants is a favorite activity among older people.

6. Windows with a view: back yard? front yard? neighbor's yard? street?

Rowles (1981) reports on the significance of the surveillance zone, the space within the visual field of home, in the lives of elderly adults. This zone allows for "watching" and "being watched." This visual reciprocity facilitates the development and maintenance of practical and social support from neighbors. It also provides an opportunity to vicariously participate in the community. This can promote the maintenance of a sense of identity and "connectedness." When touring a home, it is important to note the size and location of windows. While doing so, observe if there is one around which a favorite chair, lamp, radio, television, telephone are arranged to facilitate optimum surveillance. Also, note windows that could have this potential if the view weren't obstructed by fences, tall trees, or shrubs. The removal of such obstructions could create a surveillance zone with the potential to augment the social networks of the occupants on *both* sides of the fence.

Transition to Debriefing

Thank you for sharing your home assessments. Now, based on your mind's-eye observations and our discussion, I would like you to draw some conclusions about your home.

Please take the next few minutes to respond to the questions on your Debriefing Sheet (allow three to five minutes).

Debriefing

1. Are there any changes you think are indicated to enhance an older person's functioning optimally in this home?
2. If so, what approach would you use to make these suggestions to the older residents?

Suggestions of any structural or safety changes to enhance daily functioning and safety must be made with appropriate timing and emotional support. To recognize any needed compensatory changes or repairs, the elderly person must also recognize a declining ability to function, a deterioration of the home, or both. This may be a difficult process and may take time. It is important to remember that the elderly resident has the ultimate decision-making power for any changes in the home.

3. Based on your knowledge of the residents in this home, what do you think are their most prized possessions in it?
4. When you were living in this home, what were or are your most treasured possessions?
5. What did you, or will you, take with you when you move?

Thank you for sharing about your personal possessions. You've certainly demonstrated the point that everyone, regardless of age, has possessions they treasure and want to keep "forever." In most instances, the subjective value of these items has no positive correlation with their objective, monetary value. Yet, in the eyes of their possessors, these objects are "priceless." It is important to remember this when interacting with people in their home environment. These special possessions can become even more significant to people as they grow older. They provide the elderly continuity with the past and the security of sameness as they cope with changes in their present. In addition, they can trigger significant reminiscences for the visitor.

Summary

This activity has certainly demonstrated the uniqueness of your "visualized" homes and neighborhoods and some of their similarities to others. Each of you took the opportunity to look at your selected neighborhood and home in an objective way, focusing on the safety of the physical environment and indicators of the resident's lifestyle, activities, and social support system. Based on your observations, we discussed supportive interventions that could enhance the safety and security of elderly people in their homes. We also talked about the importance of acknowledging the items that reflect older adults' psychosocial worlds, especially their treasured possessions.

I hope that by participating in this activity you have enhanced your appreciation of the value of a home assessment visit and feel prepared to make one. Clearly, an assessment of the home environment can be the initial step in working with elderly people to devise ways to create an individualized, supportive, safeguarded setting in which they can remain as long as they choose.

Evaluation

Please take a few moments now to complete the evaluation.

Home Assessment, Worksheet

Background Information on Home

1. Style: ☐Early American ☐Modern Other_____
2. Type: ☐Single dwelling ☐Duplex ☐Townhouse ☐Condo ☐Apartment ☐Mobile home Other_____
3. Structure: ☐One story ☐Two story Other_____
4. Age of home:_____
5. Location: ☐City ☐Suburb ☐Rural Other_____
6. Length of time resident has lived in home:_____

Physical Environment

1. *Neighborhood*
   a. Safety: ☐Routine police patrols ☐ Neighborhood watch ☐Buddy system for outings?
   b. Demographic Changes
      i. Generational: ☐Mostly older people ☐Mixed generations ☐Mostly young families
      ii. Ethnic: Predominate culture_____? Diverse cultures_____?
   c. Services within walking distance (four to six blocks): ☐Grocery store ☐Liquor store ☐Drug store ☐Post office ☐Bank ☐Beauty shop ☐Barber shop ☐Laundromat ☐Restaurants ☐Fast foods ☐Cleaners ☐Library ☐Educational institutions
   d. Activities: ☐Multipurpose community center ☐Store fronts ☐Religious institutions ☐Civic programs ☐Parks
   e. Public transportation accessible: ☐Bus ☐Dial-a-Ride ☐Minibus for seniors
   f. Terrain: ☐Hilly ☐Flat
   g. Traffic: ☐Heavy ☐Light

2. *Outside Home*
   a. In good repair: ☐Paint ☐Stucco ☐Roof
   b. Describe yards and include: Size: ☐Small ☐Large ☐Fruit trees ☐Flowers ☐Shrubs ☐Dog house ☐Bird feeder ☐Patio ☐Pool Fences: ☐High ☐Low ☐None
      i. Front:

Home Assessment, Worksheet (Continued)

    ii. Back:

  c. Describe garage: ☐For car ☐Workshop ☐Game room ☐Storage ☐Clutter ☐Well lit ☐Automatic door opener ☐Open directly into the home

  d. Is there a car present ☐Yes ☐No ☐More than one
Model:_____ Year:_____

  e. Safety
    i. Sidewalk: ☐Is there one ☐Uneven ☐Raised ☐Cluttered ☐Overhanging trees ☐Bushes
    ii. Stairs: ☐Nonskid treads ☐Edge of tread painted with contrasting strip ☐Edge of top and bottom stairs painted in another color ☐Handrails
    iii. Windows: ☐Usually open ☐Locked when no one home ☐Screens ☐Blinds ☐Drapes
    iv. Porch: ☐Outdoor carpeting ☐Nonskid doormats
    v. Mail box: ☐Slot in door ☐Close to door ☐At curb
    vi. Screens: ☐Doors ☐Windows
    vii. Front door: ☐Working doorbell ☐Locked ☐Open ☐Deadbolt ☐Peephole
    viii. Outdoor lighting: ☐Street lights ☐Yard ☐Stairs ☐Porch ☐Carport or garage
    ix. ☐Alternate exit from home

3. Interior of Home
  a. Assessment of Safety
    i. General
- Flooring: ☐Wood ☐Tile ☐Linoleum ☐Waxed ☐Carpet
- Scatter rugs: ☐Loose ☐Firmly anchored ☐Rubber backed
- Electrical cords: ☐In good repair (especially heating pad) ☐Across walk areas ☐Outlets overloaded
- Clutter: ☐Low-lying objects ☐Low-hanging ceiling lights
- Storage space: ☐Easily accessible ☐Too high ☐Too low

Home Assessment, Worksheet (Continued)

- Furniture: ☐Sturdy enough to give support ☐Arms to facilitate ambulation ☐Sharp corners
- Doors: ☐Open and close easily ☐Have locks ☐Safety release ☐Door knobs ☐Levers
- ☐Smoke detectors
- ☐Alarm system
- Weatherizing: ☐Storm windows ☐Weather stripping
- Location of washer and dryer: ☐Kitchen ☐Laundry room ☐Garage ☐None
- Water heater: ☐Temperature set at 120°F or less.

ii. Heat and ventilation
- ☐Heater properly ventilated
- ☐Temperature regulated at 70°–75°F.
- ☐Cross-ventilation

iii. Lighting
- ☐Adequate in each room
- ☐Wall switches that glow in dark
- ☐Night lights in each room
- ☐Lighted path between bedroom and bathroom
- ☐On stairways ☐Halls ☐Always on

iv. Phone
- Location: ☐Kitchen ☐Bedroom ☐Living room ☐Cordless ☐Answering machine
- Emergency numbers: ☐911 posted ☐Doctor ☐Relatives

v. Kitchen
- Stove: Type:_____ ☐Clean ☐Well-functioning ☐Pilot light ☐Light above stove
- In case of fire: ☐Baking soda ☐Fire extinguisher
- Refrigerator: ☐Clean ☐Working well
- Sink: ☐Draining well ☐Garbage disposal ☐Nonskid mat
- Food: ☐Stored properly ☐Adequate for nutritional needs
- Trash: ☐Taken out regularly
- Cupboards: ☐Easily accessible
- ☐Sturdy step stool

vi. Bathroom
- ☐Faucets easy to turn on and off
- Electrical outlets: ☐Properly placed ☐Grounded
- Medicine cabinet: ☐Good lighting ☐Drugs labeled with large letters ☐Magnifying glass close by

Home Assessment, Worksheet (Continued)

- Grab bars: ☐Beside toilet ☐Tub
- Nonskid strips: ☐In bathtub ☐Shower
- ☐Skid-proof mats on floor

4. *Preparedness for emergency/disaster*

   a. Location of shutoffs for gas, water, electricity
   b. ☐Pipe and crescent wrenches
   c. ☐Portable radio with extra batteries
   d. ☐Two flashlights with extra batteries
   e. ☐Extra batteries for wheelchair, hearing aid
   f. ☐Whistle
   g. ☐First aid box
   h. ☐List of current medications
   i. ☐Cloth or paper bag for medications
   j. ☐Paper and pencil
   k. ☐Emergency canned food and water for two days
   l. ☐Water purification tablets
   m. ☐Mechanical can opener
   n. ☐Plastic bags for toilets

Evidence of Relationships/Activities/Interests

1. Family and friends: ☐Pictures ☐Handicrafts ☐Collectibles ☐Cards Other:_____
2. Past and present activities: ☐Awards ☐Certificates ☐Journals ☐Church bulletins ☐Art work ☐Musical instruments ☐Sports equipment ☐Travel brochures Other:_____
3. ☐Clocks ☐Calendars ☐Mirrors
4. Pets: ☐Food dishes ☐Pet toys and bones ☐Aquarium ☐Bird feeder
5. ☐Plants ☐Flowers
6. Windows with a view: ☐Back yard ☐Front yard ☐Neighbor's yard ☐Street

Home Assessment, Debriefing Sheet

1. Based on your assessment, are there any changes you think are indicated to enhance an older person's functioning optimally in this home?

2. If so, what approach would you use to make these suggestions to the older residents?

3. Based on your knowledge of the residents in this home, what do you think are their most prized possessions in it?

4. When you were living in this home, what were or are your most treasured possessions?

5. What did you or will you take with you when you move?

Home Assessment, Evaluation

1. Did this activity increase your appreciation of the value of a home assessment visit?

Not much		Some		A lot
1	2	3	4	5

2. Identify four things to assess for home safety.

   _____
   _____
   _____
   _____

3. Identify four interventions to provide a more supportive environment.

   _____
   _____
   _____
   _____

4. Identify four indicators of an elderly person's lifestyle, interests and psychosocial supports.

   _____
   _____
   _____
   _____

5. Based on this activity, are you prepared to assess a home environment? ☐Yes ☐No
   Why?

6. Give at least one example of how this activity will affect your interactions with older adults.

11 Relocation

Rationale for Activity

Most older Americans have lived in their present dwellings for more than twenty years. Homes can be a symbol of independence, a focal point for family gatherings, a link to the neighborhood and a symbol of standing in the community (Atchley 1987). It is extraordinarily significant to many older persons—a part of their identity, a place where things are familiar, and a place to maintain autonomy and control (Butler and Lewis 1982). A home can be a link to the past, containing such precious memories as the laughter of young children or the planting of a four-inch tree that now has grown to thirty feet. It is their personalized private space.

It is understandable why many older adults elect to remain in their homes as long as possible. However, the lives and circumstances of elderly people change over the years and in many cases relocation becomes necessary. It is usually based on several interrelated factors, including financial issues, physical or mental decline or both, insufficient informal or formal supports to remain in their present residence, or a decline of the neighborhood with resulting safety issues.

Relocation has the potential to place additional stress on the lives of the elderly because it sets into motion yet another change that requires coping and adaptation skills. The actual impact of the move varies according to each individual's situation. However, based on their review of the relocation literature, Schultz and Brenner (1977) and Hasselkus (1978) concur that the greater the choice the individual has in being relocated and the more predictable the new environment, the less negative the effects of the relocation.

It is timely that those who interact with older people develop ways to implement these findings so that relocation can promote an improvement in the elderly's physical and psychosocial functioning.

This activity provides participants with an opportunity to increase their appreciation of the importance of older people's involvement in all phases of their relocation and to enhance their understanding of ways to facilitate an optimum relocation process.

Participants: This activity is appropriate for graduate and undergraduate students and professionals in mental health, social work, health care and gerontology, administrators and staff of long-term care facilities, other service providers, and family caregivers.

Objectives

Upon completion of this activity participants will:

1. Have an increased appreciation of the importance of older people's involvement in all phases of their relocation.
2. Be able to identify four ways to reduce stress associated with the relocation process.
3. Be able to give at least one example of how this activity will affect their interactions with older adults.

Class Size: Open

Time: Forty-five to fifty-five minutes. Allow ten extra minutes if you include Pointers for Long-Term Care Facilities.

> Fifteen minutes: introduction and activity
> Ten minutes: small group discussion
> Fifteen to twenty-five minutes: debriefing
> Five minutes: evaluation

Materials: Relocation Worksheets, Evaluation Sheets.

Teaching Notes

1. This activity works well for small-group sharing before a general debriefing. The group members are usually very supportive of each other. They seem to benefit from discovering the commonalities of their feelings and they enjoy sharing about their treasured possessions and finding out that everybody has a special one.
2. The participants are usually surprised at the intensity of their feelings related to their difficult moves. Most of these moves occurred when they were teenagers or younger and were not of their choice. Their overriding feeling was one of loss, and for some this feeling of loss was still not totally resolved. They need time to share these feelings and receive supportive feedback from other participants.

Introduction to Activity

1. Relocation is a potentially stressful event in anyone's life, but can be especially so for the elderly who may also be coping with the concurrent stresses of loss of loved ones and roles, financial problems, and declining health. Older adults usually change their living arrangements when their health or their support systems or both have declined to a point where they can no longer manage in their present situation.
2. The effect of the move on the person varies according to each individual's situation. However, based on their review of the relocation literature, Schulz and Brenner (1977) and Hasselkus (1978) concur that the greater the choice the individual has in being relocated and the more predictable the new environment, the less negative the effects of the relocation. Amenta, Weiner, and Amenta (1984) reported from their study that a reasonable amount of preparation that includes many opportunities for choice during the relocation process can provide geriatric residents with increased autonomy, stimulation, and renewed interest in mental and social activities.
3. Given these findings and supporting the premise that the purpose of any relocation is to improve the elderly's physical and psychosocial functioning, it would seem important to be certain the following be included in any relocation process:
   a. Maximizing the elderly's active involvement.
   b. Offering choices regarding relocation.
   c. Giving the elderly opportunities to assess and become familiar with the proposed new environment.
4. Unfortunately, in reality, this is not always done for a variety of reasons, some valid, some not. With the growth of our elderly population and the increasing range of housing options available to them, relocations will likely become more frequent in the future. Thus, it is timely to explore ways to assist the elderly in making positive relocations.
5. To help you appreciate the impact of relocation, I would like you to participate in the following activity.

Instructions to Participants

1. Place your Relocation Worksheet in front of you.
2. Now close your eyes and take a few deep breaths.
3. Think back over your life and the relocations you've experienced.
   a. Have you moved a lot?
   b. Think about the different kinds of moves you've experienced.
      i. What ages were you?
      ii. Did you have a choice regarding the moves?
      iii. Think about a difficult move. How did you feel about it?
      iv. Think about your best move. How did you feel about it?

c. In the moves you've made, what did you find most difficult in breaking with the past?
d. What treasured possession has gone with you in every move?
4. Now open your eyes and respond to the questions on your worksheet.

Transition to Debriefing

1. Now that you've recalled some of the relocations in your lives, before we debrief as a group, I would like you to share your experiences with some of the other participants.
2. So please divide up into groups of five to seven and do a compare and contrast on your relocation experiences (allow ten minutes).
3. Now, let's debrief as a group.

Debriefing

1. How many times have you moved in your lifetime?
   Possible range: Zero to thirty times
2. If you've moved a lot, does it get easier? If so, why?

   Responses may include: We moved so much, I never allowed myself to get really close to people. I don't keep collectibles anymore, so I can pack easier. I meet strangers easier. I adjust better to new places and foods. I feel more self-sufficient. I don't mind moving as long as I'm the one to decide.

   From what you've shared it would seem that there are both pros and cons of moving a lot, and each of you handled it differently. However, the issue of choice is an important one. If you can't control the move, at least you will choose how you will interact with new people or what you will take with you.

3. Describe your most difficult relocation.

   Responses may include: When I moved away from my grandmother. When I was sent to live with friends after my mother died. When I left my homeland and familiar customs. When my parents got divorced and we left my dad behind. When I moved from a big house into a small apartment because of finances. When I had to move into a dorm with five other girls and lost my privacy. When I had to move after my divorce.

4. How did you feel about it?

   Responses may include: I was sad and I felt lonely. I felt grief over loss of part of myself that was left behind. I felt helpless and out of control. I was angry that I had no choice. I was scared because I didn't know anybody. I felt overwhelmed and I was abandoned.

Loss is certainly a theme in your difficult moves: loss of loved ones, home, privacy. With these losses you experienced, you *still* remember the pain, grief, lack of control, helplessness—a very difficult period in your lives. Thank you for sharing these feelings.

5. Describe your best relocation.

> Responses may include: *When I started college two thousand miles from home. When we moved to a new family home with lots of space. When we got married and moved to California. When I got promoted. When we moved into a better neighborhood.*

6. How did you feel about it?

> Responses may include: *I felt excited to be in control of my life. I was happy to meet new people. I was enthusiastic to get settled. I felt anxious over making condo payments. I was glad to have my own space. I felt ambivalent. I wanted both the security of the old and the challenge of the new. I felt responsible for my own life.*

The contrast is striking. Most of your best moves include growth of self, expansion of space, exploring new horizons, new relationships, challenges. Your feelings were happy, *in control*, competent, high self-esteem, sometimes ambivalent yet forging ahead.

7. In the moves you've made, what did you find most difficult in breaking with the past?

> Responses may include: *When I left my friends. When I gave up familiar and trusted stores, my doctor, and dentist. When I lost my own space. When I left my neighbors behind, I really missed them. Leaving the security of knowing where you are. I had no one to call for advice. I had to adjust to a different lifestyle. When I had to leave my familiar room that I had just decorated.*

Even positive moves involve some losses and it takes time to adjust, adapt and "grow into" a new environment, get reconnected with needed services, and develop new relationships.

8. What treasured possessions have always gone with you in every move?

> Responses may include: *Family pictures. My books. My doll. My stuffed teddy bear. My pillow. My toy soldiers. My stereo and tapes. My mother's quilt. A mother's day gift my son made for me.*

These treasured possessions are part of you—they are representations of your unique identity, your heritage, your childhood, your music, your relationships. They are special and you are protective of them.

Transition to Pointers

Thank you for sharing about your relocations. They are all unique, but your feelings associated with them reflect our humanness with the sadness and joys of moving away from our past and into our future. Please remember these feelings as we discuss relocation in relation to the elderly.

To meet the relocation needs of the elderly there are a growing number of alternatives for different levels of functioning, including independent living, semi-supportive care, and comprehensive care.

Relocation can be:

a. From a single dwelling home to another independent living option (duplex, mobile home, condominium, apartment, shared housing).
b. From independent living to:
   i. A semisupportive environment involving congregate care (senior housing, retirement hotel, board and care, foster homes, retirement community).
   ii. Directly to comprehensive care.
c. From semisupportive care to comprehensive supportive environment (intermediate care, skilled nursing, acute care, hospice).
d. The reverse of any of the above.
e. Between health care facilities.
f. Within a health care facility.
g. Temporary or permanent, depending on the status of the elderly person, the housing or both.

Because of these multiple options and the potential to move among them, it is essential to take the necessary time to locate the one best suited to meet the elderly person's individual environmental, physical, and psychosocial needs at any given point in their lives. However, because these needs may change with the elderly's advancing years, so may their needs for a type of housing. With *each* relocation the following pointers need to be considered.

Pointers to Promote a Positive Relocation Process

1. The process needs to start with the elderly people themselves. They should undergo a comprehensive medical and functional assessment. This is important for many reasons:

a. It can reveal any physical problems or undiagnosed illnesses, which can then be remedied before the relocation (Mullen 1977).
b. Vision and hearing evaluations are essential so that impairments can be corrected. Adequate vision and hearing are critical in facilitating the adjustment to a new environment. Lack of adequate sensory input can be one of the significant causes of relocation stress and maladjustment. If sensory impairments cannot be corrected, special compensatory plans must be made for orientation to the new environment (Wolanin 1978).
c. It can be the major guideline for selecting which level of living arrangement (independent, semisupportive, or comprehensive care) would be most appropriate. This can minimize the potential problem of older adults who overestimate their ability to function, relocate in a semisupportive environment, find they cannot cope, and then have to re-relocate into a higher level of care. Or, on the other hand, families may underestimate their older relatives' abilities to function and place them in too high a level of care. This can cause premature dependency or acting-out behavior on the part of the elderly. In either case, such an inappropriate relocation can cause needless additional stress and strains on both the elderly and their families. For all concerned, it is extremely important that older people reside in the least restrictive environment possible (Borup 1983).
2. The challenge is to have older people realistically appraise and *accept* their functioning level and then be given the time and assistance needed to find the most appropriate housing option to meet their individual needs. Berland and Poggi (1981) learned from their study that older people considered their move into a retirement home the *last real choice* they would have to move. So, significantly, they wanted the move to be free of coercion from family or friends and they wanted to take their own time.
3. Once the type of housing option has been selected, it is important that the elderly and their family seek out a reasonable number of choices of that type of housing. Too many choices may be confusing to the elderly person and result in a decision that is not carefully weighed. Too few choices may result in an option that is taken begrudgingly. Both conditions might result in an unsuccessful relocation (Beaver 1979). Once a list is developed, they should obtain initial information about these housing options. This information can include brochures, information about costs and services, history of facility, availability of tours, reputation in the community, and maps of surrounding areas. Then, as the selection narrows to one or two, the older person should spend time in the proposed environments to become familiar with them. For example, in a congregate care setting, they could:
a. Have meals with the residents; meet with the staff; visit activity programs; stay overnight; assess facility's involvement in the

community; compare and contrast their lifelong habits and routines with those of the proposed residence.
   b. Compare and contrast their current living conditions with the proposed living quarters: floor space, windows, location in relation to sun, location of bathroom, ground floor or high-rise, view of garden or concrete parking lot.
   c. Assess availability of services: beauty shop, gift shop, nearby stores, banks, post office, theatre, library.
   d. Assess surrounding neighborhood for attractiveness, safety for walking, noise level; compare and contrast with their current neighborhood.

Such comprehensive interactions reduce the stress of the unknown and promote cognitive mastery of the environment. Ebersole and Hess (1985) discuss the importance of cognitive maps or the perceptual image of one's environment. Older people need maps, personalized tours, and visual points of reference to help them orientate to new surroundings. These interactions also allow the elderly time to do an assessment of the proposed residence's assets and limitations in relation to meeting their specific needs. Thus, they will be able to make an informed choice based on the reality of the situation. This in turn promotes a positive relocation.

If the elderly person is too frail or ill to participate in the assessment process, two alternative methods can help them to be involved. First, the family can do the assessment and discuss its findings with the elderly. Secondly, a staff member from the proposed residence can bring brochures and other information to the elderly person, and serve as the contact person.

4. Once the elderly person has decided to relocate, the staff and administration of the new residence have the challenge to provide an environment that will respond to and support the resident's efforts to "settle in" to his or her new home. This includes encouraging self-determination and reinforcing coping skills. This is critical for a successful relocation. The best preparatory efforts will be negated if the new environment does not promote the optimum physical and psychosocial functioning of the elderly person.

Ways for Adminstration and Staff of Long-Term Care Facilities to Assist in a Positive Relocation

1. Learn as much as possible about the elderly person's previous environment, lifestyle, and routines so that the new residence can be made as similar to the former one as possible.
2. Be aware of the factors that precipitated the move, such as loss of a significant other, loss of own home, declining health. These con-

comittant events add to the stresses of relocation. The resident may need extra support.
3. Inquire if this is the first move made in many years or the first time in congregate living. If so, the resident may need more initial assistance.
4. Individualize the admission process by:
   a. Providing privacy so that confidentiality will be protected regarding questions related to personal health, social, and financial matters.
   b. Asking the new resident how he or she wishes to be addressed and using the preferred name frequently.
   c. Giving initial explanations of routines and procedures.
   d. Providing the new resident with a "summary page" (large print with dark letters) of important information: daily routines and activities, use of telephones, visiting hours, doctors visits, etc.
   e. Providing or reinforcing "cognitive maps" with individualized tours.
   f. Introducing the new resident to staff and other residents when the timing is right.
   g. Being sensitive to avoid information overload.
5. Let the resident move in incrementally, if possible. This allows more time to adjust and adapt.
6. Make every effort, during the actual move, to have residents and their possessions separated for the least time possible (Kowalski 1981). If possible, let them pack some of their special keepsakes, carry them to the new location, unwrap, and place them. This helps the person maintain his or her sense of identity during the transition (Dimon 1979).
7. Let the residents have enough time to decide on the placement of their possessions. Berland and Poggi (1981) found in their study that this placement occupied almost all the elderly's attention during the first week or two. Only after they had organized their living space could they redirect their attention to new people and new places in their environment.
8. Encourage as much personalization of space as possible to provide a sense of life's continuity. Items can include treasured pieces of furniture, figurines, family pictures, hobbies, books. Be tolerant of their "organized clutter"—they have a reason for it (ask them!).
9. Recognize and support the resident for handling so many things simultaneously, including:
   a. Losses associated with the move such as former home, belongings sold or given away, neighbors and service providers in their former community, former routines and lifestyle, and declining health.
   b. Adjusting to constricted life space, living in close proximity to

others, perhaps having a roommate for the first time, new routines, services, and staff.
   c. Establishing new interaction patterns with their family and friends.

   In addition to recognizing their coping strengths and resilience, the staff also needs to remember the importance of letting the elderly set their own pace and prioritize where they want to spend their energies. Also, understand that it takes time to change lifelong habits, especially if they've served the individual well for decades.

10. Always explain what you are doing, why you are doing it, where you're taking them, and when their appointments are, as you provide services and care for the residents.
11. Have key staff members available to answer any questions or solve problems as they arise (Mirotznik and Ruskin 1985). Encourage residents to express their *feelings* about the *meaning* of the event and neutralize any threatening meanings with realistic ones (Rosswurm 1983).
12. The importance of privacy and personal space cannot be overemphasized.
    a. Each of us needs some private space where we can escape the attention of others, relax, replenish our energies and be ready for the stresses of more interactions (Porter, Rasmussen, and Burnside 1981). If one is under constant surveillance, there is a necessity to always "be on," and this can be psychologically exhausting (Newcomer and Caggiano 1981). This can be even more stressful for elderly people whose previous lifestyle may have involved only minimal day-to-day contact with people.
    b. Lack of privacy and insufficient personal space with the resultant stress and anxiety can be readily converted into illness, sexual disturbances, aggression, anger or submissiveness, and withdrawal (Trierweiler 1978).
    c. Ways to respect and protect resident's personal space and privacy:
        i. Always knock on door before entering.
        ii. Approach resident slowly enough so you can be acknowledged and given implied consent to come closer if need be (Louis 1981).
        iii. Ask resident's permission before touching any belongings. If it's not possible to ask, at least explain why.
        iv. Ask permission before going into a person's closet or drawers.
        v. Praise for personalization of their space.
        vi. Never read resident's mail unless requested to do so.
        vii. Keep their personal belongings safe yet accessible for their use.

d. Those whose privacy, personal space, and possessions are respected have their identity reinforced, relate better to others, and feel more secure.

Ways for Administration to Involve Families and Community to Establish an Ongoing Positive Psychosocial Environment Following Relocation

1. Smith and Bengtson (1979) concluded from their study that institutionalization of an elderly parent can result in a strengthening of family ties and renewed closeness between parent and child. The major reason is the alleviation of strain and pressure caused by the multiple physical and mental problems of the parent. Families are responsive to suggestions for their ongoing involvement in the resident's life. Suggestions could include taking their relative out for regular engagements, keeping the resident updated on family activities, bringing in pictures and tape recordings of special events, continuing to do traditional remembrances, and encouraging their "senior" member to reminisce and tape record family history.
2. Develop programs for families such as "rap" sessions for peer support and staff updates, a family council to serve in advisory capacity, and a volunteer program.
3. Involve the community. Invite service clubs to do special events, have community college extension courses on site, involve preschool and grade-school students in sharing music and arts and crafts. Holiday times can be very special. For example, hold a valentine poster contest with the theme "Love is _____" in relation to an old person.

In one facility where such a valentine poster contest was held, the responses from the fourth and fifth grade children of a neighboring school were the focus of attention for several weeks. More than forty posters were hung in the halls of the facility. There were smiles and feelings of warmth from everyone who saw the posters, which were brightly colored drawings of old and young people together. Some were outside scenes, some were in homes, and some were in hospitals. Some examples of their poster theme "Love is _____" included:

- Bringing flowers to an old woman.
- Walking with your grandma in the park.
- Sharing.
- Letting someone try.
- Taking time to call.
- Caring about old people.
- Singing to grandma.
- Helping grandpa plant flowers.

- Being with a sick friend.
- Visiting an old man.

Such statements, stated so simply, reflect needs that are common to all of us throughout our life cycle:

- The need to be recognized as an individual.
- The need to have meaningful relationships with others.
- The need to continue to risk, to grow, and be competent.
- The need to feel that what we are doing is worthwhile.
- The need to feel secure in our environment.

Summary

With the growth of our elderly population and the increasing range of housing options available to meet its needs, relocations by older adults will likely be more frequent in the coming years. To help older people make a successful relocation is a multidimensional challenge. The research is clear that the elderly's active involvement in the assessment and selection of their new location facilitates a positive move. As part of this process, older people need to assess *both* their own strengths and limitations as well as those of their potential new home so that the best "optimum fit" will be made.

During this relocation period, adequate support from the family, relevant professionals, and a supportive facility staff can reinforce the elderly's coping strategies, help them maximize their choices, and maintain a sense of control over their lives.

Because the main purpose of any relocation is to provide the elderly with a more appropriately supportive environment, it is vital that the staff and administration of the new facility meet the challenge of optimizing each older adult's physical and psychosocial functioning. Maintaining an environment that encourages independence, constructive activities, social interaction and access to the outside community stimulates alertness, participation, and a sense of well-being (Amenta, Weiner, and Amenta 1984).

I hope that by participating in this activity you have increased your appreciation of the importance of older people's involvement in all phases of their relocation and enhanced your understanding of ways to facilitate their optimum relocation.

Evaluation

Please take a few moments now to complete an evaluation.

Relocation, Worksheet

1. How many times have you relocated in your lifetime?

2. If you've moved a lot, does it get easier?

   If so, why?

3. Describe your most difficult relocation.

4. How did you feel about it?

5. Describe your best relocation.

6. How did you feel about it?

Relocation, Worksheet (Continued)
---

7. In the moves you've made, what did you find most difficult in breaking with the past?

8. What treasured possession has always gone with you in every move?

Relocation, Evaluation

1. Did this activity increase your appreciation of the importance of older people's involvement in all phases of their relocation?

   Not much   Some   A lot
   1 2 3 4 5

2. Identify four ways to reduce stress associated with the relocation process.

   _____
   _____
   _____
   _____

3. Give one example of how this activity will affect your interactions with older adults.

PART 4

PSYCHOSOCIAL CONSIDERATIONS

12 Recognition Day

Rationale for Activity

Everyone likes to be recognized by others. This basic human need for recognition is constant throughout our life cycle. Such acknowledgement of our existence provides us with our identity, self-esteem, and sense of belonging.

In the full lives of many young and middle-aged people, verbal and nonverbal recognition happens so frequently that it is accepted as "a given." However, for many older adults this is not the case. Their social worlds have shrunk due to losses of meaningful relationships, and fewer opportunities to socialize because of limited income, poor health, or both. Thus, the elderly can be deprived of needed ongoing recognition.

Those who interact with the elderly need to make a conscious effort to use every opportunity to give individualized recognition to them. Such recognition will help to compensate for older adult's reduced social opportunities to receive reinforcement of their personhood. This activity provides the participants with an opportunity to increase their appreciation of the importance of giving individualized recognition to older people and to enhance their understanding of ways to provide such recognition.

Participants: This activity is appropriate for graduate and undergraduate students and professionals and paraprofessionals in mental health, social work, health care, gerontology and adult education, other service providers, and volunteers.

162 • *Understanding Older Adults*

Objectives

Upon completion of this activity participants will:

1. Have an increased appreciation of the importance of giving individualized recognition to elderly people.
2. Be able to identify four ways to give recognition to older adults.
3. Be able to give at least one example of how this activity will affect their interactions with older adults.

Class Size: Open

Time: Thirty minutes.

> Ten minutes: introduction and activity
> Fifteen minutes: debriefing
> Five minutes: evaluation

Materials: Recognition Day Worksheets, Evaluation Sheets.

Teaching Notes

1. This activity can either be integrated into a presentation on communication with the elderly or completed as a separate activity. I have always elected to use it early in my presentation on communication techniques. It helps to spark interest in a "common" topic like communication, which is sometimes greeted with an "ho hum" attitude by participants. It also serves to set a good pace for the presentation and gets people involved.
2. The worksheet for this activity is quite comprehensive. If time permits, I "walk" the participants through each section. If time is tight, I may focus on selected categories depending on the background of the participants and their roles in working with the elderly.
3. When I ask the participants to think back over a twenty-four-hour period, I make it a weekday so that the participants will recognize how their multiple roles result in many forms of personal recognition.
4. Overall, the participants are surprised at how many times they receive individualized recognition in any twenty-four-hour period. However, some have had only a few social contacts outside the workplace. Thus, I usually do not divide the class into small discussion groups because I do not think a "have" versus a "have-not" dialogue would be of benefit to the participants and could be detrimental to their self-esteem.
5. In my work with health and human service providers to the elderly, I generally have found them to be committed individuals who carry

out their duties because they want to "help people," and they obtain personal and professional satisfaction from doing it. In many cases, they are frustrated because they perceive that their tight time schedules do not allow them enough time with their elderly clients. These providers need to be helped to recognize that they can simultaneously do their functional caregiving tasks while also giving individualized recognition to people. If they can understand how much this interaction means to their clients, they may be more motivated to carry out this dual caregiving role.

Introduction to Activity

1. Everybody likes to be recognized. Such acknowledgement by others provides us with our identity, self-esteem, and sense of belonging. These are basic and ongoing human needs. Maslow (1970) places them third on his hierarchy of basic needs. He places physiological and safety needs first. However, in contrast to these needs, which may be fulfilled by older people themselves, the need to be recognized can only be fulfilled by another person. It requires interaction with and feedback from others. A dictionary definition of recognition is "the perception of something or someone existing."
2. Ways to acknowledge that someone exists include:
   a. Calling people by their name.
   b. Giving a general greeting: Hello! Hi! Good morning! How are you?
   c. Commenting on their appearance: Attire, hair.
   d. Using nonverbal signs: Touch, smile, wave, nod.
3. For most of us, this happens so frequently in a day we do not really focus on it, to be so recognized is "a given." We don't think about how much our "knowing we're alive" is based on other people's recognition of us.
4. To help you recognize this "given" in our lives, I invite you to participate in the following activity.

Instructions to Participants

1. Place your Recognition Day Worksheet in front of you.
2. Now, close your eyes and think back over the last twenty-four hours and the people who came and went or stayed in your life during that period (allow two to three minutes).
3. Now, open your eyes and on your worksheet, list those people and indicate the ways they gave you recognition: called you by name, gave you a general greeting, commented on your appearance, or acknowledged your presence nonverbally.
   a. For family, role names such as mom, brother, etc. or terms of affection are equivalent to your first name.

b. A "friend in the workplace" would be someone you also socialize with outside work.
c. If you interact with many co-workers or elderly residents frequently in one day (such as in a nursing home) you may estimate your contacts by number.
4. Now list the recognitions you expected and didn't receive. If we think about it, most of us have at least one "missed recognition" a day. For example:
a. A co-worker passed you by first thing in the morning and didn't even nod.
b. You didn't receive a birthday card from a good friend.
c. You were wearing a new tie and no one even noticed.
d. Your neighbor drove off and didn't wave.
5. When you have finished your list, total your recognitions (received and not received) at the bottom of the page.

Debriefing

1. How many of you had recognition from:
   a. Your family?
   b. Friends outside school/workplace?
   c. Friends in school/workplace?
   d. Classmates/co-workers?
   e. Acquaintances?
   f. Who were the other people?

   > Responses may include: *Mailperson. Grocery store checker. Video rental store manager. Bank teller. Girl at MacDonald's. Gas station attendant.*

2. In what ways did you receive recognition?
   a. By others using your name: In person? phone? mail?
   b. Notice of your appearance?
   c. General greeting?
   d. Nonverbal: Touch? smile? wave? nod?

It is certainly evident that many of you have social networks which provide you with individualized recognition, verbal and nonverbal. As is to be expected, during any twenty-four-hour period contacts with that network will vary. Also, because each of you is in a different place in the life cycle and have your own lifestyles, the members of your recognition network will be different as will their methods of recognizing you.

3. When you added up the number of people who gave you recognition, were there:
   a. More than you expected?
   b. Less than you would have liked?

c. How many of you had too much recognition?
d. How many of you had "missed" recognitions?

It is interesting to note, but not surprising, how many of us take the recognition of our existence for granted, because we've always had it! We should feel very secure in our "belongingness."

Yet how did you feel when you received less recognition than you would have liked or someone missed giving you a recognition?

Responses may include: I felt slighted. Did I do something wrong? Is my new dress too tight to wear to work? Did my friend not send me a card because I forgot to send her one? Is my neighbor angry with me? I felt hurt.

Remember how quickly these feelings of insecurity, alienation, and hurt arose and how these perceived rejections made you question yourself and your behaviors as we move on to discuss ways to give individualized recognition to the elderly.

Pointers to Promote Recognition of the Elderly

1. Remember that the older people become, the more unique they are as individuals because they have had a lifetime to establish relationships and patterns of socialization and activities that fit their needs and lifestyle.
2. Recognize their individuality by first asking how they would like to be addressed (by first name or surname). Then use that name every time you interact with them. Combine it with a general greeting when appropriate.
3. Recognize and comment on their visits, phone calls, and mail from relatives and friends. This can reinforce their feelings of self-esteem and belonging.
4. Invite them to share with you what their relationships, activities, and related roles have been, are, and would like them to be. This recognition of the continuum and continuance of their lives can serve to remind older adults of their accumulated experience, skills, and coping abilities. This in turn can revitalize their positive adaptation to current changes in their lives. Based on her review of models of the psychophysiology of aging, Woodruff (1975) concluded that old people are extremely adaptable, and although some physiological functions decline, the lifestyles of the elderly may not have to change dramatically.
5. The challenge for caregivers may be not only to recognize and reinforce the older person's ability to adapt but also do everything possible to adapt the environment to the older person's lifestyle. This in turn recognizes the importance their lifestyle has to them.
6. Notice and give the elderly feedback on their appearance. It reflects their femininity or masculinity. Throughout our life cycle, other

roles and relations come and go, but from the moment of conception until the day we die, we have a gender identity. This identity is reinforced through our socialized behaviors and appearance. It is a major part of our personhood. Encourage and recognize its expression through older adults' behaviors, attire, jewelry, make-up, hairstyle, perfume, or aftershave.
7. Consciously use nonverbal communication at every opportunity. Eye contact reinforced by a nod, wave, and smile is an important nonverbal way to convey individualized recognition. However, neither verbal or nonverbal recognition can ever take the place of touch.

Touch, an Essential Means of Recognition

1. Touch is our first form of human communication and remains a basic human need throughout our lives. Our ongoing desire to maintain contact with people is apparent in figurative terms like: "kiss and make it better," "soft-touch," "thin-skinned," "rubbing someone the wrong way," "keep in touch," "handle with care," "reach out and touch someone."
2. The need for touch may even be intensified in old age because of changes that occur in that part of the life cycle, including:
   a. Changes in one's body image heighten the need to be recognized (Hollinger 1980). In our youth-oriented society, elderly need reassurance that their aging bodies still "have the skin you love to touch" and that when people "reach out to touch someone..." it will include them.
   b. Decreased vision and hearing and impaired functional capacity reduces environmental input and information (Seaman 1982). Touch can be used to help compensate for these other sensory and mobility impairments, thus keeping the elderly "grounded" and increase their feelings of "being-in-the-world." Also, multiple sensory stimulation like touch, eye contact, and speech can enhance communication (Burnside 1981).
   c. The elderly have fewer opportunities to be touched because of reduced contact or losses of family and friends (Tobiason 1981). Those caregivers who are in contact with older adults need to be aware of these losses and provide appropriate compensatory touch.
3. Multiple positive effects of touch on nurse-client relationships have been reported. It has calmed agitated patients (Seaman 1982), increased nonverbal responses from confused clients (Langland and Panicucci 1982), made patients more cooperative and receptive to learning (McCoy 1977), and enhanced patients' self-appraisal (Copstead 1980). Touch can establish empathy, stimulate perception, and increase communication (Hollinger 1980). It can convey inter-

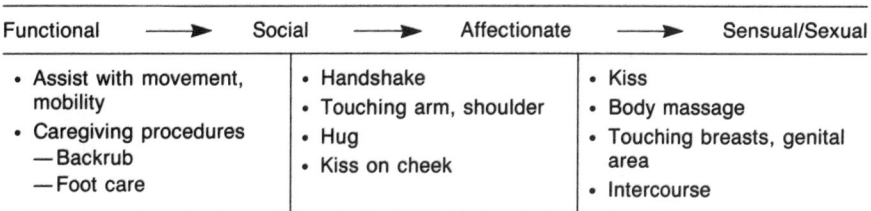

Figure 12-1. Range of Touching

est rather than influence, approval rather than disapproval, and respect rather than contempt (McCoy 1977).

4. Types of touch can range from functional to sexual, as shown in figure 12-1. Functional touch is task-oriented and usually related to physical care procedures. Social touch involves amenities and customs. Affectionate touch expresses caring, concern, and friendship. Sensual, sexual touch expresses love and intimacy.

5. Age does not change our need for touch, but it may change the way these needs are met. For example, if sexual needs can no longer be met because of poor health or lack of a partner, one way to help a person compensate for these needs is through increasing affectionate touch which expresses care and concern.

6. It is important to know how the caregiver and the client have been socialized to view and react to touch. This is based on family, culture, and previous experiences (Hollinger 1980). Burnside suggests to proceed slowly and be sensitive to cues. She suggests starting with a gentle handshake (Burnside 1981).

7. Be aware of the institutional barriers to touch. Geriatric chairs, wheelchairs, and bed rails wall off the elderly from physical contacts with others (Burnside 1981). Also, prolonged bed rest or being in a wheelchair does not allow people the same sense of movement as walking because they are not touching the ground (Hollinger 1980). These conditions that can deprive older people from touch need to be acknowledged and appropriate touch used for compensation.

8. In summary, touch verifies a person's existence and value, provides important recognition, and enhances communication. We should *not* be thrifty with touch.

Summary

Your participation in this activity certainly has demonstrated the need we all have for ongoing recognition. We need interaction and feedback from others on a daily basis. We depend on others to validate our existence and provide us with a sense of belonging.

This need for recognition begins with birth and ends with death. As people proceed along the life cycle, their support systems become smaller. Thus, anyone who interacts with older adults is challenged to optimize every opportunity to recognize their unique personhood.

I hope that by participating in this activity you have increased your appreciation of the importance of giving individualized recognition to older people and enhanced your understanding of ways to provide such recognition.

Evaluation

Please take a few moments now to complete an evaluation.

My 24-Hours Recognition Day Worksheet

Name	Used my name			Noticed my appearance (attire, hair)	General greeting (Hello! Hi! How are you? Good morning)	Non-verbal recognition				Missed recognition
	In person	Phone	Mail			Touch	Smile	Wave	Nod	
Family										
Friends outside school, workplace										
Friends in school, workplace										
Classmates/ Co-workers										
Acquaintances (clubs, church, activities, neighbors)										
Others (identify)										
Totals										

Recognition Day, Evaluation

1. Did this activity increase your appreciation of the importance of giving individualized recognition to the elderly?

Not much		Some		A lot
1	2	3	4	5

2. Identify four ways to give recognition to older adults.

   _____
   _____
   _____
   _____

3. Give at least one example of how this activity will affect your interactions with older adults.

13 Reminiscing

Rationale for Activity

Reminiscing, or the act of remembering one's past, is a universal process throughout the life cycle that can become increasingly adaptational and significant in the later years. Its psychosocial and adaptational functions for the elderly include: stimulating thought processes and long-term memories needed for life review, providing a sense of continuity of life, maintaining self-esteem and identity, reactivating dormant strengths and coping strategies, promoting family interactions, increasing socialization, and developing peer relationships.

In addition to enhancing the older person's psychosocial functioning, those who reminisce with the elderly can gain a better understanding of each older person's uniqueness. This, in turn, can help them provide more individualized and appropriate care and services. The process of reminiscing can enhance older people's functioning directly and indirectly.

Reminiscing can be beneficial to elderly people regardless of their physical impairments and levels of cognitive functioning. It can be conducted individually or in groups in a variety of settings by professionals or supervised students and volunteers.

Given the importance of reminiscing as a process to enhance the elderly's psychosocial functioning and its continual availability to be used, it is important that those who work with and care for older adults be aware of this potential resource.

This activity provides participants with an opportunity to increase their appreciation of the process of reminiscing and to enhance their understanding of its usefulness, and to prepare themselves to facilitate an elderly person's reminiscence.

Participants: This activity is appropriate for graduate and undergraduate students and professionals and paraprofessionals in mental health, social work, health care, gerontology and adult education, other service providers, volunteers, and family caregivers.

However, for maximum effectiveness it will have to be adapted to the educational level of the participants and the settings in which they work. As an example, following this activity, I have included a thirty-minute inservice developed for the paraprofessional staff of a geriatric center. It is titled "Reminiscing Over the Holidays." Depending on your participants, you can use it as an example to review and discuss or you can use it as an additional activity.

Objectives

Upon completion of this activity participants will:

1. Be able to identify four reasons why reminiscing is a significant activity for the elderly.
2. Have an increased appreciation of the range of feelings that can be aroused during the reminiscing process.
3. Have increased knowledge of topics which can facilitate reminiscing.
4. Be able to facilitate an elderly person's reminiscence.
5. Be able to give at least one example of how this activity will affect their interactions with the elderly.

Class Size: Open. If small discussion groups are desired, see Teacher Notes for suggestions regarding selection of a reminiscing topic.

Time: Forty to fifty-five minutes, depending on class size and debriefing format.

Fifteen minutes: introduction
Twenty minutes: activity and debriefing (if the class breaks into small discussion groups, allow an addi- fifteen minutes)
Five minutes: evaluation

Materials: Reminiscing Worksheets or blank paper, Evaluation Sheets.

Teaching Notes

1. General Suggestions for Conducting this Activity

a. This activity can be used to "set the stage" for a discussion on any topic related to the life cycle. For example, if the overall class topic is "friendship in the later years," participants could reminisce about their friendships at different stages of their life cycle. This reminiscing experience makes the topic more meaningful and enhances learning. Also, it can be used in conjunction with developing interviewing skills.

b. When the development of group process is an important objective of a workshop, I may select and assign a reminiscing topic to facilitate a nonthreatening discussion. In this case, I select a topic such as: describe what you enjoyed doing as a child, favorite song, favorite vacation, best friend, or happiest memory. Participants generally enjoy sharing these topics in small group discussions. They can stimulate insightful conversations on both the similarities and uniqueness of common human experiences.

c. People vary in their level of participation in any activity. This is especially so when it involves sharing personal experiences. In debriefing as a class, I emphasize that everyone make his or her own decision regarding the sharing of memories. I acknowledge in a general way those who shared and those who did not, making the point that there are times we feel like sharing memories and times we do not and so it is with the elderly. We need to respect the elderly's selection of a time to share. Also, I always give the participants of ongoing classes the option of sharing the memories they have written on their worksheets with me with the understanding that they will be returned. Many do, some do not. I never give the participants points toward a grade for sharing their memories. The value of the activity is in the experience and the feelings aroused by it and the participants are frequently surprised at the intensity of these feelings. It is this personal, affective experience that facilitates the participants' appreciation of the importance of this activity for the elderly.

d. I usually suggest that the participants consider sharing their memory with a relative or close friend following the class. Such sharing can further enrich a relationship.

2. Selecting Reminiscing Topics

a. For a class discussion format, I give the introduction, then dictate the list of potential reminiscing topics and let them select one, or ask them to describe the first memory that comes to mind before dictating the list. Both approaches allow the participants choices and control, as they self-select their memories. Even given this control, some choose not to share verbally with the class during the debriefing.

b. I dictate the list of topics rather than give it as a handout because I have observed that in the process of writing down the list, the participants give nonverbal signs of beginning to remember certain events. These signs can include a smile or chuckle, a look of sadness, or a twinkle in the eye. This process helps to focus their attention on the activity and give it significance.

c. In structured reminiscing, the topics need to be selected with objectivity and sensitivity. Ebersole, a recognized leader in this field, has suggested that it is usually better to begin with topics which describe events, since those are less threatening than sharing feelings of fears and failures (Ebersole and Hess 1985). In response to that suggestion, I have categorized the sample reminiscing topics into societal events, education/work/activities, relationships, and other personal experiences. This categorization was based on reminiscing topics that participants have self-selected over the years in which I have conducted this activity. The frequency of these self-selected topics was: societal events 10 percent; education/work/activities 15 percent; relationships 60 percent; other personal experiences 15 percent. The importance of relationships in our lives is clearly evident. When these memories are voluntarily shared with the group, the support and empathy based on the commonalities of the human condition becomes a growth experience for all those present.

3. Follow-up Assignment for Participants

a. If the reminiscing activity is part of an ongoing class, I follow it up with an assignment that requires the student to conduct a reminiscing session with an adult over sixty-five years old. The content of this session has varied depending on the level of the class. Assignments have included either letting the elderly person select the reminiscing topic or having the topic preselected in order to focus on a specific event in the elderly person's life.

b. In some cases I select the interviewees. If this is a first interview for the students or their first experience with an elderly person, I select an individual with whom the establishment of rapport will be easy. In my experience, this first connection can be very significant. In other cases, I let the students select their own interviewees. Their ages have ranged from sixty-five to 101 years. Frequently students choose family members and inevitably learn new things about these relatives. Comments have included:

> *My grandmother let me become part of her memories; it brought us closer. I learned new things from my grandmother that are a part of my heritage—like my family's pioneer spirit that led to their survival in a new land. My grandfather is a survivor. I never knew of his struggles before; I learned a lot.*

c. Overall, these intergenerational assignments have been very successful. These students gain a memorable first-hand experience in hearing about the trials and triumphs of aging. As a result, they discard many of society's negative stereotypes of the elderly. Their comments have included:

> *I got the picture of a very adaptive person. He had experienced hardships but carried on; he's a good lesson in living. We should sit down and listen to the aged and reassess their potential to activate change. I learned that we all, as human beings, share many basic characteristics yet we are all unique. This assignment was not only educational in a schol-*

arly aspect but also a true learning experience of life itself. The elderly can be our best teachers in problem solving and adaptation. Old people have gone through and experienced many changes and coped remarkably well. I would never have believed a one hundred-year-old lady could be so alert and at the end of my interview, asked my opinion about current world issues.

4. Reminiscing Groups for the Elderly

a. As with your classes, reminiscing with older people can be conducted on an individual basis or in groups. Ideally, elderly people would have access to both methods. Groups have several advantages including: more people can be helped at one time; they provide an opportunity for increased socialization; they create a potential for the development of peer relationships beyond the group session.

b. As a group activity, reminiscing can be conducted in a variety of settings, including churches, libraries, community centers, nutrition sites, residential care homes, day treatment centers, rehabilitation units, nursing homes, and psychiatric facilities.

c. The prime qualifications to lead a reminiscing group include an interest in the elderly, an appreciation for the uniqueness of each individual, excellent listening skills, a supportive, empathetic approach, and an interest in learning group process skills and gerontological content. This type of group can be led by supervised students and volunteers as well as professionals.

d. A reminiscing group is primarily supportive. It is not necessary or even advisable to confront or interpret what the elderly share (Ebersole 1978a). If the leader determines that a group member is distressed because of a memory, immediate recognition of the feelings needs to be given and the elderly person assured that there will be appropriate follow-up after the session on an individual basis.

e. As a reminiscing group develops, it is important to conduct an ongoing assessment of both the group's and its individual members' growth and changing needs (Remnet 1978). As a group progresses it may diversify its discussions to include past and present events, evolve into another type of group, or there may be spinoff activities to meet other needs and interests (Remnet 1974).

It is beyond the scope of this activity to cover any more guidelines for forming and conducting a reminiscing group. However, there are excellent resources available, including Adams 1979; Ebersole 1976, 1978a, 1978b; Ebersole and Hess 1985; and Hartford 1980.

Introduction to Activity: Overview of Reminiscing

1. Life Review and Reminiscing

Robert Butler, in his classic article, The Life Review: An Interpretation of Reminiscence in the Aged (1963), introduced the life review concept as a naturally occurring universal mental process characterized by recalling and reviewing past experiences, including conflicts and disappointments. This gives people the opportunity to come to terms with their imperfections and failures so that a balanced life perspective can be developed. Reminiscing can give new meaning and significance to one's life and reduce the fear and anxiety of death. Butler perceives reminiscing as an integral part of the life review process. It provides the material for the life review. Though reminiscing is seen in other age groups, it becomes more intense in old age as the elderly strive toward putting their lives in order (Butler and Lewis 1982).

2. Reminiscing throughout Life

Based on her review of the literature, Adams (1979) reported conflicting and inconclusive research concerning the amount of time older people spent reminiscing. Thus, one is cautioned not to infer that there is a linear relationship between age and time spent in reminiscing. Merriam and Cross (1982) report from their research that increasing age merely offers more life about which to reminisce. They concluded that adults of all ages reminisce about events throughout their entire lives.

3. Recent Research Findings

In 1980, based on her review of research on the concept and function of reminiscence, Merriam cautioned that more groundwork had to be done to conceptualize the phenomenon of reminiscence and its relationship to ego integrity and psychological adjustment (Merriam 1980). Recent studies on group reminiscing have provided some of this needed groundwork and have reported that this activity has had a positive effect on the psychosocial functioning of the elderly. These groups have been conducted with elderly people who have had a range of physical impairments and were at various levels of cognitive functioning. The settings included nursing homes (Cook 1984; Ellison 1981; Lappe 1987; Perschbacher 1984); geriatric day care centers (Baker 1985; Dietsche 1979); a health center (Huber and Miller 1984); and a state psychiatric institute (Lesser, Lazarus, Frankel, and Havasy 1981). In one study (Perschbacher 1984) nursing home residents used their life experience to teach an oral history class to third grade students. It is evident that reminiscing can be a beneficial activity for a broad spectrum of older people from the well, cognitively alert elderly to those coping with a range of physical and mental impairments.

Transition to Activity

Reminiscing, as part of the life review, is a necessary healthy process in daily life as well as in the mental health care of the elderly. It is important that those who interact with the elderly appreciate the process of reminiscing and provide opportunities for it to occur.

Questions to stimulate reminiscing are endless. The suggestions that follow may trigger many more of your own. The questions have been categorized by their potential to trigger affective memories, beginning with those having the least potential (societal events) to those with more potential (personal experiences).

Reminiscing Topics

1. Societal Events   In relation to our society and world, in your lifetime describe:
   a. The most significant historical event.
   b. The greatest disaster.
   c. The greatest accomplishment for mankind.

2. Education/Work/ Activities.
   a. In relation to your educational experiences, describe your first day at:
      - Nursery school
      - Preschool
      - Kindergarten
      - Grade school
      - Junior high
      - High school
      - College
   b. In relation to your work/career experiences, describe:
      - Your first job
      - Your best promotion
      - A time you left a job
   c. In relation to your activities, describe:
      - A favorite toy
      - What you enjoyed doing as a child
      - Your first car
      - Your favorite song/hymn
      - Your best vacation
      - Your favorite food
      - What event in your early life impressed you the most

3. Relationships
   a. Describe your earliest memory.
   b. In relation to friendship, describe your best friend in:
      - Kindergarten
      - Grade school
      - Junior high
      - Adolescence
      - Early adulthood
      - Middle years
      - Later years
   c. Describe your first date.
   d. Who was or is the most influential person in your life?

e. In relation to your family.
- Describe your favorite home
- Describe your most memorable holiday:
  - New Year's
  - Valentine's Day
  - Passover
  - Easter
  - July Fourth
  - Thanksgiving
  - Hanukkah
  - Christmas
- What is the most vivid memory of your:
  - Mother
  - Father
  - Brother
  - Sister
  - Aunt
  - Uncle
  - Cousins
  - Grandmother
  - Grandfather

4. Other Personal Experiences

a. What is your greatest regret?
b. Describe your most embarrassing experience.
c. Describe your most frightening experience.
d. When have you felt most alone?
e. What has been your greatest disappointment?
f. What have been the major turning points in your life?
g. Describe your funniest memory.
h. What has been your most significant experience?
i. When have you felt life has been most challenging?
j. What has been your greatest accomplishment?
k. Describe your proudest day.
l. Describe your happiest memory.

Instructions to Participants

1. Now that you have a list of potential reminiscing topics, I would like you to review the list and select a memory you would either like to draw or describe.
2. Place you Reminiscing Worksheet in front of you.
3. Close your eyes for a few moments, think about your selected memory and why it is special to you and how you *feel* when you think about it.
4. Now open your eyes and describe the memory and your feelings about that memory on your worksheet. After you've finished, close

your eyes again and try to hold onto the feelings your memory aroused. When everyone is finished, those who would like to share with the class will have an opportunity to do so (allow five to seven minutes).

Suggestions for Debriefing

1. It is important not to give the impression of being rushed because participants are focusing on a significant experience in their lives. So after five minutes, check and see if everyone has finished. If not, allow a few more minutes.
2. Then ask who would like to share a memory.
   a. Encourage as many people as possible to participate and give each of them enough time to share their memories.
   b. As each person finishes, acknowledge the content and empathize with the feelings which may be positive, negative or both.
   c. Also, give recognition to the other participants' attention and nonverbal support for those who shared (sharing of memories can promote the development of group camaraderie).
3. After all who wish to share have finished, your summary statement could be, "We appreciate those who chose to share; we are all richer because of it. We also respect those who decided not to share for everyone deserves the right to select when, what, and where they share."

Transition to Functions of Reminiscing

Now that we've personalized the process of reminiscing, let's discuss how it can enhance the psychosocial functioning of the elderly, directly and indirectly.

Functions of Reminiscing

1. Reminiscing, or the act of remembering one's past, is a universal process throughout the life cycle that can become increasingly important in the later years. The activity of reminiscing involves an emotional experience in which significant past events are brought back into mind and re-experienced and savored. It has both intrapersonal and interpersonal adaptational significance for the person (Pincus 1970). It can enhance the psychosocial functioning of the elderly directly through their own experiences and indirectly through helping their caregivers gain a greater understanding of them.

2. In relation to helping the elderly directly, reminiscing has multiple functions. It can provide older adults with opportunities:
   a. To get in touch with their feelings. Memories are sensitive and can be intense and as such add a vital dimension to the quality of life. Every person has a unique treasure of memories—some are happy, some are sad. All are important if they are selected to be shared.
   b. To stimulate the long-term memories needed for the life review. The life review, in turn, facilitates the reliving of past events in terms of present reality which leads to greater self-understanding, an acceptance of the past, a sense of the continuity of life, and the achievement of the developmental task of ego integrity. For example, Boylin, Gordon, and Nehrke (1976) reported that the participants in their study who reminisced most frequently scored higher on the measure of ego integrity. Ego integrity involves the older person's reconciling "what might have been" with "what actually is" (Erikson 1963).
   c. To remember and reactivate their dormant strengths and coping strategies. Today's elderly have "made it through" the multiple, major changes of this century. They are survivors and need to be so recognized!
   d. To make meaningful intergenerational connections:
      i. With families as they discuss, write, or tape record their knowledge of their culture, family and selves so that these can contribute to the generations to follow.
      ii. With students of all ages and educational levels so they use their own historical and individual experiences to teach about the realities of aging.
   e. To participate in peer groups where they can overcome their reluctance to interact with people of their own age. Through sharing their losses, tribulations, accomplishments, viewpoints, and commonalities, feelings of camaraderie can develop (Ebersole 1978a).
   f. To have increased socialization and with it a renewed sense of identity and self-esteem through the validation of their life experiences by others. Such socialization can also allay anxiety associated with the aging process and help mitigate fear of death.
3. In relation to helping the elderly indirectly, older people's reminiscences can also be beneficial to those who work with and provide care to them. It can help these caregivers develop a therapeutic relationship with older individuals through insights gained from the elderly sharing parts of themselves which are no longer observable to others. It can:
   a. Provide information about older people's current state. Spontaneous reminiscing changes with current affective experiences. For example, if people reminisce about food, they could be hungry.

b. Provide useful insights regarding the elderly's self-images, use of relationships and general adaptive functioning (Carlson 1984).
c. Help the caregivers learn about the elderly's past life with its struggles, losses, fears, triumphs, and strengths (Ebersole 1976). Erikson (1964) identifies the strengths of hope, will, purpose, competence, fidelity, love, care, and wisdom as safeguards for psychosocial survival.
d. Help clinicians, students, family, and friends who participate with the elderly in their reminiscing and life reviews obtain a rich supply of information and models for their own eventual old age.

Summary

Today we've felt how our emotions are stimulated when we reminisce about our unique experiences. It is these emotions that provide a vital dimension to the *quality* of our lives. When we recapture the past, experience the present or anticipate the future—we *feel* alive.

As we've experienced, reminiscing is meaningful for all of us, regardless of our stage in the life cycle. However, because it has increasing adaptational significance in the later years it is vital to provide opportunities for reminiscing in our interactions with the elderly. These opportunities can occur spontaneously when initiated by either the older person or a professional, student, family, or friend on a one-to-one basis. Also, reminiscing can occur as a structured group experience. The important thing is that it occur!

I hope that this activity has increased your appreciation of the reminiscing process, its adaptational role in lives of elderly people and the need to provide opportunities for it to take place.

Evaluation

Please take a few moments now to fill out the evaluation.

Reminiscing, Worksheet

Memory Topic:

Describe your memory and feelings aroused by it:

Reminiscing, Evaluation

1. Based on this activity, identify four reasons why reminiscing is an important activity for the elderly.

   _____

   _____

   _____

   _____

2. Did this activity increase your appreciation of the range of feelings that can be aroused during the reminiscing process?

Not much		Some		A lot
1	2	3	4	5

3. Did this activity increase your knowledge of topics that can facilitate reminiscing?

Not much		Some		A lot
1	2	3	4	5

4. Based on this activity, are your prepared to facilitate an elderly person's reminiscence? ☐ Yes ☐ No
   Why?

5. Give at least one example of how this activity will affect your interTactions with older adults.

Example of an Inservice Training Session
Reminiscing over the Holidays

Objectives

At the completion of this activity the participants will:

1. Be able to define reminiscing.
2. Have an increased appreciation of the importance of reminiscing during the holiday season.
3. Be able to give at least one example of how this activity will affect their interactions with their elderly patients.

Class size: Open

Time: Thirty minutes.

> Five minutes: introduction
> Twenty minutes: activity and debriefing
> Five minutes: evaluation

Materials: Reminiscing over the Holidays Worksheets, Evaluation Sheets.

Teaching Notes

Review the Reminiscing Activity that precedes this exercise for additional information you may wish to include.

Introduction to Activity

1. Today we're going to use the time we have together to discuss an activity that is important for all of us at any age, but is even more so for the residents here in the geriatric center. This activity is "reminiscing."
2. What does the word "reminiscing" mean?

> Responses may include: *Memories. Recalling the past. Telling stories about the family. Talking about past experiences. Sharing "the good old days."*

As you have suggested the process of reminiscing involves thinking about experiences we've had in our lives. It is the process of remembering one's past. Some of our remembrances are happy; some are sad. When we think of these special memories, we also *feel* them, relive them, savor them. We all reminisce throughout our lives about our special and unique memories. These memories grow in number as we become older.

3. The holiday season can be a special time of bittersweet reminiscing

---
*Example of an Inservice Training Session
Reminiscing over the Holidays
(Continued)*
---

    for all of us but especially for the elderly. They remember both the happy times they've spent over the years with loved ones and also the sadness of being separated from some of them by distance or death.
4. It is important that all of us who work with the elderly be sensitive to the importance and intensity of their memories so that we can be appropriately supportive.
5. In order to increase your appreciation of the importance of reminiscing, I'd like you to participate in an activity that will give you the opportunity to share some of your special holiday memories.

Instructions to Participants

1. Place your Reminiscing over the Holidays Worksheet in front of you.
2. Close your eyes for a few moments and think about the holidays:
    a. What makes them special to you?
    b. What's your favorite holiday food
    c. Who do you miss during the holidays?
3. Now open your eyes and answer those questions on your worksheet (allow three to five minutes).

Suggestions for Debriefing

The participant's responses to the questions on the worksheet can be used:

1. To make the observation of how animated some of the participants are when they share their holiday experiences with others who are *listening* to them. They are re-experiencing and savoring the events just as their elderly patients would like the opportunity to do.
2. To reinforce that holidays focus on family and friends, giving and receiving, food, and festivities. Thus, it is important that they, as caregivers, do as much as possible to provide their elderly patients with opportunities: to share memories of the past and to savor the present with staff, friends, and family; to give and receive cards and presents; and to enjoy familiar foods and festivities.
3. To support reminiscing about their family members and friends who are not able to be with them. Such memories may be bittersweet and probably intense. However, it will help them to appreciate the importance of giving their patients an opportunity to validate and savor the experiences they've had in meaningful past relationships. Such emotions provide a vital affective *quality* to life.

Example of an Inservice Training Session
Reminiscing over the Holidays
(Continued)

Debriefing

1. What makes the holiday season special for you?

   Responses may include: *Happiness at being with my family. Being with people I really care about. Sharing gifts. Making gifts for grandchildren. Getting cards from friends. Singing favorite songs and hymns that bring back memories.*

2. What is your favorite holiday food and why?

   Responses may include: *Turkey and dressing because my mom made it. Tamales my grandmother made. Pies because all my sisters get together and make them. Shortbread because my grandmother sends it from Scotland.*

3. Who do you miss during the holidays?

   Responses may include: *My mother. My dad. My children. My close friend. My sister. My aunt. My grandparents. My husband. My grandchild.*

   Thank you for sharing your special memories. Their importance to you was very obvious. When your memories were happy your eyes sparkled, your voice was joyful, and your positive body movements reinforced your pleasure. For those of you who shared sad memories, your facial expressions were doleful, your voice was soft, and your body was still.

   I was impressed by the way you all really listened to each other, sharing in the joys and sadness. It's evident you are caring people.

   Again, thank you for sharing.

Transition to Summary Points

I selected this activity today for two reasons:

a. I wanted you to get in touch with your own special memories so that you could share them with your co-workers and families.
b. Also, through your sharing today, I hope it will remind you to help your patients share their holiday memories with you. You may be the *only* person to listen.

Summary Points

When your patients do share, remember these points:

1. In recalling past holidays spent with loved ones, their memories may be bittersweet because they involve people who may no longer

---

Example of an Inservice Training Session
Reminiscing over the Holidays
(Continued)

---

be alive or they may not be able to be with the patient during the holidays.
2. Memories do not have to be happy to be therapeutic. If they talk about their losses, listen and be empathetic. Encourage rather than inhibit the expression of emotion.
3. Through sharing special memories with others, individuals feel more connected to each other and feel important because someone has cared enough to *really* listen, as you did for each other today.
4. Remember that helping a person reminisce can be your *year-long* gift to them. By helping older people get in touch with their past experiences you are giving them recognition that their lives have been worthwhile, and showing that you care about them and their uniqueness.

So, at the same time you provide physical care for each of your elderly patients, also care for their mental health by reminiscing with them.

Evaluation

Please take a few moments now to fill out the evaluation.

Reminiscing over the Holidays, Worksheet

1. What makes the holiday season special for you?

2. What is your favorite holiday food and why?

3. Who do you miss during the holidays?

Reminiscing over the Holidays, Evaluation

1. Define reminiscing.

2. Did this activity increase your appreciation of the importance of reminiscing during the holiday season?

Not much		Some		A lot
1	2	3	4	5

3. Give at least one example of how this activity will affect your interactions with your elderly patients.

14 Family Interactions

Rationale for Activity

The primary social support system for most people, including elders, is the family and extended kin network (Herr and Weakland 1979). The importance and viability of this family network in the lives of the elderly has been well-documented in gerontological literature (Brody 1985; Cicirelli 1981; Frankfather, Smith, and Caro 1981; Hagestad 1981; Horowitz and Shindelman 1983; Troll and Stapley 1985).

It is important for those who interact with the elderly to not only view them as individuals but also as an integral part of their dynamic family system. Relationships and roles in this family system are never fixed. They are always "in process," changing as members grow older and as society affects each of their lives. Two major societal influences on the family system are changing demographics and economic trends.

The older population is the most rapidly growing segment of our society. By 1980 there were 24 million older people living in the United States. By 1990 there will be 28 million and by the year 2020 there will be 40 million (Atchley 1987). These changing demographics are affecting the structure of the family system and increasing its responsibilities for the care of its older members.

Other demographic changes are also affecting the family structure. There has been an increase in the number of elderly women compared to elderly men. Present predictions state that women can expect to live about eight years longer than men (National Institute on Aging 1977). This demographic change has implications for middle-aged caregivers who will have more responsibility for elderly widows (Cicirelli 1981). In addition, the caregiving role may now come at a time when middle-aged adults still have responsibilities for their own children. Data from the 1980 Current Population Survey show that women are having their first children later in life (United States Bureau of the

Census 1984). This trend can increase the need for middle-aged adults to provide care for two generations simultaneously.

Responsibility for the older generation is increased even more because there are fewer adult children to provide the care needed. Because of the severe economic conditions during the Depression years, there were more one- and two-child families, more childless marriages, and more unmarried adults (United States Bureau of the Census 1972). As a result, a smaller nuclear family unit is currently involved with varying levels of responsibility for more older relatives including parents, uncles, aunts, and siblings. More "young-old" adults, fifty-five to seventy-four years old, are responsible for the care of their "old-old" relatives, seventy-five years and older (Brody 1981). Also, because of their advancing years, the elderly over seventy-five require progressively more care and other supportive services to assist them in maintaining their optimum level of functioning. Thus, the young-old adults will be concurrently dealing with their own aging issues including their work, financial state, children, and health, as well as with their aging parents' needs.

Inflationary economic trends that have been decreasing the economic resources of all generations have a particularly serious effect on the elderly who are less able to make compensatory adjustments. In addition, the middle-aged generation's adjustments also have an effect on the elderly. The purchase of smaller cars and homes makes it more difficult to provide transportation and housing for aging relatives. A two-worker income is becoming essential for an increasing number of families to maintain the family's standard of living. There has been a progressive increase in women working outside the home. Between 1940 and 1979, the proportion of working married women rose from 11 percent to almost 56 percent. Sixty-two percent of all women between the ages of forty-five and fifty-four now work, as do 42 percent of those who are fifty-five to sixty-four (Brody and Schoonover 1986).

It is evident that with these current societal trends consisting of a rapidly increasing elderly population, fewer potential family caregivers, and shrinking economic resources, more family systems will be prone to increasing stresses and role conflicts as they struggle to maintain their traditional role of caring for all of their members and adapt to both husband and wife working outside the home.

Those who work with the elderly have the ongoing challenge to be as understanding and supportive as possible to the family as it endeavors to cope with these major changes. This activity will provide participants an opportunity to increase their understanding of elderly people within the context of their family system. It focuses on interaction patterns among family members and some psychodynamic aspects of family relationships.

Participants: This activity is appropriate for graduate and undergraduate students and professionals in mental health, social work, health care, and gerontology.

Objectives

Upon completion of this activity, participants will:

1. Have an increased understanding of the family as a "system in process."
2. Be able to identify three ways to examine family interaction patterns.
3. Be able to give at least one example of how this activity will affect their interactions with intergenerational families.

Class Size: Open. If a large class, break up into small groups of five to seven so participants can compare and contrast their family systems' interaction patterns.

Time: Fifty-five minutes.

> Fifteen minutes: introduction and activity
> Ten minutes: small group discussion
> Twenty-five minutes: debriefing
> Five minutes: evaluation

Materials: Family Interaction Worksheets, Evaluation Sheets.

Teaching Notes

1. I have found this activity effectively highlights the complex interrelationships within a family system. A spirit of camaraderie seems to develop as the participants compare and contrast the interaction patterns of their family systems.
2. I have included many references in the debriefing section. I wanted to provide you with a wide range of resources for this important topic.
3. If you are interested in obtaining more resources which are available to respond to the needs of families with older members, two suggestions are:
   a. Programs to assist professionals in conducting workshops for family caregivers include: As Parents Grow Older Program (Silverman, Brahce, and Zielinski 1981); Aging Parents: Whose Responsibility? (Goodman 1980); Help for Families of the Aging (Pierskalla and Heald 1982); The Natural Supports Program (Rzetelny and Mellor 1981); Hand in Hand (Bressler 1984).
   b. Books to help adult children in their caregiving roles include those written by: Andrus Volunteers 1985; Bloomfield 1985; Bumagin and Hirn 1979; Cohen and Gans 1978; Grollman and Grollman 1978; Hooyman and Lustbader 1986; Horne 1985; La Buda 1985; Otten and Shelley 1977; Silverstone and Hyman

1982; Springer and Brubaker 1984. These self-help books provide information about aging, caregiving relationships, and available community resources.

Introduction to Activity

1. For most individuals, including the elderly, the family is the primary social support system. The affectional and supportive functions of the family continue to emerge as most crucial to the security of the elderly and are a means to intergrate the elderly in American society (Puner 1974; Tobin and Kulps 1980). Troll (1971) has written that family ties are the last social stronghold to which the elderly adhere. Families continue to function as the greatest resource of elderly persons for social, emotional, economic, and health needs and as a source of emergency aid (Bild and Havighurst 1976; Seelbach and Hansen 1980).
2. However, despite the continuing importance of family support systems for the aged, Treas (1977) reported that historical changes have created new constraints on families in caring for aging kin. Demographics have reflected the reduced number of descendants to whom an older person may turn for assistance. Changes in women's roles, particularly the rise in work outside the home, have fostered obligations that compete with duties toward aging parents. Thus, kin resources are readily becoming overextended because there are fewer adult children to share the care of aging relatives, and these adult children have more obligations and constraints in other areas.
3. Given these changing family dynamics, it is important that those who interact with the elderly gain an understanding of the elderly from both an individual and family system's perspective.
4. Looking at elderly people within the context of their family system provides the opportunity to examine the dynamic nature of the family and how interaction patterns among members have a ripple effect throughout the entire system.
5. To help you become better acquainted with this approach, I would like you to participate in the following activity.

Instructions to Participants

1. Place your Family Interaction Patterns Worksheet in front of you.
2. Let's work through the components together:
   a. Proximity:
      i. How far do you live from your parents (in travel time)?
      ii. Approximately how often do you see them: daily? twice a week? weekly? monthly? other?

b. How do you perceive your family's boundaries?

Boundaries mean the openness of your family to nonfamily members:

    i. Closed—nonfamily members are not invited to participate in family activities.
    ii. Semipermeable—partially open.
    iii. Open—family members hardly recognize the difference between relatives and nonrelatives.

c. What are some of your family's rules?

Family rules are attitudes and values that families develop to define how family members should interact with one another. These rules are handed down from generation to generation, with each generation making functional and pragmatic changes (Herr and Weakland 1979). Such rules can include:

    i. Communication patterns: verbal/nonverbal, loud/quiet.
    ii. Expression of affection: verbal/nonverbal, demonstrative/nondemonstrative.
    iii. Roles: fixed or flexible, males assigned instrumental (task-oriented), women assigned expressive (emotional support).
    iv. Attendance at family rituals: birthdays, weddings, funerals, holidays, family reunions, picnics.
    v. Approaches to family problems: avoidance, family meeting, keep in family, discuss with friends.
    vi. Acceptance of help from outsiders: friends, neighbors, medical, church, community resources.

d. Identify what members fulfill what roles in your family. There may be more than one member in each role. Fulfillment of these interlocking roles keeps the family system in balance. When a member ceases to perform a role or tries to take over someone else's, the whole system is shaken up. Members will make any adjustments necessary to bring the system back into equilibrium.

    i. Leader: Represents security, strength, makes and maintains family boundaries, and maintains contact with the world (Peterson 1980).
    ii. Decision maker: In some families one person makes all the decisions; in others, all decisions are shared; in yet others, it depends on the subject.
    iii. Mobilizer: Focuses the family's energies to accomplish its tasks and meet its goals.
    iv. Joker: Provides the comedy relief; usually has a funny story or joke.
    v. Provoker of conflict: Presents "the other side" of every issue, provokes arguments, gets bored if the system is running smoothly and likes to stir things up.
    vi. Peacemaker: The family negotiator, a good communicator whose goal is to keep the family system running smoothly.

vii. Kinkeeper: A pivotal role in the family system; takes the responsibility of keeping family members connected through letters, cards, phone calls, visits; knows the family background, present functioning, and future plans. If the person in this role dies and is not replaced, it can be a serious threat to the survival of the system.

e. In the area of mutual aid:
   i. Whom do you go to for help?

Help can include emotional support, problem solving, financial aid, help with chores, picking out clothing, etc.

   ii. Who comes to you?

Transition to Debriefing

1. Now that you've identified some of your own family interaction patterns, before we debrief as a group, I would like you to share your families' interaction patterns with some of the other participants.
2. So please divide up into groups of five to seven and do a compare-and-contrast on your family interaction patterns (allow ten minutes).
3. Now, let's debrief as a group.

Debriefing

1. How many of you live an hour or less from your parents? Two to three hours? More?

In her review of more than twenty-five studies on residential proximity between older parents and their adult children, Troll (1971) found that older people prefer to live "near" their children, near being defined functionally in terms of travel time rather than geographic distance. Rosenmayr (1977) supported Troll's findings. From his critical review of empirical research studies, he concluded that "intimacy at a distance" in matters of housing, help, and communication corresponded to the wishes of both generations.

2. How frequently do you see your parents: daily? weekly? other?

Based on his review of the literature, Cicirelli (1983) reports that from 78 percent to 90 percent of all older people with children see them once a week or more often and are in contact with them by phone at about the same frequency. However, the quality of these contacts is another issue and is based on the older person's perception. The importance of perception is evident in Ward, Sherman, and LaGory's (1984) study. They reported that elderly people's perception of enough contact with their children and that it had the desired quality was more important to their well being than whether they had enough interaction in the objective sense.

3. How many of you have: Closed family boundaries? Semipermeable? Open?

Each family has its established "boundaries." Some family boundaries are closed to nonfamily members and participation in activities outside the family are not encouraged. Other families with permeable boundaries hardly recognize the difference between family and nonfamily (Troll 1980). These differences between open and tight knit families play a major role in intergenerational families' interaction (or lack of it) with formal support systems.

4. What are some of your family's rules?
    a. Communication patterns: verbal? nonverbal? loud? quiet?
    b. Ways to express affection: verbal? nonverbal? touch? demonstrative? nondemonstrative?
    c. Roles: fixed? flexible? gender-assigned?
    d. Attendance at family rituals: mandatory? optional?
    e. Approaches to family problems: avoidance? family meetings? keep in family? discuss with friends? seek professional help?
    f. Acceptance of help from outsiders: never? friends? neighbors? medical care? church? community resources?

These rules, because they involve attitudes and values and are "givens" in every person's family of origin, are powerful determinants of behavior. Blending families and rules can be an ongoing challenge.

5. Regarding roles in your families: Can you identify the leader? Decision maker? Does the decision maker change with the topic? Mobilizer? Joker? Provoker of conflict: Hell-raiser? Pot-stirrer? Peacemaker? Kinkeeper?

As we discussed earlier, these designated roles keep the family system in balance. The loss of any member or change in any member's fulfillment of a role puts the family in a state of flux. To regain its equilibrium, the system requires a reorganization of roles and tasks and a realignment of power and interaction patterns.

6. Regarding patterns of mutual aid in your family: How many of you have more family members coming to you than you go to others? Do you give financial assistance? Emotional support? How many of you have reciprocity with certain family members regarding giving and receiving help?

Thank you for sharing about your family and its rules, roles, relationships, and patterns of mutual aid. You have certainly demonstrated the uniqueness of each family system.

I would like to keep focused on patterns of mutual aid for a few moments because discussing some of the influences involved in the development of these patterns can serve to enhance your understanding of the intergenerational family. Such influences include: the family's history, perceptions of its members, types of aid provided, reciprocity between the generations, and changes in the health of its members.

Influences on Patterns of Aid

1. Family History   Every family has a unique history and the adaptive abilities of elderly individuals and their family systems to the changes associated with aging are influenced by it. This history consists of the family's cultural heritages and the life experiences of its members. These factors have shaped their views on family relations, expectations of kin support, and how to interact with public agencies and bureaucratic institutions (Hareven 1982). This history can facilitate or impede a relative's attempt to fulfill caregiving responsibilities (Horowitz and Shindelman 1983). Also it can influence the older person's receptivity of the care. Although family history can never be rewritten, attitudes and perspectives may be modfied so that problems can be approached more effectively (Silverstone and Hyman 1982).

2. Family Perceptions   Each member of a family system is perceived differently by every other family member. Factors contributing to this include age and developmental stage of members during interactions, roles played, selective memories, residential proximity, and current situations. These different perceptions can have a major impact on an intergenerational family's assessment of and care plan for one of its older members. For example, Remnet (1987) reported from her study that when aging parents reentered their adult children's lives after several years of separation there were many incongruencies in their expectations of each other because these expectations had been based on "how each had been in the past" rather than how "each was in the present." It is important that the family system be aware of and give recognition to the dynamic nature of its members' health, lifestyle, needs, and expectations.

Intergenerational differences in perception can be related to Bengtson and Kuypers' (1971) term "generational stakes," which they used to describe how each generation has a different developmental stake in the other. Parents are prone to minimize the differences between themselves and their children while their children maximize these differences. Bengtson and Treas (1980) found that, while the elderly reported higher levels of affection, they minimized the amount of assistance or exchange of services with their adult children. This is congruent with their greater "stake" in the relationship, in which the dimension of affect or sentiment is more important than the instrumental dimension of assistance or help. However, this may lead to a reluctance to request assistance from adult children, because such demands put the older member at a disadvantage in terms of exchange.

3. Types of Aid

The type of mutual aid that flows between older adults and their middle-aged children varies with sex, marital status, social class, and health of each generation. Aid from the older generation frequently includes babysitting, light housework, advice on jobs and life's problems, moral support, and financial aid and gifts. Aid from the middle generation includes transportation, shopping, heavy housework, home repairs, advice, moral support, gifts, and bureaucratic mediation.

As a general rule, it would seem that parents continue to give to their adult children as long as they are able (Atchley and Miller 1980; Cicirelli 1981). Also they try to maintain their own households as long as possible, retaining their autonomy and enabling the younger family to develop and pursue its own aspirations (Tibbitts 1979).

Brody (1979) stated that old people do not want money or concrete services as much as concern, affection, caring, and being able to continue to contribute to as well as receive from their family. A study by Hildreth, Van Lannen, Kelley, and Durant (1980) supported that perspective. They concluded that the non-task activities such as getting together for a family meal, telling stories to the grandchildren and other family *quality* interactions in which the elderly could get involved were more enjoyed by them than task-oriented activities such as cleaning and shopping.

4. Reciprocity betweeen Generations

Based on her study, Wentowski (1981) reported that reciprocity had great personal significance for preserving the self-esteem of older people. Participation in balanced exchanges of a long period of time was considered a major means of guaranteeing security in old age through building up "credit" to draw on later. This "deferred exchange" was seen to strengthen kinship bonds.

However, when parents do attain advanced age with its frailties, the balance of mutual support shifts, and adult children provide greater amounts of aid (Atchley and Miller 1980; Cicirelli 1981). This shift creates new challenges for the adult child/aging parent relationship because one of the consequences of caregiving for aging relatives is that there is no predictable end. The caregiver faces sustained or increasing dependency on the part of the elderly family member (Archbold 1982).

5. Changes in the Health of Family Members

Health is one of the most important variables affecting the family life of older people. Consequently, it becomes the catalyst in relation to a number of aspects of family life: kin interactions, residential patterns, economic support, and on occasion, legal implications (Streib and Beck 1980). A study conducted by Stoller and Earl (1983) supported these allocations. They found that the family-helping networks increased in both size and scope as the functional capacity of the elderly member declined. However, this was at a cost to the physical, psychological, and financial resources of the caregivers, particularly the adult daughters, who were facing increasing employment and family responsibilities.

Based on their interviews with professionals who worked with neglect and abuse of the elderly, Hickey and Douglass (1981) suggested from their findings that the sudden or unwanted dependency of a parent was a key factor in understanding neglect or abuse of older family members. When such mistreatment exists, it may either reflect a real unwillingness to accept dependency or the family's incapability of being caretaker for highly dependent older family members or a combination of both.

It is evident that the older generations' health, both perceived and actual, and the family's attitudes and response to it can have a ripple effect through the multigenerational family. This, in turn, can change its pattern of types of aid.

Transition to Pointers

Given the multiple factors influencing the intergenerational families' patterns of aid to its elderly members and the importance of health care and service providers developing plans to support these patterns, let us now discuss pointers that can help you to examine family interaction patterns.

Assessment Pointers

1. Assess family members' proximity and frequency of contact, while remembering that such figures only measure quantitative, not qualitative interactions. With the elderly person's permission, ask family members who are not currently involved in caregiving if and how they would like to be.
2. Assess the family's "boundaries" before attempting to problem-solve with the members. If it is a family with tight boundaries, the identified "leader" or "mobilizer" of the system would need to be included in any problem-solving discussions.
3. Identify "family rules" regarding interactions among members. If rules keep people in roles when not appropriate or deter important problem solving communication, the family may need help to negotiate changes (Herr and Weakland 1979).
4. Assess how the elderly family member's problems have affected the family systems' established interaction patterns such as communication, activities, roles, and exchange of services.

5. Assess the family system regarding responsibilities for caregiving:
   a. What functions each member is fulfilling.
   b. What they can realistically continue to do.
   c. What needs to be shared with other members.
6. Differentiate between a caregiver and a caretaker.
   a. Caregivers can be seen as the individuals who are responsible *to* the older person. In this capacity they can do their best to fulfill their responsibilities to their elderly family member while also recognizing their own needs which have to be met (care of own physical and mental health and family, demands of workplace, etc.) in order to have the inner and outer resources to continue to fulfill their caregiving role. The caregivers recognize and support older people having the ultimate control and responsibility for their own well being.
   b. In contrast, caretakers assume this control and become (or try to become) responsible *for* the older person. In this role, caretakers are more prone to neglect their own needs in their efforts to take care of the elderly relative. This heavy burden of responsibility makes them more prone to feel resentment and frustration if elderly relatives don't comply with their care plans.
7. Assess each member's perception of the situation and proposed solutions. However, don't assume just because one member of a family is seeking help that either that person or anyone else in the system really wants a solution. Old problems are predictable, whereas proposed solutions require changes in behavior or changes in perception of behavior.
8. Avoid being pulled into an alliance by some family members; this can make other members adversaries.
9. Give recognition and support to the caregivers. Archbold (1982) has suggested the following for caregiver's support: screening and treatment for caregiver's health, help in coping and managing problems encountered in caregiving, provision of comprehensive information and referral services, respite care, and psychosocial supports.

Summary

It is evident that families remain the most important support system for our nation's older people, especially in time of need (Shanas 1979). Each family system has its own unique response to these needs based on its structure and the interaction patterns of its members. Factors that motivate families to provide long-term care for their elderly members include the continuity of the generations, reciprocity, filial responsibility, and facing one's own old-age dependency needs (Kingson, Hirshorn, and Cornman 1986).

Caregiving within the family is common, accepted, and preferred. Most individuals within the family system will receive care from and give care to other members (Kingson, Hirshorn, and Cornman 1986). However, though the family remains the main social support system for its aging members, because of changes in the economy, affectional and supportive functions have supplanted economic aid as crucial family resources. These functions are facilitated by residential proximity and intergenerational mutual aid. Types of aid vary according to social class, perceptions of family boundaries, and caregiving modalities.

It is the adult children, usually women, who continue to carry out these responsibilities for their aging relatives. This can be based on feelings of obligation, feelings of attachment, or both. However, it will become increasingly difficult for women to continue this because they are being caught in the middle of competing and multiple demands of traditional roles and employment outside the home. Such societal value conflicts cause intergenerational stress. Stress becomes more evident when aging relatives expect more attention and support because of their changing social and physical states.

The intergenerational family has not been prepared to cope optimally with these growing issues resulting from increased longevity, fewer caregivers, and increasing numbers of women in the work force. Some model programs and resources have been developed to begin to respond to the growing needs of families endeavoring to care for their elderly members. However, much more needs to be done, not only in the development of programs and services but also in effectively reaching out to the intergenerational family.

The family system is in constant change. It is our challenge as supporters of that system to facilitate its change to promote its optimum functioning. I hope that participating in this activity has enhanced your ability as a facilitator of change by increasing your understanding of the family as "a system in process" and providing you with ways to examine family interaction patterns.

Evaluation

Please take a few minutes now to complete the evaluation.

Family Interactions, Worksheet

1. **Proximity:** Distance from parents (approximate hours in travel time):_____
2. **Frequency of contact:** ☐daily ☐twice/week ☐weekly ☐monthly ☐other_____
3. **Boundaries:** ☐closed ☐semipermeable ☐open
4. **Rules**

    Communication patterns:_____

    Ways to express affection:_____

    Role flexibility:_____

    Attendance at family rituals:_____

    Approaches to family problems:_____

    Acceptance of help from outsiders:_____

    Overall, are these rules flexible: ☐no ☐somewhat ☐yes

5. **Family Roles**

    The leader_____

    The decision maker(s)_____

    —social activities_____

    —medical_____

    —finances_____

    —vacations_____

    The mobilizer(s)_____

    The joker_____

    The provoker of conflict (hell raiser, pot stirrer)_____

    The peacemaker_____

    The kin keeper_____

6. **Mutual Aid**

    Who do I go to for help?

    Who comes to me?

Family Interactions, Evaluation

1. Did this activity increase your understanding of the family as a "system in process"?

Not much		Some		A lot
1	2	3	4	5

2. Identify three ways to examine a family's interaction patterns.

   _____

   _____

   _____

5. Give at least one example of how this activity will affect your interactions with intergenerational families.

15 An Unexpected Role

Rationale for Activity

Health is one of the most important variables affecting the family life of older people. If an older family member's health deteriorates physically or mentally, it may precipitate new kinds of intergenerational family involvement (Streib and Beck 1980).

The commitment of families to become involved as caregivers to their older members has been well documented (Brody 1985; Cicirelli 1981; Hagestad 1981; Horowitz and Shindelman 1983; Troll and Stapley 1985). However, their effectiveness in fulfilling this commitment will be influenced by their availability to fulfill this caregiving role. Johnson (1983) has stated, in keeping with societal and family expectations, adult children establish their independence well before the time when parents need their help. Their lives are increasingly full and time is always at a premium. When an unexpected caregiving role is thrust upon these intergenerational family members, strain and stress are likely to result.

It is important for those who work with intergenerational families to understand the effect an additional role can have on an individual member and on the family system. This activity provides participants with an opportunity to gain increased understanding of the impact of an unexpected caregiving role being thrust on a family member.

Participants: This activity is appropriate for graduate and undergraduate students and professionals and paraprofessionals in mental health, social work, health care, and gerontology.

Objectives

Upon completion of this activity participants will:

1. Have more understanding of the effect of being thrust into an unexpected caregiving role.
2. Be able to identify three ways to enhance an intergenerational family's ability to adapt to an unexpected caregiving role.
3. Be able to give at least one example of how this activity will affect their interactions with intergenerational families.

Class Size: Open

Time: Forty minutes.

> Twenty minutes: introduction and activity
> Fifteen minutes: debriefing
> Five minutes: evaluation

Materials: Adaptation to an Unexpected Role Worksheets #1 and #2, Evaluation Sheets.

Teaching Notes

1. If you wish to expand the content of this activity in relation to the intergenerational family system's response to an elderly member's needs, the Family Interactions Activity (chapter 13) is a good resource.
2. I have found this to be a very good activity to bring into focus the multiple feelings involved in making "trade-off" decisions about role changes necessary to care for an elderly relative. As the participants discuss how they feel, they are reminded that feelings that result from situations beyond our control are usually mixed.
3. Depending on the group, I sometimes comment on their nonverbal behaviors as they listen to and think about the unexpected situation to which they have to respond. Their initial behaviors may include restlessness, anxiety over their mind's "going blank," looking at the worksheets of people on either side of them to see how they are adapting to the change, scratching their heads, rubbing their eyes, or taking a drink of water. Then they begin to "settle in," assess their situation and begin to develop an adaptation plan. Their behavior can be used as a mild example of Hans Selye's "flight-fight" stress response. Faced with an unexpected challenge, some people's first thoughts are of flight—they don't want to deal with "one more thing" in their lives. Then they begin to assess the situation and adapt to it. A person's great capacity for adaptation

is what makes life possible on all levels of complexity. It is the basis of homeostasis and of resistance to stress (Selye 1974).

Introduction to Activity

1. Aging brings change. What may be insufficiently recognized is that changes associated with aging present challenges to the family as well as to the individual. Confronting these challenges, such as sudden dependency, is often difficult (Bengtson and Kuypers 1985). Adding to the difficulty is the full life of the family with each member's multiple and interrelated roles and responsibilities.
2. However, regardless of the difficulties, family members do respond to an unexpected caregiving role by trying to make the necessary adjustments in other roles of their lives. This usually involves constricting some roles, putting others on hold, and/or eliminating some. Though the extent of these adaptations varies with individual circumstances, all involve changes in routines and relationships. Coping with such changes involves people's feelings as well as their intellect.
3. To help you gain a greater understanding of the impact of being thrust into an unexpected caregiving role, I would like you to participate in the following activity.

Instructions to Participants: Current Roles

1. Place your Unexpected Role Worksheet #1 in front of you.
2. Close your eyes and take a few deep breaths.
3. Begin to think of all the different roles and responsibilities you handle in any given day or week. Such roles may include your involvement in: relationships (family members, friend, neighbor), work, clubs, organizations, church, home management, physical fitness, recreational activities, gardening, or shopping.
4. Now that you have your multiple roles in your mind's eye, open your eyes and focus on your worksheet. On the left side, under the words "I am," list all your current roles (allow two to three minutes).
5. Now look at the circle on your worksheet. It represents 100 percent of the time you have to fulfill your roles (excluding time to eat and sleep, which probably fluctuates depending on what time is left!)
6. Consider your circle like a pie and divide it into sections corresponding to the amount of time you spend in each of your roles in any average month. For example, one quarter of the circle would be designated as "work" if you spent 25 percent of your time in the workplace (allow two to three minutes).

208 • Understanding Older Adults

Transition to Debriefing: Current Roles

Now that you've taken a few minutes to recognize and appreciate yourselves for handling your multiple roles, let's see what general trends we have in this group.

Debriefing: Current Roles

1. How many of you have five roles you're fulfilling? Between six and ten? Between eleven and fifteen? More?

   As you can see, you're a very busy group. None of you is underloaded; rather, some of you could be considered overloaded.

2. Given your current level of roles and responsibilities:
   a. How many of you would like to eliminate some of your roles?
   b. How many of you would like to take on an extra role to fill in any spare time you may have?

   In many instances in our lives, we have the control over which roles we take on and which we eliminate. For example, as adults we have some control over advancing our education, selecting employment, joining organizations, participating in activities, and maintaining our health. We also make choices regarding selecting our spouse and other significant people in our lives. However, in spite of our best efforts to control continuity and change in our lives, at various times we will be confronted with unexpected changes that "always comes at a bad time" because, as we've just shared, our lives are already full.
3. Nevertheless, prepared or not, a challenge can confront you at any time. Here is such a challenge now!

Background for Role Adaptation

When you arrive home today, you receive a phone call from your dearest, oldest relative (or friend if you don't have a relative). She's calling from a nearby hospital where she has been since she fractured her hip and arm in a bad fall. Her discharge plans have fallen through, and she is asking if she can come and live with you for five weeks until she can make a more permanent arrangement for herself.

You can't turn her down. She was always there for you and now she needs you! She feels very bad about having to ask you because she knows how busy you are. However, she feels you are the best one to help her.

She'll be arriving by ambulance tomorrow afternoon. How do you feel about this news?

Responses may include: *I feel overwhelmed. I feel unprepared. How am I going to cope? I feel like running away. I feel bad for both of us. Why now? Angry, not at her, "but at the situation we're both in." Very stressed!*

Thank you for sharing. These immediate feelings are normal. Given such a challenge most people are immobilized, usually only briefly, but it depends on individuals' reaction patterns, coping skills, and support systems.

Instructions to Participants: Adaptation to New Role

1. I'm assuming that you are quick mobilizers, so let's see what adaptations you're going to make.
2. First, review the roles in your "current pie."
   a. How big a slice will this new role of caregiver take?
   b. How can you arrange your other roles and responsibilities?
   c. Which roles will have to be constricted?
   d. Which roles will have to be put on hold?
   e. Will you have to eliminate any of your roles?
3. Now make these necessary adjustments in your second pie (allow two to three minutes).
4. Now, please respond to the questions on Worksheet #2 (allow three to five minutes).

Debriefing: Adaptation to New Role

1. How many of you could make the changes easily? Would some of you share why?
2. How many of you found it difficult? Would some you you share why?

   Responses may include: *I'd use it as an excuse to quit work. I am glad to help. I couldn't do it without help but I don't like asking for it. I'm upset about having to drop my classes. I feel frustrated that I can't do it all. I love my mom, yet feel resentful at having to make changes. It would jeopardize my job; I'm working overtime now.*

   Thank you for sharing. These varied and ambivalent feelings usually accompany any adaptations that have to be made in response to unexpected changes.

4. How many of you will use your informal support systems? Which ones?

   Responses may include: *Specific family members, friends, colleagues, neighbors.*

5. How many of you will use community resources?

> Responses may include: *Home Health Care Agencies, Home Health Care Equipment Rental, Homemakers Service, Meals on Wheels.*

Though the situation I gave you was the same for all of you, each of you made individualized changes in your "current roles" pie and used different resources depending on your own set of circumstances. Research studies concur that the same circumstances faced by different people will have effects that vary depending on their individual coping responses and their use of psychosocial resources (Pearlin 1982).

The important thing is to get the supports you perceive you need to provide the best care you can for your elderly family member, and also allow you to keep a healthy balance in your life. Keep in mind the metaphor, "If your cup is empty, it's impossible to give someone else a drink!"

Transition to Pointers

Let's move on to points to consider when helping people adapt to unexpected health changes in the lives of their elderly family members.

Points on Adaptive Strategies

1. People's Initial Response to Unexpected Roles

Pearlin (1982) has said most people do not remain passive in the face of forces that affect them. They actively react by:

a. Seeking to alter the situation.
b. Attempting perceptually and cognitively to reshape the meaning of the change in a way that reduces its threat.
c. Using their inner strengths and employing social support networks to enable them to live with the change without being overwhelmed by it.

2. Timing of Supportive Interventions

Golan (1981) has presented a framework to examine transitions and to promote problem-solving and success in passing through transitions. This framework focuses on two areas: material-arrangement (instrumental) tasks and psychosocial (affective) tasks. She says that shifts in roles, status, or habitual behavior upsets a person's equilibrium and motivates the person to find new ways to cope. Pearlin (1982) concurs that individuals facing new conditions for which they have neither prior experience nor opportunities to develop coping skills are most disposed to seek access to community resources such as educational and support services. Thus, when a family system is faced with adapting to an unexpected role, the timing to introduce supportive interventions would seem to be optimum.

3. Supportive Interventions

A priority would be to deal with the immediate adaptations needed to cope with the current unexpected change in the health of an elderly relative. These adaptations include enhancing communication and problem-solving skills and increasing use of appropriate community resources.

a. Communication Skills

Effective communication promotes clarity of expectations and appropriate responses to meet needs (Quinn and Keller 1983). Effective communication among all involved family members promotes clarification of each members' expectations and increases the probability of each members' needs being met in the most appropriate way. This can help offset problems Johnson (1983) reported from her study. She found that adult children were willing to do what they could to help their aging parents but were more likely to report conflict and ambivalence in assuming duties that were not clearly defined. This had a negative effect on the quality of their support.

In relation to enhancing communication and problem-solving skills, specific areas to focus on include:

i. Finding out *each* family member's *perception* of the unplanned situation and their role in it;
ii. Discussing any discrepancies to arrive at a consensus on how to deal with the situation;
iii. Examining as many alternatives and choices as possible, letting each person involved have appropriate decision-making power;
iv. Setting as goals what is realistically possible given the elderly person's physical and mental status, the family system's capacity to provide support, and available financial and community resources.

b. Problem-Solving Skills

A prevalent problem in today's fast-paced society is the shortage of time. Many families do not seem to have enough time to perform their multiple and interrelated roles. When the unexpected role of caregiver arises, with its associated time commitments, it has a ripple effect throughout the family system. Based on their study on the opinions and preferences of three generations of women, Brody, Johnsen, and Fulcomer (1984) reported that adjustment of family schedules and help with the costs of professional health care were seen as appropriate for adult children, but adjustment of work schedules and sharing of households was not.

Remnet (1985) reported from her study that an aging relative's sudden change from perceived health to illness had a major impact on the relationship with the adult children. These adult children made the necessary adjustments in their home and work routines and other responsibilities to be available to their relative. However, they perceived these transitions to be temporary and time-limited, and therefore manageable. In prolonged situations, as Johnson and Bursk (1977) noted in their study, the parent's increasing dependency caused some resentment on the part of the adult child and frustration on the part of the parent.

It is important to solve the time issue by involving as many family members as possible in the discussion and planning for:

i. Changes in time allocation for any roles that involve family members.
ii. Anticipated time that will be spent in various caregiving activities.
iii. Time changes in established family routines and activities.
iv. Anticipated length of time in the caregiving role, even if it is anticipated to be open-ended.
v. Ways to maintain a regular schedule for frequent reassessments of these various time allocations so that appropriate changes can be made.

c. Community Resources

In relation to increasing the caregivers' knowledge of relevant community resources, it is helpful to discuss which approach they plan to use in meeting their elderly relatives' needs:

i. A care provider identifies which services are needed and then provides them herself.
ii. A care manager identifies the needed services and then manages their provision by others (Archbold 1983).
iii. A caregiver identifies needed services and then does some direct provision of care and manages other needed services.

This information will influence the types of supports needed by the family members. For example, the care provider may need respite care support whereas the care manager may need home health care resources.

4. Preparation for Future Changes

Once the immediate situation is under control, the members of the family need to be encouraged to continue their educational efforts to prepare themselves for other inevitable changes as they and other family members age. Education for the later stages of relationships with aging kin is essential to successfully negotiate late-life transitions of family members and one's own old age (Weishaus 1979). McMahon and Ames' (1983) study on educational programming for midlife adults with parent-caring responsibilities found that information related to the aging process was of greatest concern. Other priority topics included dealing with chronic illness, coping with stress, community resources, physical care of the elderly, emotional needs of self/elderly, and intergenerational relationships.

In her review of the literature on middle age and its implications for educational intervention, Merriam (1978) agreed with the importance of such supportive programming. Remnet (1987) concurs. The middle-aged adults in her study identified three areas where they wanted to enhance their proficiencies. One area was to develop skills in anticipatory planning. In various ways they indicated that, although they recognized the value of this planning, they found it difficult to approach their relatives directly to discuss age-related issues. Secondly, they identified two areas of knowledge that could assist them in their understanding of and responding appropriately to their relatives. They wanted to gain information on normal and abnormal aging and become aware of community resources available to their aging relatives.

The need for educational programs has been identified. It is the challenge of those of us in the health care and service professions to find creative ways to provide such supportive interventions.

Summary

Family stress and strain can be minimized and the Kuyper's and Bengtson's (1983) family support cycle can be developed by using "teachable moments" (Havighurst 1952) to enhance the aging family's communication and problem-solving skills, use of appropriate resources, and knowledge of the aging process. This will promote the optimum functioning of the aging relative in the community and thus avoid inappropriate dependency, the development of the social breakdown syndrome (Bengtson 1973), and increased potential for premature institutionalization. In addition to improving the quality of life for the intergenerational family, there can also be an economic benefit to society because the family will be able to use health care and other community support services in more efficient and effective ways.

I hope that by participating in this activity you have increased your understanding of the effect of being thrust into an unexpected caregiving role and your knowledge of ways to enhance an intergenerational family's ability to adapt to an unexpected caregiving role.

Evaluation

Please take a few moments now to complete the evaluation.

214 • *Understanding Older Adults*

An Unexpected Role, Worksheet #1

Current Roles

I am:

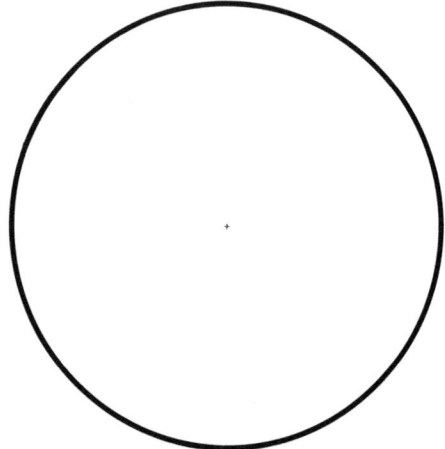

Adapted Roles

I will reduce the time I spend in:

I will put on hold:

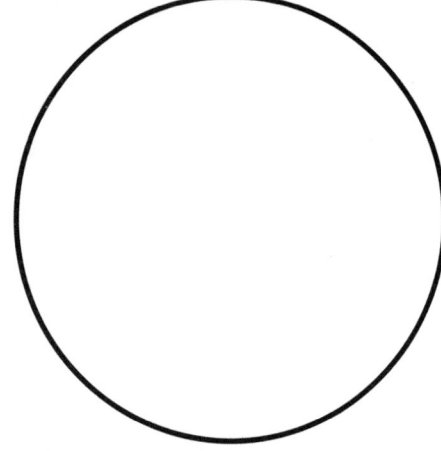

I will eliminate:

An Unexpected Role, Worksheet #2

1. In relation to adapting to this unexpected role, was it easy or difficult and why?

2. Will you use your informal support systems to help you (family, friends, neighbors, church members)?

3. Will you use community resources? Which ones?

An Unexpected Role, Evaluation

1. Did this activity increase your understanding of the effect of being thrust into an unexpected caregiving role?

Not much		Some		A lot
1	2	3	4	5

2. Identify three ways to enhance an intergenerational family's ability to adapt to an unexpected caregiving role.

   _____

   _____

   _____

3. Give at least one example of how this activity will affect your interactions with intergenerational families.

Appendix: Answer Key for Activities

Answer Key numbers correspond to the fill-in questions on each chapter's Evaluation Sheet

Chapter 2: *Anticipating Your Future Self*
1. General facts about elderly people.
    a. Physical: Visual and hearing changes occur in the later years; multiple chronic conditions are common among elderly; most elderly people function independently in the community.
    b. Environmental: Older people do not relocate as often as younger people; most older people own their own home.
    c. Socialization: There are more widows than widowers; most older people live close to their adult children and maintain intergenerational ties; a confidant is a significant source of psychosocial support; pets are important sources of companionship.
    d. Activities: Many older people work part-time but the positions are usually low-paying; church membership is the most common community activity; life-long learners continue to pursue educational activities; older adults' patterns of activities remain rather constant over the life cycle; available transportation is a key factor in maintaining an elderly person's independence.

Chapter 3: *Needs and Services: Optimum Fit*
1. Major categories of services that may be used to assist older adults: basic services; supportive services; adjustment and integrative services/ programs; congregate care services; protective services.

Chapter 4: *First Impressions*
None.

Chapter 5: *Pacing and Patience*
2. Ways to help an older person learn a new task: Preferably prepare people in advance for the task; give instructions that are clear and concise in an appropriate vocabulary; if possible, allow self-pacing; give time to get focused on the task; let the person examine any equipment; demonstrate the task to be completed; let the individual practice; review and discuss

printed instructions; at each step ask for feedback; give positive recognition for successful efforts.

Chapter 6: *Developing Trust*

1. Ways to earn an elderly person's trust by using a PEN TIP: *P*raise the elderly person's efforts to do things for self; tell the person what to *E*xpect; help the person when he or she *N*eeds you; use *T*ouch to express caring and concern and give support and security; *I*dentify the person by name, identify surroundings by describing them; *P*ractice pacing and patience. Also, communicate effectively and compensate appropriately for sensory impairments.

Chapter 7: *A Surprise Snack*

4. Ways to promote an enjoyable eating experience for older adults: Promote good oral hygiene; create a positive dining environment; prepare an appealing meal; compensate for sensory impairments; encourage socialization during mealtime.

Chapter 8: *Maintaining Mobility*

1. Changes in the musculoskeletal system: Decrease in skeletal bone mass or osteopenia; degenerative or osteoarthritic changes; thinning and flattening of vertebral discs; reduction in size of muscles; gait changes; proneness to flexion or bending of joints.
3. Strategies to promote maintenance of strength and mobility: Regular individualized exercise program; daily routines that provide frequent changes of body position and pacing of activities; well-balanced diet; maintenance of good posture and proper weight; use of good body mechanics; supportive shoes; safeguarded environment.

Chapter 9: *Skin Sensitivity*

4. Ways to promote good skin care: Be gentle when touching older people's skin; prevent sudden changes or extremes in temperatures; avoid overuse of soaps; use emollients frequently; protect skin from the sun; encourage good personal hygiene; promote frequent changes of body position; encourage an optimum dietary intake and a regular exercise program.

Chapter 10: *Home Assessment*

2. Things to assess for home safety: Scatter rugs, electrical cords, clutter, furniture, security measures, alarm system, water heater, heating system, lighting, phone, kitchen, bathroom.
3. Interventions to provide a more supportive environment: Nonskid scatter rugs; keep traffic pathways clear; sturdy furniture; smoke alarm; hot water heater at 120° F or less; adequate lighting; night lights; phone in handy location with emergency numbers posted; kitchen appliances in good condition; safety supports in bathroom.
4. Indicators of an elderly person's lifestyle: Pictures, albums, scrapbooks, children's handicrafts, greeting cards, newspapers, magazines, journals, church bulletins, awards and certificates, musical instruments, sports equipment, travel brochures, clocks, calendars, mirrors, pets, plants, flowers, windows with a view.

Chapter 11: *Relocation*

2. Ways to reduce stress associated with the relocation process: The elderly person needs to have a comprehensive medical and functional assessment and any problems addressed; the person should have an active involvement in the relocation process, including having choices regarding the relocation and opportunities to assess and become familiar with the proposed new environment; the staff needs to know the older person's background and circumstances of the move; personalization of space should be encouraged; the elderly person should be given as much recognition as possible and have adaptive capabilities praised; there should be respect for the person's privacy and personal space.

Chapter 12: *Recognition Day*

2. Ways to give individualized recognition to older adults: Use their preferred name every time you interact with them; notice and give positive comments on their appearance and personal possessions such as pictures or handicrafts; acknowledge adaptability and skills; use appropriate touch and other nonverbal behaviors such as a smile, nod, and wave.

Chapter 13: *Reminiscing*

1. Reasons why reminiscing is a significant activity for the elderly: Gets in touch with feelings; stimulates long-term memories needed for life review; provides a sense of continuity of life; promotes ego integrity, identity, and self esteem; encourages reactivation of coping skills; promotes intergenerational connection; encourages peer interactions; increases socialization.

Chapter 14: *Family Interactions*

2. Ways to examine family interaction patterns: Assess proximity and frequency of contact among members; assess family boundaries; identify family rules; assess impact of the elderly member's problem on the family system's interaction patterns; assess responsibilities and approaches to caregiving; solicit each family member's perception of the situation and proposed solutions.

Chapter 15: *An Unexpected Role*

2. Ways to enhance an intergenerational family's ability to adapt to an unexpected caregiving role: Increase the members' communication and problem-solving skills, their use of appropriate community resources, and their knowledge of the aging process.

References

Chapter 1

Atchley, R.C. 1987. *Aging: Continuity and Change*, 2d ed. Belmont, Calif.: Wadsworth Publishing Co.

Austin, D.R. 1985. "Attitudes Toward Old Age: A Hierarchical Study." *The Gerontologist* 25(4): 431–434.

Benson, E.R. 1982. "Attitudes Toward the Elderly: A Survey of Recent Nursing Literature." *Journal of Gerontological Nursing* 8(5) (May): 279–281.

Boren, N., J. Johnson, and G. Pawlson. 1982. "Community-Based Settings for Training in Geriatric Medicine." *Educational Gerontology* 8(6): 585–595.

Brock, A.M. 1977. "Improving Nursing Care for the Elderly: An Educational Task." *Journal of Gerontological Nursing* 3(1): 26–28.

Brower, H.T. 1981. "Social Organization and Nurses' Attitudes Toward Older Persons." *Journal of Gerontological Nursing* 7(5) (May): 293–298.

Brown, G.I. 1975. *The Live Classroom*. New York: The Viking Press.

———. 1971. *Human Teaching for Human Learning: An Introduction to Confluent Education*. New York: The Viking Press.

Butler, R.N., and M.I. Lewis. 1982. *Aging and Mental Health*, 3d ed. St. Louis: C.V. Mosby Co.

Darkenwald, G.G., and S.B. Merriam. 1982. *Adult Education: Foundations of Practice*. New York: Harper and Row.

Galbraith, M.W., and S.M. Suttie. 1987. "Attitudes of Nursing Students Toward the Elderly." *Educational Gerontology* 13(3): 213–223.

Glass, J.C., Jr., and E.S. Knott. 1982. "Effectiveness of a Workshop on Aging in Changing Middle-Aged Adults' Attitudes Toward the Aged." *Educational Gerontology* 8(4): 359–372.

Gordon, S.K., and D.S. Hallauer. 1976. "Impact of Friendly Visiting Program on Attitudes of College Students Toward the Aged." *The Gerontologist* 16(4): 371–376.

Hart, L.K., M.I. Freel, and C.M. Crowell. 1976. "Changing Attitudes Toward the Aged and Interest in Caring for the Aged." *Journal of Gerontological Nursing* 2(4): 10–16.

Heller, B.R., and F.J. Walsh. 1976. "Changing Nursing Student's Attitudes Toward the Aged and Interest in Caring for the Aged." *Journal of Nursing Education* 15(5): 9–17.

Holtzman, J.M., J.D. Beck, and P. Coggan. 1978. "Geriatrics Program for Medical Students II. Impact of Two Educational Experiences on Student Attitudes." *Journal of the American Geriatrics Society* 26(8): 355–359.

Holtzman, J.M., J.D. Beck, and R.L. Ettinger. 1981. "Cognitive Knowledge and Attitudes Toward the Aged of Dental and Medical Students." *Educational Gerontology* 6(2-3): 195-207.

Klausmeier, H.J., and W. Goodwin. 1975. "Learning and Human Abilities." *Educational Psychology*, 4th ed. New York: Harper and Row.

Knowles, M. 1978. *The Adult Learner: A Neglected Species*, 2d ed. Houston: Gulf.

Muldary, T.W. 1983. *Interpersonal Relations for Health Care Professionals*. New York: Macmillan.

Murphy-Russell, S., A.H. Die, and J.L. Walker, Jr. 1986. "Changing Attitudes Toward the Elderly: The Impact of Three Methods of Attitude Change." *Educational Gerontology* 12(3) (December): 241-251.

Pullias, E.V., and J.D. Young. 1977. *A Teacher is Many Things*. Bloomington, Ind.: University Press.

Seltzer, M. 1977. "Differential Impact of Various Experiences in Breaking Down Age Stereotypes." *Educational Gerontology* 2(2): 183-189.

Steinaker, N.W., and M.R. Bell. 1979. *The Experiential Taxonomy: A New Approach to Teaching and Learning*. New York: Academic Press.

Tobiason, S.J., F. Knudsen, J.C. Stengel, and M. Giss. 1979. "Positive Attitudes Toward Aging: The Aged Teach the Young." *Journal of Gerontological Nursing* 5(3) (May/June): 18-23.

Towle, C. 1954. *The Learner in Education for the Professions*. Chicago: University of Chicago Press.

Tyler, R.W. 1949. *Basic Principles of Curriculum and Instruction*. Chicago: The University of Chicago Press.

White, R.W. 1981. "Humanitarian Concern." In *The Modern American College*, edited by A.W. Chickering and Associates. San Francisco: Jossey-Bass.

Wilson, J.F., and F.W. Hafferty. 1983. "Long-Term Effects of a Seminar on Aging and Health for First-Year Medical Students." *The Gerontologist* 23(3): 319-324.

Chapter 2

Atchley, R.C. 1987. *Aging: Continuity and Change*, 3d ed. Belmont, Calif.: Wadsworth.

———. 1980. *The Social Forces in Later Life*, 3d ed. Belmont, Calif.: Wadsworth.

Butler, R.N., and M.I. Lewis. 1982. *Aging and Mental Health*, 3d ed. St. Louis: C.V. Mosby Co.

Ebersole, P., and P. Hess. 1985. *Toward Healthy Aging*. St. Louis: C.V. Mosby Co.

Ham, R.J., L.G. Kerzner, and M.R. Smith. 1983. "Altered Presentations of Disease in the Elderly." In *Primary Care Geriatrics*, edited by R.J. Ham. Boston: John Wright, P.S.G. Inc.

Ham, R.J. and M.L. Marcy. 1983. "Normal Aging: A Review of Systems/The Maintenance of Health." In *Primary Care Geriatrics*, edited by R.J. Ham. Boston: John Wright, P.S.G. Inc.

Harris, C.S. 1978. *Fact Book on Aging*. Washington, D.C.: The National Council on the Aging, Inc.

Kimmel, D.C. 1980. *Adulthood and Aging*, 2d ed. New York: John Wiley and Sons.

Monea, H.E. 1976. *Instructor's Manual to Accompany Nursing and the Aged*. New York: McGraw-Hill.

Peterson, D.A. 1983. *Facilitating Education for Older Learners*. San Francisco: Jossey-Bass.

Robinson, J. 1986. "Retirement." In *The Process of Human Development*, 2d ed., edited by C.S. Schuster and S.S. Ashburn. Boston: Little, Brown.

Williams, T.F. 1983. "Diabetes Mellitus in Older People." In *Clinical Aspects of Aging*, 2d ed., edited by W. Reichel. Baltimore: Williams and Wilkins.

Chapter 3

Austin, C. 1983. "Case Management in Long-Term Care: Options and Opportunities," *Health and Social Work* 8(1) (Winter): 16–30.

Brill, N.I. 1985. *Working with People*, 3d ed. New York: Longman, Inc.

Erikson, E.H. 1963. *Childhood and Society*, 2d ed. New York: W.W. Norton.

Grau, L. 1984. "Case Management and the Nurse," *Geriatric Nursing* 5(8) (November/December): 372–375.

Kane, R.A., and R.L. Kane. 1981. *Assessing the Elderly*. Lexington, Mass.: Lexington Books.

Nelson, J.C. 1975. "Dealing with Resistance in Social Work Practice," *Social Casework* 56(10) (December): 587–592.

Perlman, H.H. 1957. *Social Casework*. Chicago: University of Chicago Press.

Steinberg, R.M., and G.W. Carter. 1982. *Case Management and the Elderly: A Handbook for Planning and Administering Programs*. Lexington, Mass.: Lexington Books.

Williams, T.F. 1983. "Assessment of the Geriatric Patient in Relation to Needs for Services and Facilities." In *Clinical Aspects of Aging*, 2d ed., edited by W. Reichel. Baltimore: Williams and Wilkins.

Chapter 4

Asburn, S.S., and C.S. Schuster. 1986. "Cognitive Development During Infancy." In *The Process of Human Development*, 2d ed., edited by C.S. Schuster and S.S. Ashburn. Boston: Little, Brown.

Brill, N.I. 1985. *Working with People*, 3d ed. New York: Longman, Inc.

Kane, R.A., and R.L. Kane. 1981. *Assessing the Elderly*. Lexington, Mass.: Lexington Books.

Chapter 5

Bengtson, V.L. 1973. *The Social Psychology of Aging*. Indianapolis: Bobbs-Merrill.

Eisdorfer, C. 1977. "Intelligence and Cognition in the Aged." In *Behavior and Adaptation in Late Life*, 2d ed., edited by E. Busse and E. Pfeiffer. Boston: Little, Brown.

Greenberg, B. 1973. "Reaction Time in the Elderly." *American Journal of Nursing* 23(12) (December): 2056–2058.

MacRae, P.B. 1986. "The Effects of Physical Activity on the Physiological and Psychological Health of the Older Adult." In *Education and Aging*, edited

by D.A. Peterson, J.E. Thorton, and J.E. Birren. Englewood Cliffs, N.J.: Prentice-Hall.
Moody, H.R. 1986. "Late Life Learning in the Information Society." In *Education and Aging*, edited by D.A. Peterson, J.E. Thorton, and J.E. Birren. Englewood Cliffs, N.E.: Prentice-Hall.
Peterson, D.A. 1983. *Facilitating Education for Older Learners*. San Francisco: Jossey-Bass.
Schaie, K.W. 1980. "Intelligence and Problem Sovling." In *Handbook of Mental Health and Aging*, edited by J.E. Birren and R.B. Sloane. Englewood Cliffs, N.J.: Prentice-Hall.
Welford, A.T. 1977. "Motor Performance." In *Handbook of the Psychology of of Aging*, edited by J.E. Birren and K.W. Schaie. New York: Van Nostrand Reinhold.

Chapter 6

Butler, R.N., and M.I. Lewis. 1982. *Aging and Mental Health*, 3d ed. St. Louis: C.V. Mosby.
Ernst, M., and H. Shore. 1976. *Sensitizing People to the Processes of Aging: The In-Service Educator's Guide*, 2d printing. Denton, Texas.: Center for Studies in Aging, North Texas State University.
Greenberg, B. 1973. "Reaction Time in the Elderly." *American Journal of Nursing* 23(12) (December): 2056–2058.
Lieberman, M.A., and S.S. Tobin. 1983. *The Experience of Old Age*. New York: Basic Books.

Chapter 7

Alfin-Slater, R.B., and R. Friedman. 1978. "Nutrition and Aging: Are We What We've Eaten?" In *Aging in the 21st Century*, edited by C.F. Jarvik. New York: Gardner Press.
Beattie, B.L., and V.Y. Louie. 1983. "Nutrition and Health in the Elderly." In *Clinical Aspects of Aging*, 2d ed., edited by W. Reichel. Baltimore, Williams and Wilkins.
Brill, N.I. 1985. *Working with People*, 3d ed. New York: Logman, Inc.
Dassenko, S. 1981. "Nutrition and the Elderly." *Long Term Care* 1(2) (August): 1, 8.
Ernst, M., and H. Shore. 1976. *Sensitizing People to the Processes of Aging: The In-Service Educator's Guide*, 2d printing. Denton, Texas, Center for Studies in Aging, North Texas State University.
Ham, R.J., and M.L. Marcy. 1983. "Normal Aging: A Review of Systems/The Maintenance of Health." In *Primary Care Geriatrics*, edited by R.J. Ham. Boston: John Wright, P.S.G. Inc.
Kalish, R.A. 1982. *Late Adulthood: Perspectives on Human Development*, 2d ed. Monterey, Calif.: Brooks/Cole Publishing Co.
Weg, R.B. 1980. "Prolonged Mild Nutritional Deficiencies: Significance for Health Maintenance." *Journal of Nutrition for the Elderly*, Spring 1(1): 3–22.
Yen, P.K. 1981. "Eating Habits—Chance or Choice?" *Geriatric Nursing*, July/August: 278–299.

Chapter 8

Benison, B., and M.O. Hogstel. 1986. "Aging and Movement Therapy." *Journal of Gerontological Nursing* 12(12) (December): 8–16.

Ebersole, P., and P. Hess. 1985. *Toward Healthy Aging*. St. Louis: C.V. Mosby.

Grob, D. 1983a. "Prevalent Joint Diseases in Older Persons." In *Clinical Aspects of Aging*, 2d ed., edited by W. Reichel. Baltimore: Williams and Wilkins.

———. 1983b. "Common Disorders of Muscles in the Aged." In *Clinical Aspects of Aging*, 2d ed., edited by W. Reichel. Baltimore: Williams and Wilkins.

Ham, R.J., and M.L. Marcy. 1983. "Evaluation of the Elderly Patient." In *Primary Care Geriatrics*. Boston: John Wright & P.S.G. Inc.

Harris, R. 1983. "Exercise and Physical Fitness for the Elderly." In *Clinical Aspects of Aging*, edited by W. Reichel. Baltimore: Williams and Wilkins.

Milde, F.K. 1988. "Impaired Physical Mobility." *Journal of Gerontological Nursing* 14(3) (March): 20–24.

Saxon, S.V. and M.J. Etten. 1978. *Physical Change and Aging*. New York: The Tiresias Press.

Sullivan, M. 1987. "Atrophy & Exercise." *Journal of Gerontological Nursing* 13(7) (July): 26–31.

Wiswell, R.A. 1980. "Relaxation, Exercise, and Aging." In *Handbook of Mental Health and Aging*, edited by J.E. Birren and R.B. Sloan. Englewood Cliffs, N.J.: Prentice-Hall.

Chapter 9

Ham, R.J., and M.L. Marcy. 1983. "Normal Aging: A Review of Systems/the Maintenance of Health." In *Primary Care Geriatrics*, edited by R.J. Ham. Boston: John Wright, PSG Inc.

Iverson-Carpenter, M.S. 1988. "Impaired Skin Integrity." *Journal of Gerontological Nursing* 14(3) (March): 25–29.

Tindall, J.P. 1983. "Geriatric Dermatology." In *Clinical Aspects of Aging*, 2d ed., edited by W. Reichel. Baltimore: Williams and Wilkins.

Chapter 10

American Red Cross. 1984. *Safety and Survival in an Earthquake*, 2d ed. Los Angeles: American Red Cross.

Andrus Volunteers. 1985. *Who Cares? Helpful Hints for Those who Care for a Dependent Older Person at Home*. Los Angeles: Andrus Gerontology Center, University of Southern California.

Antunes, G.E., F.L. Cook, T.D. Cook, and W.G. Skogan. 1977. "Patterns of Personal Crime Against the Elderly: Findings From a National Survey." *The Gerontologist* 17: 321–327.

Atchley, R.C. 1987. *Aging: Continuity and Change*, 2d ed. Belmont, Calif.: Wadsworth Publishing Co.

Brickel, C.M. 1980–1981. "A Review of the Role of Pet Animals in Psychotherapy and with the Elderly. *International Journal of Aging and Human Development* 12: 119–128.

Butler, R.N., and M.I. Lewis. 1982. *Aging and Mental Health*, 3d. ed. St. Louis: C.V. Mosby.

Clark, M.C., and M.S. Gaide. 1986. "Choosing the Right Device." *Generations* 11: 18–21.

Craven, R., and P. Bruno. 1986. "Teach the Elderly to Prevent Falls." *Journal of Gerontological Nursing* 12: 27–33.

Ebersole, P., and P. Hess. 1985. *Toward Healthy Aging*, 2d ed. St. Louis: C.V. Mosby.

Gray-Vickrey, M. 1984. "Education to Prevent Falls." *Geriatric Nursing* May/June: 179–183.

Greenstein, D. 1985. "Home Repair Programs." *Generations* 9: 52–54.

Ham, R.J., and M.L. Marcy. 1983. "Normal Aging: A Review of Systems/The Maintenance of Health." In *Primary Care Geriatrics*, edited by R.J. Ham. Boston: John Wright, P.S.G. Inc.

Harris, C.S. 1978. *Fact Book on Aging*. Washington, D.C.: The National Council on the Aging, Inc.

Hartford, M.E. 1985. *Making the Best of the Rest of Your Life*, Leader's Guide. Pacific Palisades, Calif.: Personal Strengths Publishing Inc.

Hayter, J. 1980. "Hypothermia, Hyperthermia in Older Persons." *Journal of Gerontological Nursing* 6: 65–68.

Heymann, A.D. 1979. "The Effect of Incidental Hypotermia on Elderly Surgical Patients." *Journal of Gerontology* 32: 46–48.

Howell, S. 1985. "Home: A Source of Meaning in Elders' Lives." *Generations* 9: 58–60.

Kolanowski, A.M., and L.M. Gunter. 1983. "Thermal Stress and the Aged." *Journal of Gerontological Nursing* 1: 13–15.

La Buda, D.R., ed. 1985. *The Gadget Book: Ingenious Devices for Easier Living*. Glenview, Ill.: Scott, Foresman and Company.

Lafferty, L. 1986. *Preparedness Guide for Earthquakes and Other Disasters*. La Canada, Calif.: Lafferty and Associates, Inc.

Newman, S.J. 1985. "Housing and Long-Term Care: The Suitability of the Elderly's Housing to the Provision of In-home Services." *The Gerontologist* 25: 35–40.

O'Bryant, S.I. 1982. "The Value of Home to Older Persons." *Research on Aging* 4: 349–363.

Price, J.H. 1978. "Unintentional Injury Among the Aged." *Journal of Gerontological Nursing* 4: 36–41.

Regnier, V. 1975. "Neighborhood Planning for the Urban Elderly." In *Aging: Scientific Perspectives and Social Issues*, edited by D. Woodruff and J. Birren. New York: D. Van Nostrand.

———. 1983. "Housing and Environment." In *Aging: Scientific Perspectives and Social Issues*, 2d ed., edited by D. Woodruff and J. Birren. New York: D. Van Nostrand.

Remnet, V. 1981. "The Home Assessment." In *Nursing and the Aged*, 2d ed., edited by I.M. Burnside. New York: McGraw-Hill.

Rodstein, M. 1983. "Accidents Among the Aged." In *Clinical Aspects of Aging*, 2d ed., edited by W. Reichel. Baltimore: Williams and Wilkins.

Rowles, G.D. 1981. "The Surveillance Zone as Meaningful Space for the Aged." *Gerontologist* 21: 304–311.

Thatcher, R.M. 1983. "98.7 F., What is Normal?" *Journal of Gerontological Nursing* 9: 22–27.

Toseland, R. 1979. "More Than Just a Home." *Generations* 3: 20–21.

Chapter 11

Amenta, M., A. Weiner, and D. Amenta. 1984. "Successful Relocation of Elderly Residents." *Geriatric Nursing* 5(8), November/December: 356–360.

Atchley, R.C. 1987. *Aging: Continuity and Change*, 2d ed. Belmont, Calif.: Wadsworth Publishing Co.

Beaver, M.L. 1979. "The Decision-Making Process and Its Relationship to Relocation Adjustment in Old People." *The Gerontologist* 19(6): 567–574.

Berland, D.A., and R.L. Poggi. 1981. "Establishing a Newcomers' Group." In *Nursing and the Aged*, 2d ed., edited by I. Burnside. New York: McGraw Hill.

Borup, J.H. 1983. "Relocation Mortality Research: Assessment, Reply, and the Need to Refocus on the Issues." *The Gerontologist* 23(3): 235–242.

Butler, R.N., and M.I. Lewis. 1982. *Aging and Mental Health*, 3d ed. St. Louis: C.V. Mosby.

Dimon, J. 1979. "A Geriatric Relocation: Transplantation Shock." *Journal of Gerontological Nursing* 5(5) September/October: 17–20.

Ebersole, P., and P. Hess. 1985. *Toward Healthy Aging*, 2d ed. St. Louis: C.V. Mosby.

Hasselkus, B.R. 1978. "Relocation Stress and the Elderly." *American Journal of Occupational Therapy* 32(10) November-December: 631–636.

Kowalski, N.C. 1981. "Institutional Relocation: Current Programs and Applied Approaches." *The Gerontologist* 21(5): 512–519.

Louis, M. 1981. "Personal Space Boundary Needs of Elderly Persons: An Empirical Study." *Journal of Gerontological Nursing* 7(7) July: 395–400.

Mirotznik, J., and A.P. Ruskin. 1985. "Inter-Institutional Relocation and Its Effects on Psychosocial Status." *The Gerontologist* 25(3): 265–270.

Mullen, E. 1977. "Relocation of the Elderly: Implications for Nursing." *Journal of Gerontological Nursing* 3(4) July-August: 13–18.

Newcomer, R.J., and M.A. Caggiano. 1981. "Environment and the Aged Person." In *Nursing and the Aged*, 2d ed., edited by I.M. Burnside. New York: McGraw-Hill.

Porter, J.E., T.J. Rasmussen, and I.M. Burnside. 1981. "Developing a Working Relationship with a Confused Client." *Nursing and the Aged*, 2d ed., edited by I.M. Burnside. New York: McGraw-Hill.

Rosswurm, M.A. 1983. "Relocation and the Elderly." *Journal of Gerontological Nursing* 9(12) December: 632–637.

Schultz, R., and G. Brenner. 1977. "Relocation of the Aged: A Review and Theoretical Analysis." *Journal of Gerontology* 32(3): 323–333.

Smith, K.F., and V.L. Bengtson. 1979. "Positive Consequences of Institutionalization: Solidarity Between Elderly Parents and Their Middle-Aged Children. *The Gerontologist* 19(5): 438–447.

Trierweiler, R. 1978. "Personal Space and its Effects on an Elderly Individual in a Long-Term Care Institution." *Journal of Gerontological Nursing* 4(5), September/October: 21–23.

Wolanin, M.O. 1978. "Relocation of the Elderly." *Journal of Gerontological Nursing* 4(3) May/June: 47–50.

Chapter 12

Burnside, I.M. 1981. "The Therapeutic Use of Touch." In *Nursing and the Aged*, 2d ed., edited by I.M. Burnside. New York: McGraw-Hill.

Copstead, L.C. 1980. "Effects of Touch on Self-Appraisal and Interaction Appraisal for Permanently Institutionalized Older Adults." *Journal of Gerontological Nursing* 6(12) (December): 747–752.

Hollinger, L.M. 1980. "Perception of Touch in the Elderly." *Journal of Gerontological Nursing* 6(12) (December): 741–745.

Langland, R.M., and C.L. Panicucci. 1982. "Effects of Touch on Communication with Elderly, Confused Clients." *Journal of Gerontological Nursing* 8(3) (March): 152–155.

Maslow, A.H. 1970. *Motivation and Personality*, 2d ed. New York: Harper and Row.

McCoy, P. 1977. "Further Proof that Touch Speaks Louder than Words." *R.N.* 40(11) (November): 43–46.

Seaman, L. 1982. "Affective Nursing Touch." *Geriatric Nursing* 13(3) (May/June): 162–164.

Tobiason, J.B. 1981. "Touching is for Everyone." *American Journal of Nursing* 81(4) (April): 728–730.

Woodruff, D.S. 1975. "A Psychological Perspective of the Psychology of Aging." In *Aging: Scientific Perspectives and Social Issues*, edited by D.S. Woodruff and J.E. Birren. New York: Van Nostrand.

Chapter 13

Adams, E.B. 1979. "Reminiscence and Life Review in the Aged: A Guide for the Elderly, Their Families, and Service Providers." Center Studies Series, 15. Denton, Texas: North Texas State University.

Baker, N.J. 1985. "Reminiscing in Group Therapy for Self-Worth." *Journal of Gerontological Nursing* 11(7): 21–24.

Boylin, W., S.K. Gordon, and M.F. Nehrke. 1976. "Reminiscing and Ego Integrity in Institutionalized Elderly Males." *The Gerontologist* 16(2): 118–124.

Butler, R.N. 1963. "The Life Review: An Interpretation of Reminiscence in the Aged." *Psychiatry* 26(1) February: 65–76.

Butler, R.N., and M.I. Lewis. 1982. *Aging and Mental Health*, 3d ed. St. Louis: C.V. Mosby.

Carlson, C.M. 1984. "Reminiscing Toward Achieving Ego Integrity in Old Age." *Social Casework* 65(2) February: 81–89.

Cook, J.B. 1984. "Reminiscing: How it can Help Confused Nursing Home Residents." *Social Casework* 65(2) February: 90–93.

Dietsche, L.M. 1979. "Facilitating the Life Review Through Group Reminiscence." *Journal of Gerontological Nursing* 5(4) July/August: 43–46.

Ebersole, P. 1978a. "Establishing Reminiscing Groups." In *Working with the Elderly: Group Processes and Techniques*, edited by I. Burnside. North Scituate, Mass.: Duxbury Press.

———. 1978b. "A Theoretical Approach to the Use of Reminiscence." In *Working with the Elderly: Group Processes and Techniques*, edited by I. Burnside. North Scituate, Mass.: Duxbury Press.

———. 1976. "Reminiscing." *American Journal of Nursing* 76(8) August: 1304–1305.

Ebersole, P., and P. Hess. 1985. *Toward Healthy Aging.* St. Louis: C.V. Mosby.

Ellison, K.B. 1981. "Working with the Elderly in a Life Review Group." *Journal of Gerontological Nursing* 7(9) September: 537–541.

Erikson, E.H. 1963. *Childhood and Society,* 2d. ed. New York: Norton.

———. 1964. *Insight and Responsibility.* New York: Norton.

Hartford, M.E. 1980. "The Use of Group Methods for Work with the Aged." In *Handbook of Mental Health and Aging,* edited by J.E. Birren and R.B. Sloane. Englewood Cliffs, N.J.: Prentice-Hall.

Huber, K., and P. Miller. 1984. "Reminisce with the Elderly: Do It!" *Geriatric Nursing* March/April: 84–87.

Lappe, J.M. 1987. "Reminiscing: The Life Review Therapy." *Journal of Gerontological Nursing* 13(4) April: 12–16.

Lesser, J., L.W. Lazarus, R. Frankel, and S. Havasy. 1981. "Reminiscence Group Therapy with Psychotic Geriatric Inpatients." *The Gerontologist* 21(3): 291–296.

Merriam, S. 1980. "The Concept and Function of Reminisce: A Review of the Research." *The Gerontologist* 20(5): 604–609.

Merriam, S., and L.H. Cross. 1982. "Adulthood and Reminiscence: A Descriptive Study." *Educational Gerontology* 8(3): 275–290.

Perschbacher, R. 1984. "An Application of Reminiscence in an Activity Setting." *The Gerontologist* 24(4): 343–345.

Pincus, A. 1970. "Reminiscence in Aging and Its Implications for Social Work Practice." *Social Work* 15 July: 47–53.

Remnet, V.L. 1978. "The Eclectic Approach to Group Work." In *Working with the Elderly: Group Processes and Technique,* edited by I. Burnside. North Scituate, Mass.: Duxbury Press.

Remnet, V.L. 1974. "A Group Program for Adaptation to a Convalescent Hospital." *The Gerontologist* 14(4) August: 336–341.

Chapter 14

Andrus Volunteers. 1985. "Who Cares: Helpful Hints for Those who Care for a Dependent Older Person at Home." Los Angeles: Andrus Gerontology Center, University of Southern California.

Archbold, P.G. 1982. "All-Consuming Activity: The Family as Caregiver." *Generations* 7(2) (Winter): 12–13, 40.

Atchley, R.C. 1987. *Aging: Continuity and Change,* 2d ed. Belmont, Calif.: Wadsworth Publishing Co.

Atchley, R.C., and S.J. Miller. 1980. "Older People and Their Families." In *Annual Review of Gerontology and Geriatrics,* edited by C. Eisdorfer. New York: Springer Publishing Co.

Bengtson, V.L., and J.A. Kuypers. 1971. "Generational Differences and the Developmental Stake." *Aging and Human Development* 2(4): 249–260.

Bengtson, V.J., and J. Treas. 1980. "The Changing Family Context of Mental Health and Aging." In *Handbook of Mental Health and Aging,* edited by J.E. Birren and R.B. Sloane. Englewood Cliffs, N.J.: Prentice-Hall.

Bild, B.R., and R.J. Havighurst. 1976. "Family and Social Support." *The Gerontologist* 16(1): 63–69.

Bloomfield, H.H. 1985. *Making Peace with Your Parents.* New York: Ballentine Books.

Bressler, D.S. 1984. *Hand in Hand,* edited by R.J. Loewinsohn and L.E. Baldwin. Washington, D.C.: American Association of Retired Persons.

Brody, E.M. 1985. "Parent Care as a Normative Family Stress." *The Gerontologist* 25(1) (February): 19–29.

———. 1981. "Women in the Middle' and Family Help to Older People." *The Gerontologist* 21(5): 471–480.

———. 1979. "Social, Economic and Environmental Issues Relating to Aging, with Some Thoughts About 'Women in the Middle.'" *Aging: Research and Perspectives* 3: 37–45.

Brody, E.M., and C.B. Schoonover. 1986. "Patterns of Parent-Care When Adult Daughters Work and When They Do Not." *The Gerontologist* 26(4) (August): 372–381.

Bumagin, V.E., and K.F. Hirn. 1979. *Aging is a Family Affair.* New York: Thomas Y. Crowell.

Cicirelli, V.G. 1983. "Adult Children and Their Elderly Parents." In *Family Relationships in Later Life,* edited by T.H. Brubaker. Beverly Hills, Calif.: Sage Publications.

———. 1981. *Helping Elderly Parents.* Boston: Auburn House Publishing Co.

Cohen, S.Z., and B.M. Gans. 1978. *The Other Generation Gap.* New York: Warner Books.

Frankfather, D.L., M.J. Smith, and F.G. Caro. 1981. *Family Care of the Elderly.* Lexington, Mass.: Lexington Books.

Goodman, J.G. 1980. *Aging Parents: Whose Responsibility?* New York: Family Service Association of America.

Grollman, E.A., and S.H. Grollman. 1978. *Caring for Your Aged Parents.* Boston: Beacon Press.

Hagestad, G.O. 1981. "Problems and Promises in the Social Psychology of Intergenerational Relations." In *Aging: Stability and Change in the Family,* edited by R.W. Fogel, E. Hatfield, S.B. Kiesler, and E. Shanas. New York: Academic Press.

Hareven, T.K. 1982. "The Life Course and Aging in Historical Perspective." *Aging and Life Course Transitions: An Interdisciplinary Perspective,* edited by T.K. Hareven and K.J. Adams. New York: Guilford Press.

Herr, J.J., and J.H. Weakland. 1979. *Counseling Elders and Their Families.* New York: Springer Publishing Co.

Hickey, T., and R. Douglass. 1981. "Neglect and Abuse of Older Family Members: Professionals' Perspectives and Case Experiences." *The Gerontologist* 21(2): 171–176.

Hildreth, G.J., G. Van Lannen, E. Kelley, and T. Durant. 1980. "Participation in and Enjoyment of Family Maintenance Activities by Elderly Women." *Family Relations* 29(3): 386–390.

Hooyman, N.R., and W. Lustbader. 1986. *Taking Care.* New York: The Free Press.

Horne, J. 1985. *Caregiving: Helping an Aged Loved One.* Glenview, Ill.: Scott, Foresman.

Horowitz, A., and L.W. Shindelman. 1983. "Reciprocity and Affection: Past Influences on Current Caregiving." *Journal of Gerontological Social Work* 5(3) (Spring): 5–20.

Kingson, E.R., B.A. Hirshorn, and J.M. Cornman. 1986. *Ties that Bind*. Washington, D.C.: Seven Locks Press.

La Buda, D.R. 1985. *The Gadget Book: Ingenious Devices for Easier Living*. Glenview, Ill.: Scott, Foresman.

National Institute on Aging. 1977. "Our Future Selves: A Research Plan Toward Understanding Aging." Washington, D.C.: Department of Health, Education and Welfare, National Institute on Aging.

Otten, J., and F.D. Shelley. 1977. *When Your Parents Grow Old*. New York: The New American Library.

Peterson, J.A. 1980. "Social-Psychological Aspects of Death and Dying and Mental Health." In *Handbook of Mental Health and Aging*, edited by J.E. Birren and R.B. Sloane. Englewood Cliffs, N.J.: Prentice-Hall.

Pierskalla, C.S., and J.D. Heald. 1982. *Help for Families of the Aging*. Swarthmore, Penn.: National Support Center for Families of the Aging.

Puner, M. 1974. *To the Good Long Life: What We Know About Growing Old*. New York: Universe Books.

Remnet, V.L. 1987. "How Adult Children Respond to Role Transitions in the Lives of Their Aging Parents." *Educational Gerontology* 13(4): 341–355.

Rosenmayr, L. 1977. "The Family: A Source of Hope for the Elderly?" In *Family, Bureaucracy and the Elderly*, edited by E. Shanas and M.B. Sussman. Durham, N.C.: Duke University Press.

Rzetelny, H., and J. Mellor. 1981. *Support Groups for Caregivers of the Aged*. New York: Community Service Society.

Seelbach, W.C., and C.J. Hansen. 1980. "Satisfaction with Family Relations Among the Elderly." *Family Relations* 29(1): 91–95.

Shanas, E. 1979. "Social Myth as Hypothesis: The Case of the Family Relations of Old People." *The Gerontologist* 19(1): 3–9.

Silverman, A.G., C.I. Brahce, and C. Zielinski. 1981. *As Parents Grow Older*. Ann Arbor, Mich.: University of Michigan Press.

Silverstone, B., and H.K. Hyman. 1982. *You and Your Aging Parent*. New York: Pantheon Books.

Springer, D., and T.H. Brubaker. 1984. *Family Caregivers and Dependent Elderly*. Beverly Hills: Sage Publications.

Stoller, E.P., and L.L. Earl. 1983. "Help with Activities of Everyday Life: Sources of Support for the Noninstitutionalized Elderly." *The Gerontologist* 23(1): 64–70.

Streib, G.F., and R.W. Beck. 1980. "Older Families: A Decade Review." *Journal of Marriage and the Family* 42(4): 937–956.

Tibbitts, C. 1979. "Can We Invalidate Negative Stereotypes of Aging?" *The Gerontologist* 19(1): 10–20.

Tobin, S.S., and R. Kulps. 1980. "The Family Services." *Annual Review of Gerontology and Geriatrics*, edited by C. Eisdorfer. New York: Springer Publishing Co.

Treas, J. 1977. "Family Support Systems for the Aged: Some Social and Demographic Considerations." *The Gerontologist* 17(6): 486–491.

Troll, L.E. 1980. "Intergenerational Relations in Later Life: A Family Systems Approach." In *Transitions of Aging*. edited by N. Datan and N. Lohmann. New York: Academic Press.

Troll, L. 1971. "The Family of Later Life: A Decade Review." *Journal of Marriage and the Family* 33(2): 263–290.

Troll, L.E., and J. Stapley. 1985. "Elders and the Extended Family System: Health, Family, Salience and Affect." In *Life-Span and Change in a Gerontological Perspective*, edited by J.M.A. Munnichs, P. Mussen, E. Olbroch and P.G. Coleman. Orlando, Fla.: Academic Press, Inc.

United States Bureau of the Census. 1984. "Current Population Report P-20, No. 385: Childspacing Among Birth Cohorts of American Women: 1905–1959." Washington, D.C.: U.S. Government Printing Office.

United States Bureau of the Census. 1972. "Current Population Reports P-23, No. 43: Projections of the Population of the United States, by Age and Sex." Washington, D.C.: Government Printing Office.

Ward, R.A., S.R. Sherman, and M. LaGory. 1984. "Subjective Network Assessment and Subjective Well-Being." *Journal of Gerontology* 39(1): 93–105.

Wentowski, G.J. 1981. "Reciprocity and the Coping Strategies of Older People: Cultural Dimensions of Network Building." *The Gerontologist* 21(6): 600–609.

Chapter 15

Archbold, P.G. 1983. "Impact of Parent-Caring on Women." *Family Relations* 32(1): 39–45.

Bengtson, V.L. 1973. *The Social Psychology of Aging.* Indianapolis, Ind.: Bobbs-Merrill.

Bengtson, V.L., and J. Kuypers. 1985. "The Family Support Cycle: Psychosocial Issues in the Aging Family." In *Life-Span and Change in a Gerontological Perspective*, edited by J.M.A. Munnichs, P. Mussen, E. Olbrich, P.G. Coleman. Orlando, Fla.: Academic Press.

Brody, E.M. 1985. "Parent Care as a Normative Family Stress." *The Gerontologist* 25(1) (February): 19–29.

Brody, E.M., P.T. Johnsen, and M.C. Fulcomer. 1984. "What Should Adult Children Do for Elderly Parents: Opinions and Preferences of Three Generations of Women." *Journal of Gerontology* 39(6): 736–746.

Cicirelli, V.G. 1981. *Helping Elderly Parents.* Boston: Auburn House Publishing.

Golan, N. 1981. *Passing Through Transitions.* New York: The Free Press.

Hagestad, G.O. 1981. "Problems and Promises in the Social Psychology of Intergenerational Relations." In *Aging: Stability and Change in the Family*, edited by R.W. Fogel, E. Hatfield, S.B. Kiesler, and E. Shanas. New York: Academic Press.

Havighurst, R.J. 1952. *Developmental Tasks and Education.* New York: David McKay.

Horowitz, A., and L.W. Shindelman. 1983. "Reciprocity and Affection: Past Influences on Current Caregiving." *Journal of Gerontological Social Work* 5(3) (Spring): 5–20.

Johnson, C.L. 1983. "Dyadic Family Relations and Social Support." *The Gerontologist* 23(4): 377–383.

Johnson, C.L., and B.J. Bursk. 1977. "Relationships Between the Elderly and Their Adult Children." *The Gerontologist* 17(1): 90–96.

Kuypers, J.A., and V.L. Bengtson. 1983. "Toward Competence in the Older Family." In *Family Relationships in Later Life*, edited by T.H. Brubaker. Beverly Hills, Calif.: Sage Publications.

McMahon, B.J., and B.D. Ames. 1983. "Educational Programming for Midlife Adults with Parent-Caring Responsibilities." *Educational Gerontology* 9 (5–6): 377–387.

Merriam, S. 1978. "Middle Age: A Review of the Literature and its Implications for Educational Intervention." *Adult Education* 29(1): 39–54.

Pearlin, L.I. 1982. "Discontinuities in the Study of Aging." In *Aging and Life Course Transitions: An Interdisciplinary Perspective*, edited by T.K. Hareven and K.J. Adams. New York: The Guilford Press.

Quinn, W.H., and J.F. Keller. 1983. "Older Generations of the Family: Relational Dimensions and Quality." *The American Journal of Family Therapy* 11(3): 23–24.

Remnet, V.L. 1987. "How Adult Children Respond to Role Transitions in the Lives of Their Aging Parents." *Educational Gerontology* 13(4): 341–355.

———. 1985. "Adult Children's Experiences with Transitions in the Lives of their Aging Relatives: Implications for Adult Educators." Unpublished doctoral dissertation, University of Southern California, Los Angeles.

Selye, H. 1974. *Stress Without Distress*. New York: Signet Books.

Streib, G.F., and R.W. Beck. 1980. "Older Families: A Decade Review." *Journal of Marriage and the Family* 42(4): 937–956.

Troll, L.E., and J. Stapley. 1985. "Elders and the Extended Family System: Health, Family, Salience and Affect. In *Life-Span and Change in a Gerontological Perspective*, edited by J.M.A. Munnichs, P. Mussen, E. Olbroch and P.G. Coleman. Orlando, Fla.: Academic Press, Inc.

Weishaus, S. 1979. "Aging is a Family Affair." In *Aging Parents*, edited by P. Ragan. Los Angeles: Andrus Gerontology Center, University of Southern California Press.

Index

Abuse, 200
Activities: accessibility of, 127; evidence of, 134–135; future self and, 16–17, 22–23
Affectionate touch, 167
Ageism, barrier presented by, 1–2
Aging, 1; perceptions of, 12–54
Appearance, giving feedback on, 165–166
Arteriosclerosis, 20
Arthritis, 20
Attitudes, 2–3; changing, 3–4, 6
Automobile, 23, 128–129

Bathroom, assessment of, 132–133
Beliefs, attitudes and, 2
Boundaries, of families, 195, 197

Cardiovascular diseases, 20
Caregiver, caretaker versus, 201
Case study, 7
Choice, relocation and, 145
Communication: nonverbal, recognition and, 166; pointers for, 74–75; unexpected role and, 211
Community: involvement of, 153; unexpected role and, 212
Community activities, 23, 127
Confidant, 22
Confluent education, 6
Coronary heart disease, 20

Debriefing, 8
Decision making, team in, 30
Demographics: family relationships and, 191–192; in neighborhood, 127
Dentures, 19
Dependency, "responsible," 67
Developing trust, 67–82; communication pointers and, 74–75; compensating for sensory changes and, 75–77; debriefing for, 71, 72–74; instructions to participants for, 71–72; introduction to, 70; objectives of, 68; preparation of participants for, 72; rationale for, 67–68; teaching notes for, 68–70; trusting relationships activity and, 70–71; trust walk activity and, 71–74
Diabetes, 20–21
Diet, 89–90

Eating: barriers to enjoyment of, 83; facilitating process of, 90–91
Economics, family relationships and, 192
Education: attitude change and, 3–4; confluent, 6; reminiscing and, 177; unexpected role and, 212–213
Educational activities, 23
Ego integrity, 180
Elderhostel, 23
Emergency preparedness, 133–134
Empathy, development of, 8–9
Employment, 22; reminiscing and, 177
Endurance, declining, 99
Environment, 120–157; for dining, 90; future self and, 16, 21; home assessment and, 121–142; relocation and, 143–157; temperature of, 131
Exercise, mobility and, 102–103
Experiential activities, 1–9; ageism and, 1–2; aging and, 1; analogies in, 7; attitudes and, 2–4; case study in, 7; development of, 4–9; empathy and, 8–9; discussion and debriefing process for, 8; learning environment for, 5–6; mental imagery in, 7; simulation in, 7; types of, 6–7

Facilitator, instructor as, 5–6, 8
Failure, fear of, reaction time and, 61
Falls, preventing, 104, 129
Family interactions, 191–204; assessment pointers for, 200–201; debriefing for, 196–198; instructions to participants for, 194–196; introduction to, 194; objectives of, 193; patterns of aid and, 198–200; rationale for, 191–192; strengthening, 153; teaching notes for, 193–194. *See also* Unexpected role
First impressions, 45–54; debriefing for, 49–51; instructions to participants for, 48–59; introduction to, 48; objectives of, 45–46; rationale for, 45; teaching notes for, 46–48
Friends, 22
Functional assessment, prior to relocation, 148–149
Future self, 13–28; debriefing for, 19–23; instructions to participants for, 17–18, 23–24; introduction to, 17; objectives of, 13–14; questions for, 18–19; rationale for, 13; teaching notes for, 14–17

Gait, age-related changes in, 100, 130
Grab bars, in bathroom, 133
Gray hair, 19
Group(s), reminiscing, 175
Group discussion, 8

Handrails, on stairs, 130
Health, 20–21; patterns of aid and, 199–200
Hearing: changes in, 20; evaluation of, prior to relocation, 149; impairment of, 76–77, 166
Home assessment: background information and, 125–126; debriefing for, 135–136; evidence of relationships, activities, and interests and, 134–135; instructions to participants for, 125; introduction to, 124–125; objectives of, 122; physical environment and, 126–134; rationale for, 121–122; teaching notes for, 122–124
Home ownership, value placed on, 121
Hypertension, 20

Independence, 21, 97
"Innocent victim" syndrome, 50–51
Instructor, 5–6, 8

Joints, mobility and, 99, 100

Kitchen, assessment of, 132

Learning environment, supportive, 5–6
Life expectancy, sex difference in, 22
Life review, 175–176, 180
Lighting: in home, 131; of stairs, 130
Living arrangement, future self and, 21
Long-term care facility: admission to, 151; privacy and personal space in, 151, 152–153

Maintaining mobility, 97–106; debriefing for, 101–102; instructions to participants for, 100–101; introduction to, 98–100; objectives of, 98; promoting and maintaining mobility and, 102–104; rationale for, 97; teaching notes for, 98
Marital status, 22
Medical assessment, prior to relocation, 148–149
Medications, 132–133
Mental imagery, 7
Mouth, dry, 85
Musculoskeletal system, age-related changes in, 97, 99–100, 102–103
Mutual aid, family patterns of, 197, 198–200

Needs, hierarchy of, 163
Needs and services: optimum fit, 29–43; case study for, 36; debriefing for, 32–34; instructions to participants for, 31–32; introduction to, 31; objectives of, 29–30; rationale for, 29; teaching notes for, 30–31
Neglect, 200
Neighborhood, assessment of, 126–128
Nutrition, promoting and maintaining, 89–91

Oral hygiene, 89
Osteoarthritic joint changes, 99
Osteopenia, 99

Pacing and patience, 57–65; compensating for changes in reaction time and, 61–62; debriefing for, 59–61; instructions to participants for, 59; introduction to, 59; objectives of, 58; rationale for, 57–58; teaching notes for, 58–59
Peer groups, reminiscing and, 180
Perceptions: of aging, 12–54; anticipating your future self and, 13–28; attitudes and, 2; of family members, 198–199; first impressions and, 45–54; needs and services: optimum fit and, 29–43

Periodontal disease, 19, 85
Personalization, of space, 151
Pets, 22
Physical aging, 56–118; developing trust and, 67–82; future self and, 16, 19–21; maintaining mobility and, 97–106; pacing and patience and, 57–65; skin sensitivity and, 107–118; surprise snack and, 83–95
Physical setting, of learning environment, 5
Posture, age-related changes in, 100
Pressure sores, 115
Privacy, importance of, 152–153
Problem-solving skills, unexpected role and, 211–212
Proximity, to family, 194, 196
Psychosocial considerations, 160–216; family interactions and, 191–204; recognition day and, 161–170; reminiscing and, 171–189; unexpected role and, 205–216

Reaction time: changes in, 61–62
Recognition day, 161–170; debriefing for, 164–165; instructions to participants for, 163–164; introduction to, 163; objectives of, 162; promoting recognition and, 165–166; rationale for, 161; teaching notes for, 162–163; touch and, 166–167
Relationships: evidence of, 134–135; future self and, 16, 21–22; reminiscing and, 177–178; trusting, 68–69, 70–71
Relocation, 143–157; assistance from staff of long-term care facilities in, 150–153; debriefing for, 146–148; instructions to participants for, 145–146; introduction to, 145; objectives of, 144; pointers for, 148–150; positive psychosocial environment following, 153–154; rationale for, 143–144; teaching notes for, 144
Reminiscing, 171–189; debriefing for, 179; functions of, 179–181; inservice training session for, 184–189; instructions to participants for, 178–179; introduction to, 175–176; objectives of, 172; rational for, 171–172; teaching notes for, 172–175; topics for, 177–178
Resistance, regarding plans, 33–34
"Responsible dependency," 67
Retirement, 22–23
Role model, instructor as, 6
Role(s): within family, 195–196, 197. *See also* Unexpected role
Rules, of families, 197

Safety: of exterior of home, 129; of neighborhood, 126–127
Services, accessibility in neighborhood, 127
Sidewalks, 129
Simulation, 7
Skin: age-related changes in, 107, 109–110; healthy, promoting, 114–115
Skin sensitivity, 107–118; debriefing for, 111–112, 113–114; instructions to participants for, 110–111, 113; introduction to, 109–110; objectives of, 108; preparation for participants for, 113; promoting healthy skin and, 114–115; rationale for, 107; teaching notes for, 108–109
Socialization: promoting at mealtime, 91; reminiscing and, 180
Stairs, 130
Surprise snack, 83–95; debriefing for, 87–89; instructions to participants for, 86; introduction to, 85–86; objectives of, 84; preparation of participants for, 86; promoting and maintaining optimum nutrition and, 89–91; rationale for, 83; teaching notes for, 84–85

Taste sense, changes in, 85
Teeth, 19, 85
Telephone, accessibility of, 131–132
Temperature: in home, 131; of water, 131
Touch, recognition and, 166–167
Transportation, accessibility of, 127
Trust walk, 69–70, 71

Unexpected role, 205–216; adaptation to new role and, 209–210; adaptive strategies and, 210–213; debriefing for, 208; initial response to, 210; instructions to participants for, 207, 209; introduction to, 207; objectives of, 206; rationale for, 205; role adapatation and, 208–209; supportive interventions and, 210–212; teaching notes for, 206–207

Values, attitudes and, 2
Vision: changes in, 19–20; evaluation of, prior to relocation, 149; impairment of, 75–76, 166
Volunteerism, 23

Water temperature, 131
Wrinkles, 19

Yard, assessment of, 128